D0164001

Textbook Outlines, Highlights, and Practice Quizzes

Environment

by Peter H Raven, 8th Edition

All "Just the Facts101" Material Written or Prepared by Cram101 Publishing

Title Page

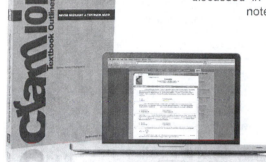

"*Just the Facts101*" is a Cram101 publication and tool designed to give you all the facts from your textbooks. Visit Cram101.com for the full practice test for each of your chapters for virtually any of your textbooks.

Cram101 has built custom study tools specific to your textbook. We provide all of the factual testable information and unlike traditional study guides, we will never send you back to your textbook for more information.

YOU WILL NEVER HAVE TO HIGHLIGHT A BOOK AGAIN!

Cram101 StudyGuides

All of the information in this StudyGuide is written specifically for your textbook. We include the key terms, places, people, and concepts... the information you can expect on your next exam!

Want to take a practice test?

Throughout each chapter of this StudyGuide you will find links to cram101.com where you can select specific chapters to take a complete test on, or you can subscribe and get practice tests for up to 12 of your textbooks, along with other exclusive cram101.com tools like problem solving labs and reference libraries.

Cram101.com

Only cram101.com gives you the outlines, highlights, and PRACTICE TESTS specific to your textbook. Cram101.com is an online application where you'll discover study tools designed to make the most of your limited study time.

By purchasing this book, you get 50% off the normal monthly subscription fee!. Just enter the promotional code **'DK73DW20924'** on the Cram101.com registration screen.

www.Cram101.com

Learning System

Environment
Peter H Raven, 8th

CONTENTS

CHAPTER OUTLINE: KEY TERMS, PEOPLE, PLACES, CONCEPTS

Antarctic ice sheet

Rachel Carson

Climate change

Greenland ice sheet

Ice sheet

Photosynthesis

Silent Spring

Natural resource

Total fertility rate

Poverty

Fossil fuel

Second law of thermodynamics

Population growth

Renewable resource

Ecological footprint

Living Planet Report

Hybrid vehicle

Air pollution

Pollution

Stewardship

Sustainable development

Tragedy of the commons

Ecology

Environmental science

MDGs

Sustainable Development Commission

Dynamic equilibrium

Ecosystem

Feedback

Scientific method

Variable

Income

Antarctic ice sheet	The Antarctic ice sheet is one of the two polar ice caps of the Earth. It covers about 98% of the Antarctic continent and is the largest single mass of ice on Earth. It covers an area of almost 14 million square km and contains 30 million cubic km of ice.
Rachel Carson	Rachel Carson was an American marine biologist and conservationist whose book Silent Spring and other writings are credited with advancing the global environmental movement.
	Rachel Carson began her career as an aquatic biologist in the U.S. Bureau of Fisheries, and became a full-time nature writer in the 1950s. Her widely praised 1951 bestseller The Sea Around Us won her a U.S. National Book Award, recognition as a gifted writer, and financial security.
Climate change	Climate change is a significant and lasting change in the statistical distribution of weather patterns over periods ranging from decades to millions of years. It may be a change in average weather conditions or the distribution of events around that average (e.g., more or fewer extreme weather events). Climate change may be limited to a specific region or may our across the whole Earth.
Greenland ice sheet	The Greenland Ice Sheet is a vast body of ice covering 1,710,000 square kilometres (660,235 sq mi), roughly 80% of the surface of Greenland. It is the second largest ice body in the world, after the Antarctic Ice Sheet. The ice sheet is almost 2,400 kilometres (1,500 mi) long in a north-south direction, and its greatest width is 1,100 kilometres (680 mi) at a latitude of 77°N, near its northern margin.
Ice sheet	An ice sheet a mass of glacier ice that covers surrounding terrain and greater than $50,000 \text{ km}^2$ (19,000 sq mi), thus also known as continental glacier. The only current ice sheets are in Antarctica and Greenland; during the last glacial period at Last Glacial Maximum (LGM) the Laurentide ice sheet covered much of North America, the Weichselian ice sheet covered northern Europe and the Patagonian Ice Sheet covered southern South America.
	Ice sheets are bigger than ice shelves or alpine glaciers. Masses of ice covering less than $50,000 \text{ km}^2$ are termed an ice cap.
Photosynthesis	Photosynthesis is a chemical process that converts carbon dioxide into organic compounds, especially sugars, using the energy from sunlight. Photosynthesis occurs in plants, algae, and many species of bacteria, but not in archaea. Photosynthetic organisms are called photoautotrophs, since they can create their own food.
Silent Spring	Silent Spring is a book written by Rachel Carson and published by Houghton Mifflin on 27 September 1962. The book is widely credited with helping launch the environmental movement.

Chapter 1. Introducing Environmental Science and Sustainability

	The New Yorker started serializing Silent Spring in June 1962, and it was published in book form (with illustrations by Lois and Louis Darling) by Houghton Mifflin later that year. When the book Silent Spring was published, Rachel Carson was already a well-known writer on natural history, but had not previously been a social critic.
Natural resource	Natural resources occur naturally within environments that exist relatively undisturbed by mankind, in a natural form. A natural resource is often characterized by amounts of biodiversity and geodiversity existent in various ecosystems.
	Natural resources are derived from the environment.
Total fertility rate	The total fertility rate of a population is the average number of children that would be born to a woman over her lifetime if (1) she were to experience the exact current age-specific fertility rates (ASFRs) through her lifetime, and (2) she were to survive from birth through the end of her reproductive life. It is obtained by summing the single-year age-specific rates at a given time.
Poverty	Poverty is the deprivation of food, shelter, money and clothing that occurs when people cannot satisfy their basic needs. Poverty can be understood simply as a lack of money, or more broadly in terms of barriers to everyday life.
	Absolute poverty or destitution refers to the state of severe deprivation of basic human needs, which commonly includes food, water, sanitation, clothing, shelter, health care, education and information.
Fossil fuel	Fossil fuels are fuels formed by natural processes such as anaerobic decomposition of buried dead organisms. The age of the organisms and their resulting fossil fuels is typically millions of years, and sometimes exceeds 650 million years. Fossil fuels contain high percentages of carbon and include coal, petroleum, and natural gas.
Second law of thermodynamics	The second law of thermodynamics is an expression of the tendency that over time, differences in temperature, pressure, and chemical potential equilibrate in an isolated physical system. From the state of thermodynamic equilibrium, the law deduced the principle of the increase of entropy and explains the phenomenon of irreversibility in nature. The second law declares the impossibility of machines that generate usable energy from the abundant internal energy of nature by processes called perpetual motion of the second kind.
Population growth	Population growth is the change in a population over time, and can be quantified as the change in the number of individuals of any species in a population using 'per unit time' for measurement.

Population growth is determined by four factors, births (B), deaths (D), immigrants (I), and emigrants (E). Using a formula expressed as

$$\Delta P \equiv (B-D)+(I-E)$$

In other words, the population growth of a period can be calculated in two parts, natural growth of population (B-D) and mechanical growth of population (I-E), in which mechanical growth of population is mainly affected by social factors, e.g. the advanced economies are growing faster while the backward economies are growing slowly even with negative growth.

Renewable resource

A renewable resource is a natural resource with the ability to reproduce through biological or natural processes and replenished with the passage of time. Renewable resources are part of our natural environment and form our eco-system.

In 1962, within a report to the committee on natural resources which was forwarded to the President of the United States, Paul Weiss defined Renewable Resources as: 'The total range of living organisms providing man with food, fibers, drugs, etc...'.

Ecological footprint

The ecological footprint is a measure of human demand on the Earth's ecosystems. It is a standardized measure of demand for natural capital that may be contrasted with the planet's ecological capacity to regenerate. It represents the amount of biologically productive land and sea area necessary to supply the resources a human population consumes, and to assimilate associated waste.

Living Planet Report

Living Planet Report is published every two years by the World Wide Fund for Nature. It is based the their Living Planet Index and ecological footprint calculations.

Hybrid vehicle

A hybrid vehicle is a vehicle that uses two or more distinct power sources to move the vehicle. The term most commonly refers to hybrid electric vehicles (HEVs), which combine an internal combustion engine and one or more electric motors. Power

Power sources for hybrid vehicles include:•On-board or out-board rechargeable energy storage system (RESS)•Coal, wood or other solid combustibles•Electricity•Electromagnetic fields, Radio waves•Compressed or liquefied natural gas•Human powered e.g. pedaling or rowing•Hydrogen•Petrol or Diesel fuel•Solar•Wind Vehicle type Two-wheeled and cycle-type vehicles

Mopeds, electric bicycles, and even electric kick scooters are a simple form of a hybrid, as power is delivered both via an internal combustion engine or electric motor and the rider's muscles.

Chapter 1. Introducing Environmental Science and Sustainability

Air pollution	Air pollution is the introduction of chemicals, particulate matter, or biological materials that cause harm or discomfort to humans or other living organisms, or cause damage to the natural environment or built environment, into the atmosphere. The atmosphere is a complex dynamic natural gaseous system that is essential to support life on planet Earth. Stratospheric ozone depletion due to air pollution has long been recognized as a threat to human health as well as to the Earth's ecosystems.
Pollution	Pollution is the introduction of contaminants into a natural environment that causes instability, disorder, harm or discomfort to the ecosystem i.e. physical systems or living organisms. Pollution can take the form of chemical substances or energy, such as noise, heat or light. Pollutants, the components of pollution, can be either foreign substances/energies or naturally occurring contaminants.
Stewardship	Stewardship is an ethic that embodies responsible planning and management of resources. The concept of stewardship has been applied in diverse realms, including with respect to environment, economics, health, property, information, and religion, and is linked to the concept of sustainability. Historically, stewardship was the responsibility given to household servants to bring food and drinks to a castle dining hall.
Sustainable development	Sustainable development is a pattern of growth in which resource use aims to meet human needs while preserving the environment so that these needs can be met not only in the present, but also for generations to come (sometimes taught as ELF-Environment, Local people, Future). The term sustainable development was used by the Brundtland Commission which coined what has become the most often-quoted definition of sustainable development as development that 'meets the needs of the present without compromising the ability of future generations to meet their own needs.' Sustainable development ties together concern for the carrying capacity of natural systems with the social challenges facing humanity. As early as the 1970s 'sustainability' was employed to describe an economy 'in equilibrium with basic ecological support systems.' Ecologists have pointed to The Limits to Growth, and presented the alternative of a 'steady state economy' in order to address environmental concerns.
Tragedy of the commons	The tragedy of the commons is a dilemma arising from the situation in which multiple individuals, acting independently and rationally consulting their own self-interest, will ultimately deplete a shared limited resource, even when it is clear that it is not in anyone's long-term interest for this to happen

Chapter 1. Introducing Environmental Science and Sustainability

Ecology	Ecology is the scientific study of the relations that living organisms have with respect to each other and their natural environment. Variables of interest to ecologists include the composition, distribution, amount (biomass), number, and changing states of organisms within and among ecosystems. Ecosystems are hierarchical systems that are organized into a graded series of regularly interacting and semi-independent parts (e.g., species) that aggregate into higher orders of complex integrated wholes (e.g., communities).
Environmental science	Environmental science is an interdisciplinary academic field that integrat physical and biological scienc, (including but not limited to Ecology, Physics, Chemistry, Biology, Soil Science, Geology, Atmospheric Science and Geography) to the study of the environment, and the solution of environmental problems. Environmental science provid an integrated, quantitative, and interdisciplinary approach to the study of environmental systems.
	Related areas of study include environmental studi and environmental engineering.
MDGs	The Millennium Development Goals (MDGs) are eight international development goals that were officially established following the Millennium Summit of the United Nations in 2000, following the adoption of the United Nations Millennium Declaration. All 193 United Nations member states and at least 23 international organizations have agreed to achieve these goals by the year 2015. The goals are:•Eradicating extreme poverty and hunger,•Achieving universal primary education,•Promoting gender equality and empowering women,•Reducing child mortality rates,•Improving maternal health,•Combating HIV/AIDS, malaria, and other diseases,•Ensuring environmental sustainability, and•Developing a global partnership for development
	Each of the goals has specific stated targets and dates for achieving those targets. To accelerate progress, the G8 Finance Ministers agreed in June 2005 to provide enough funds to the World Bank, the International Monetary Fund (IMF), and the African Development Bank (AfDB) to cancel an additional $40 to $55 billion in debt owed by members of the Heavily Indebted Poor Countries (HIPC) to allow impoverished countries to re-channel the resources saved from the forgiven debt to social programs for improving health and education and for alleviating poverty.
Sustainable Development Commission	The Sustainable Development Commission was a non-departmental public body responsible for advising the UK Government, Scottish Government, Welsh Assembly Government, and Northern Ireland Executive on sustainable development.
	It was set up by the Labour Government in June 2000 and closed by the Coalition Government in March 2011.
	Establishment

Chapter 1. Introducing Environmental Science and Sustainability

Dynamic equilibrium	A dynamic equilibrium exists once a reversible reaction ceases to change its ratio of reactants/products, but substances move between the chemicals at an equal rate, meaning there is no net change. It is a particular example of a system in a steady state. In thermodynamics a closed system is in thermodynamic equilibrium when reactions occur at such rates that the composition of the mixture does not change with time.
Ecosystem	An ecosystem is a community of living organisms (plants, animals and microbes) in conjunction with the nonliving components of their environment (things like air, water and mineral soil), interacting as a system. These components are regarded as linked together through nutrient cycles and energy flows. As ecosystems are defined by the network of interactions among organisms, and between organisms and their environment, they can come in any size but usually encompass specific, limited spaces (although some scientists say that the entire planet is an ecosystem).
Feedback	Feedback is a process in which information about the past or the present influences the same phenomenon in the present or future. As part of a chain of cause-and-effect that forms a circuit or loop, the event is said to 'feed back' into itself. Ramaprasad (1983) defines feedback generally as 'information about the gap between the actual level and the reference level of a system parameter which is used to alter the gap in some way', emphasising that the information by itself is not feedback unless translated into action.
Scientific method	Scientific method refers to a body of techniques for investigating phenomena, acquiring new knowledge, or correcting and integrating previous knowledge. To be termed scientific, a method of inquiry must be based on gathering empirical and measurable evidence subject to specific principles of reasoning. The Oxford English Dictionary says that scientific method is: 'a method or procedure that has characterized natural science since the 17th century, consisting in systematic observation, measurement, and experiment, and the formulation, testing, and modification of hypotheses.' The chief characteristic which distinguishes a scientific method of inquiry from other methods of acquiring knowledge is that scientists seek to let reality speak for itself, and contradict their theories about it when those theories are incorrect, i. e., falsifiability.
Variable	In mathematics, a variable is a value that may change within the scope of a given problem or set of operations. In contrast, a constant is a value that remains unchanged, though often unknown or undetermined. The concepts of constants and variables are fundamental to many areas of mathematics and its applications.
Income	Income is the consumption and savings opportunity gained by an entity within a specified timeframe, which is generally expressed in monetary terms.

However, for households and individuals, 'income is the sum of all the wages, salaries, profits, interests payments, rents and other forms of earnings received... in a given period of time.'

In the field of public economics, the term may refer to the accumulation of both monetary and non-monetary consumption ability, with the former (monetary) being used as a proxy for total income. Increase in income

Income per capita has been increasing steadily in almost every country.

1. _____ refers to a body of techniques for investigating phenomena, acquiring new knowledge, or correcting and integrating previous knowledge. To be termed scientific, a method of inquiry must be based on gathering empirical and measurable evidence subject to specific principles of reasoning. The Oxford English Dictionary says that _____ is: 'a method or procedure that has characterized natural science since the 17th century, consisting in systematic observation, measurement, and experiment, and the formulation, testing, and modification of hypotheses.'

The chief characteristic which distinguishes a _____ of inquiry from other methods of acquiring knowledge is that scientists seek to let reality speak for itself, and contradict their theories about it when those theories are incorrect, i. e., falsifiability.

 a. Steven Shapin
 b. The Third Culture
 c. Flammability
 d. Scientific method

2. _____ is published every two years by the World Wide Fund for Nature. It is based the their Living Planet Index and ecological footprint calculations.

 a. Millennium Ecosystem Assessment
 b. Multilateral Environmental Agreement
 c. Natural environment
 d. Living Planet Report

3. . An _____ a mass of glacier ice that covers surrounding terrain and greater than 50,000 km^2 (19,000 sq mi), thus also known as continental glacier. The only current _____ s are in Antarctica and Greenland; during the last glacial period at Last Glacial Maximum (LGM) the Laurentide _____ covered much of North America, the Weichselian _____ covered northern Europe and the Patagonian _____ covered southern South America.

_____s are bigger than ice shelves or alpine glaciers. Masses of ice covering less than 50,000 km^2 are termed an ice cap.

a. Ice sheet
b. Ice tongue
c. Icefall
d. Iceway

4. A _____ exists once a reversible reaction ceases to change its ratio of reactants/products, but substances move between the chemicals at an equal rate, meaning there is no net change. It is a particular example of a system in a steady state. In thermodynamics a closed system is in thermo_____ when reactions occur at such rates that the composition of the mixture does not change with time.

a. Fire point
b. Dynamic equilibrium
c. Flammability
d. Flash evaporation

5. The _____ of a population is the average number of children that would be born to a woman over her lifetime if (1) she were to experience the exact current age-specific fertility rates (ASFRs) through her lifetime, and (2) she were to survive from birth through the end of her reproductive life. It is obtained by summing the single-year age-specific rates at a given time.

a. Total fertility rate
b. Juglone
c. Gibbons v. Ogden
d. Iceway

ANSWER KEY
Chapter 1. Introducing Environmental Science and Sustainability

1. d
2. d
3. a
4. b
5. a

You can take the complete Chapter Practice Test

for Chapter 1. Introducing Environmental Science and Sustainability
on all key terms, persons, places, and concepts.

Online 99 Cents

http://www.epub89.6.20924.1.cram101.com/

Use www.Cram101.com for all your study needs

including Cram101's online interactive problem solving labs in

chemistry, statistics, mathematics, and more.

Chapter 2. Environmental Laws, Economics, and Ethics

CHAPTER OUTLINE: KEY TERMS, PEOPLE, PLACES, CONCEPTS

_____ Endangered Species Act

_____ Northwest Forest Plan

_____ Endangered Species

_____ General Revision Act

_____ National park

_____ Sequoia National Park

_____ Environmental history

_____ Antiquities Act

_____ Dust Bowl

_____ Soil conservation

_____ Rachel Carson

_____ Overpopulation

_____ Silent Spring

_____ Wilderness Act

_____ Environmental impact statement

_____ Environmental policy

_____ Acid rain

_____ Cost-benefit analysis

_____ Environmental justice

Chapter 2. Environmental Laws, Economics, and Ethics

CHAPTER OUTLINE: KEY TERMS, PEOPLE, PLACES, CONCEPTS

_____ | Scrubber

_____ | Air quality

_____ | Marginal cost

_____ | Cost-effectiveness analysis

_____ | Gross domestic product

_____ | Natural capital

_____ | Soil contamination

_____ | Environmental education

_____ | Basel Convention

_____ | Environmental ethics

CHAPTER HIGHLIGHTS & NOTES: KEY TERMS, PEOPLE, PLACES, CONCEPTS

Endangered Species Act	The Endangered Species Act of 1973 (Endangered Species Act; 7 U.S.C. § 136, 16 U.S.C. § 1531 et seq). is one of the dozens of United States environmental laws passed in the 1970s. Signed into law by President Richard Nixon on December 28, 1973, it was designed to protect critically imperiled species from extinction as a 'consequence of economic growth and development untempered by adequate concern and conservation.' The Act is administered by two federal agencies, the United States Fish and Wildlife Service (FWS) and the National Oceanic and Atmospheric Administration (NOAA).
Northwest Forest Plan	The Northwest Forest Plan is a series of federal policies and guidelines governing land use on federal lands in the Pacific Northwest region of the United States. It covers areas ranging from Northern California to western Washington.

Visit Cram101.com for full Practice Exams

Endangered Species	An endangered species is a species of organisms facing a very high risk of extinction. The phrase is used vaguely in common parlance for any species fitting this description, but its use by conservation biologists typically refers to those deigned Endangered in the IUCN Red List, where it is the second most severe conservation status for wild populations, following Critically Endangered. There are currently 3079 animals and 2655 plants classified as Endangered worldwide, compared with 1998 levels of 1102 and 1197, respectively.
General Revision Act	The General Revision Act of 1891 repealed the Timber Culture and Preemption Acts and authorized the President of the United States, under the Forest Reserve Act, to create forest preserves 'wholly or in part covered with timber or undergrowth, whether of commercial value or not....' about 16 million acres (65,000 km^2) of forest lands were set aside for federal use in the Yellowstone region. President Benjamin Harrison set aside 14 other areas of forest land by proclamation. After this he signed a bill preventing him, and any future president from establishing additional forest monuments.
National park	A national park is a reserve of natural, semi-natural, or developed land that a sovereign state declares or owns. Although individual nations designate their own national parks differently , an international organization, the International Union for Conservation of Nature (IUCN), and its World Commission on Protected Areas, has defined National Parks as its category II type of protected areas.
Sequoia National Park	Sequoia National Park is a national park in the southern Sierra Nevada east of Visalia, California, in the United States. It was established on September 25, 1890. The park spans 404,063 acres (631.35 sq mi; 1,635.18 km^2). Encompassing a vertical relief of nearly 13,000 feet (4,000 m), the park contains among its natural resources the highest point in the contiguous 48 United States, Mount Whitney, at 14,505 feet (4,421 m) above sea level.
Environmental history	Environmental history is the study of human interaction with the natural world over time. In contrast to other historical disciplines, it emphasizes the active role nature plays in influencing human affairs. Environmental historians study how humans both shape their environment and are shaped by it.
Antiquities Act	The Antiquities Act of 1906, officially An Act for the Preservation of American Antiquities (16 USC 431-433), is an act passed by the United States Congress and signed into law by Theodore Roosevelt on June 8, 1906, giving the President of the United States authority to, by executive order, restrict the use of particular public land owned by the federal government. The Act has been used over a hundred times since its passage. Its use frequently creates significant controversy.

Chapter 2. Environmental Laws, Economics, and Ethics

Dust Bowl	The Dust Bowl, was a period of severe dust storms causing major ecological and agricultural damage to American and Canadian prairie lands from 1930 to 1936 (in some areas until 1940). The phenomenon was caused by severe drought coupled with decades of extensive farming without crop rotation, fallow fields, cover crops or other techniques to prevent wind erosion. Deep plowing of the virgin topsoil of the Great Plains had displaced the natural deep-rooted grasses that normally kept the soil in place and trapped moisture even during periods of drought and high winds.
Soil conservation	Soil conservation is a set of management strategies for prevention of soil being eroded from the Earth's surface or becoming chemically altered by overuse, acidification, salinization or other chemical soil contamination. It is a component of environmental soil ience. Decisions regarding appropriate crop rotation, cover crops, and planted windbreaks are central to the ability of surface soils to retain their integrity, both with respect to erosive forces and chemical change from nutrient depletion.
Rachel Carson	Rachel Carson was an American marine biologist and conservationist whose book Silent Spring and other writings are credited with advancing the global environmental movement. Rachel Carson began her career as an aquatic biologist in the U.S. Bureau of Fisheries, and became a full-time nature writer in the 1950s. Her widely praised 1951 bestseller The Sea Around Us won her a U.S. National Book Award, recognition as a gifted writer, and financial security.
Overpopulation	Overpopulation is a generally undesirable condition where an organism's numbers exceed the carrying capacity of its habitat. The term often refers to the relationship between the human population and its environment, the Earth, or smaller geographical areas such as countries. Overpopulation can result from an increase in births, a decline in mortality rates, an increase in immigration, or an unsustainable biome and depletion of resources.
Silent Spring	Silent Spring is a book written by Rachel Carson and published by Houghton Mifflin on 27 September 1962. The book is widely credited with helping launch the environmental movement. The New Yorker started serializing Silent Spring in June 1962, and it was published in book form (with illustrations by Lois and Louis Darling) by Houghton Mifflin later that year. When the book Silent Spring was published, Rachel Carson was already a well-known writer on natural history, but had not previously been a social critic.
Wilderness Act	The Wilderness Act of 1964 (Pub.L. 88-577) was written by Howard Zahniser of The Wilderness Society. It created the legal definition of wilderness in the United States, and protected some 9 million acres (36,000 km²) of federal land.

The result of a long effort to protect federal wilderness, the Wilderness Act was signed into law by President Lyndon B. Johnson on September 3, 1964.

Environmental impact statement	An environmental impact statement under United States environmental law, is a document required by the National Environmental Policy Act (NEPA) for certain actions 'significantly affecting the quality of the human environment'. An is a tool for decision making. It describes the positive and negative environmental effects of a proposed action, and it usually also lists one or more alternative actions that may be chosen instead of the action described in the . Several US state governments require that a document similar to an be submitted to the state for certain actions.
Environmental policy	Environmental policy is any [course of] action deliberately taken [or not taken] to manage human activities with a view to prevent, reduce, or mitigate harmful effects on nature and natural resources, and ensuring that man-made changes to the environment do not have harmful effects on humans. It is useful to consider that environmental policy comprises two major terms: environment and policy. Environment primarily refers to the ecological dimension (ecosystems), but can also take account of social dimension (quality of life) and an economic dimension (resource management).
Acid rain	Acid rain is a rain or any other form of precipitation that is unusually acidic, meaning that it possesses elevated levels of hydrogen ions (low pH). It can have hmful effects on plants, aquatic animals, and infrastructure. Acid rain is caused by emissions of cbon dioxide, sulfur dioxide and nitrogen oxides which react with the water molecules in the atmosphere to produce acids.
Cost-benefit analysis	Cost-benefit analysis sometimes called benefit-cost analysis (BCA), is a systematic process for calculating and comparing benefits and costs of a project, decision or government policy (hereafter, 'project'). Cost benefit analysis has two purposes:•To determine if it is a sound investment/decision (justification/feasibility),•To provide a basis for comparing projects. It involves comparing the total expected cost of each option against the total expected benefits, to see whether the benefits outweigh the costs, and by how much Cost benefit analysis is related to, but distinct from cost-effectiveness analysis.
Environmental justice	Environmental justice is 'the fair treatment and meaningful involvement of all people regardless of race, color, sex, national origin, or income with respect to the development, implementation and enforcement of environmental laws, regulations, and policies.' In the words of Bunyan Bryant, 'Environmental justice is served when people can realize their highest potential.'

Chapter 2. Environmental Laws, Economics, and Ethics

Environmental justice emerged as a concept in the United States in the early 1980s; its proponents generally view the environment as encompassing 'where we live, work, and play' (sometimes 'pray' and 'learn' are also included) and seek to redress inequitable distributions of environmental burdens (pollution, industrial facilities, crime, etc).. Root causes of environmental injustices include 'institutionalized racism; the co-modification of land, water, energy and air; unresponsive, unaccountable government policies and regulation; and lack of resources and power in affected communities.'Definition

The United States Environmental Protection Agency defines as follows:'

'Environmental Justice is the fair treatment and meaningful involvement of all people regardless of race, color, national origin, or income with respect to the development, implementation, and enforcement of environmental laws, regulations, and policies. EPA has this goal for all communities and persons across this Nation.'

Scrubber	'Scrubber' systems are a diverse group of air pollution control devices that can be used to remove some particulates and/or gases from industrial exhaust streams. Traditionally, the term 'scrubber' has referred to pollution control devices that use liquid to wash unwanted pollutants from a gas stream. Recently, the term is also used to describe systems that inject a dry reagent or slurry into a dirty exhaust stream to 'wash out' acid gases.
Air quality	Air quality is defined as a measure of the condition of air relative to the requirements of one or more biotic species or to any human need or purpose. Air quality indices (I) are numbers used by government agencies to characterize the quality of the air at a given location. As the I increases, an increasingly large percentage of the population is likely to experience increasingly severe adverse health effects.
Marginal cost	In economics and finance, marginal cost is the change in total cost that arises when the quantity produced changes by one unit. That is, it is the cost of producing one more unit of a good. If the good being produced is infinitely divisible, so the size of a marginal cost will change with volume, as a non-linear and non-proportional cost function includes the following:•variable terms dependent to volume,•constant terms independent to volume and occurring with the respective lot size,•jump fix cost increase or decrease dependent to steps of volume increase In practice the above definition of marginal cost as the change in total cost as a result of an increase in output of one unit is inconsistent with the differential definition of marginal cost for virtually all non-linear functions.
Cost-effectiveness analysis	Cost-effectiveness analysis is a form of economic analysis that compares the relative costs and outcomes (effects) of two or more courses of action.

	Cost-effectiveness analysis is distinct from cost-benefit analysis, which assigns a monetary value to the measure of effect. Cost-effectiveness analysis is often used in the field of health services, where it may be inappropriate to monetize health effect.
Gross domestic product	Gross domestic product is the market value of all officially recognized final goods and services produced within a country in a given period of time. Gross domestic product per capita is often considered an indicator of a country's standard of living; Gross domestic product per capita is not a measure of personal income . Under economic theory, Gross domestic product per capita exactly equals the gross domestic income (GDI) per capita .
Natural capital	Natural capital is the extension of the economic notion of capital (manufactured means of production) to goods and services relating to the natural environment. Natural capital is thus the stock of natural ecosystems that yields a flow of valuable ecosystem goods or services into the future. For example, a stock of trees or fish provides a flow of new trees or fish, a flow which can be indefinitely sustainable.
Soil contamination	Soil contamination is caused by the presence of xenobiotic (human-made) chemicals or other alteration in the natural soil environment. This type of contamination typically arises from the failure caused by corrosion of underground storage tanks (including piping used to transmit the contents), application of pesticides, percolation of contaminated surface water to subsurface strata, oil and fuel dumping, disposal of coal ash, leaching of wastes from landfills or direct diharge of industrial wastes to the soil. The most common chemicals involved are petroleum hydrocarbons, lead, polynuclear aromatic hydrocarbons (such as naphthalene and benzo(a)pyrene), solvents, pesticides, and other heavy metals.
Environmental education	Environmental education refers to organized efforts to teach about how natural environments function and, particularly, how human beings can manage their behavior and ecosystems in order to live sustainably. The term is often used to imply education within the school system, from primary to post-secondary. However, it is sometimes used more broadly to include all efforts to educate the public and other audiences, including print materials, websites, media campaigns, etc.
Basel Convention	The Basel Convention on the Control of Transboundary Movements of Hazardous Wastes and Their Disposal, usually known simply as the Basel Convention, is an international treaty that was designed to reduce the movements of hazardous waste between nations, and specifically to prevent transfer of hazardous waste from developed to less developed countries (LDCs). It does not, however, address the movement of radioactive waste.

Chapter 2. Environmental Laws, Economics, and Ethics

Environmental ethics	Environmental ethics is the part of environmental philosophy which considers extending the traditional boundaries of ethics from solely including humans to including the non-human world. It exerts influence on a large range of disciplines including law, sociology, theology, economics, ecology and geography.
	There are many ethical decisions that human beings make with respect to the environment.

1. The _____ of 1964 (Pub.L. 88-577) was written by Howard Zahniser of The Wilderness Society. It created the legal definition of wilderness in the United States, and protected some 9 million acres (36,000 km²) of federal land. The result of a long effort to protect federal wilderness, the _____ was signed into law by President Lyndon B. Johnson on September 3, 1964.

   a. Juglone
   b. Subirrigation
   c. Sugar Mountain Farm
   d. Wilderness Act

2. An _____ under United States environmental law, is a document required by the National Environmental Policy Act (NEPA) for certain actions 'significantly affecting the quality of the human environment'. An is a tool for decision making. It describes the positive and negative environmental effects of a proposed action, and it usually also lists one or more alternative actions that may be chosen instead of the action described in the . Several US state governments require that a document similar to an be submitted to the state for certain actions.

   a. Environmental impact statement
   b. Environmental soil science
   c. Environmental Vulnerability Index
   d. In situ chemical reduction

3. . An _____ is a species of organisms facing a very high risk of extinction. The phrase is used vaguely in common parlance for any species fitting this description, but its use by conservation biologists typically refers to those deigned Endangered in the IUCN Red List, where it is the second most severe conservation status for wild populations, following Critically Endangered. There are currently 3079 animals and 2655 plants classified as Endangered worldwide, compared with 1998 levels of 1102 and 1197, respectively.

   a. Juglone
   b. Endangered Species
   c. Krakatoa

4. The _____ of 1973 (_____; 7 U.S.C. § 136, 16 U.S.C. § 1531 et seq). is one of the dozens of United States environmental laws passed in the 1970s. Signed into law by President Richard Nixon on December 28, 1973, it was designed to protect critically imperiled species from extinction as a 'consequence of economic growth and development untempered by adequate concern and conservation.'

The Act is administered by two federal agencies, the United States Fish and Wildlife Service (FWS) and the National Oceanic and Atmospheric Administration (NOAA).

a. Odyssey
b. Endangered Species Act
c. Endangered Species Act
d. Absent-minded professor

5. _____ is a set of management strategies for prevention of soil being eroded from the Earth's surface or becoming chemically altered by overuse, acidification, salinization or other chemical soil contamination. It is a component of environmental soil ience.

Decisions regarding appropriate crop rotation, cover crops, and planted windbreaks are central to the ability of surface soils to retain their integrity, both with respect to erosive forces and chemical change from nutrient depletion.

a. Soil conservation
b. Subirrigation
c. Sugar Mountain Farm
d. Sustainable Agriculture Innovation Network

1. d
2. a
3. b
4. c
5. a

You can take the complete Chapter Practice Test

for Chapter 2. Environmental Laws, Economics, and Ethics
on all key terms, persons, places, and concepts.

Online 99 Cents

http://www.epub89.6.20924.2.cram101.com/

Use www.Cram101.com for all your study needs

including Cram101's online interactive problem solving labs in

chemistry, statistics, mathematics, and more.

Chapter 3. Ecosystems and Energy

_____ | Amphibian

_____ | Estuary

_____ | Invertebrate

_____ | Meadow Vole

_____ | Salt marsh

_____ | Ecology

_____ | Ecosystem

_____ | Biosphere

_____ | Chemical energy

_____ | Hydrosphere

_____ | Landscape ecology

_____ | Lithosphere

_____ | Radiant energy

_____ | Solar energy

_____ | Thermal energy

_____ | Closed system

_____ | Kinetic energy

_____ | Open system

_____ | Thermodynamics

Chapter 3. Ecosystems and Energy

CHAPTER OUTLINE: KEY TERMS, PEOPLE, PLACES, CONCEPTS

	Entropy
	First law of thermodynamics
	Laws of thermodynamics
	Second law of thermodynamics
	Cellular respiration
	Chlorophyll
	Food web
	Hydrothermal vent
	Photosynthesis
	Sunlight
	Autotroph
	Chemosynthesis
	Energy flow
	Heterotroph
	Decomposers
	Detritivore
	Food chain
	Carbon cycle
	Path

	Krill
	Southern Ocean
	SQUID
	Biomass
	Ecological pyramid
	Climate change

CHAPTER HIGHLIGHTS & NOTES: KEY TERMS, PEOPLE, PLACES, CONCEPTS

Amphibian	Amphibians are ectothermic, tetrapod vertebrates of the class Amphibia. They inhabit a wide variety of habitats with most species living within terrestrial, fossorial, arboreal or freshwater aquatic ecosystems. Amphibians typically start out as larva living in water, but some species have developed behavioural adaptations to bypass this.
Estuary	An estuary is a partly enclosed coastal body of water with one or more rivers or streams flowing into it, and with a free connection to the open sea.
	Estuaries form a transition zone between river environments and ocean environments and are subject to both marine influences, such as tides, waves, and the influx of saline water; and riverine influences, such as flows of fresh water and sediment. The inflow of both seawater and freshwater provide high levels of nutrients in both the water column and sediment, making estuaries among the most productive natural habitats in the world.
Invertebrate	An invertebrate is an animal without a backbone. The group includes 97% of all animal species - all animals except those in the chordate subphylum Vertebrata (fish, amphibians, reptiles, birds, and mammals).
	Invertebrates form a paraphyletic group.

Chapter 3. Ecosystems and Energy

Meadow Vole	The Meadow Vole sometimes called the Field Mouse or Meadow Mouse, is a North American vole found across Canada, Alaska and the northern United States. Its range extends further south along the Atlantic coast. One subspecies, the Florida Salt Marsh Vole (M. p.
Salt marsh	A salt marsh, is a coastal ecosystem in the upper coastal intertidal zone between land and open salt water or brackish water that is regularly flooded by the tides. It is dominated by dense stands of salt-tolerant plants such as herbs, grasses, or low shrubs. These plants are terrestrial in origin and are essential to the stability of the salt marsh in trapping and binding sediments.
Ecology	Ecology is the scientific study of the relations that living organisms have with respect to each other and their natural environment. Variables of interest to ecologists include the composition, distribution, amount (biomass), number, and changing states of organisms within and among ecosystems. Ecosystems are hierarchical systems that are organized into a graded series of regularly interacting and semi-independent parts (e.g., species) that aggregate into higher orders of complex integrated wholes (e.g., communities).
Ecosystem	An ecosystem is a community of living organisms (plants, animals and microbes) in conjunction with the nonliving components of their environment (things like air, water and mineral soil), interacting as a system. These components are regarded as linked together through nutrient cycles and energy flows. As ecosystems are defined by the network of interactions among organisms, and between organisms and their environment, they can come in any size but usually encompass specific, limited spaces (although some scientists say that the entire planet is an ecosystem).
Biosphere	The biosphere is the global sum of all ecosystems. It can also be called the zone of life on Earth, a closed (apart from solar and cosmic radiation) and self-regulating system. From the broadest biophysiological point of view, the biosphere is the global ecological system integrating all living beings and their relationships, including their interaction with the elements of the lithosphere, hydrosphere and atmosphere.
Chemical energy	In chemistry, Chemical energy is the potential of a chemical substan to undergo a transformation through a chemical reaction or, to transform other chemical substans.Template:Fusion Breaking or making of chemical bonds involves energy, which may be either absorbed or evolved from a chemical system. Energy that can be released (or absorbed) because of a reaction between a set of chemical substans is equal to the differen between the energy content of the products and the reactants. This change in energy is change in internal energy of a chemical reaction.
Hydrosphere	A hydrosphere in physical geography describes the combined mass of water found on, under, and over the surface of a planet.

Chapter 3. Ecosystems and Energy

The total mass of the Earth's hydrosphere is about 1.4×10^{18} tonnes, which is about 0.023% of the Earth's total mass. About 20×10^{12} tonnes of this is in the Earth's atmosphere (the volume of one tonne of water is approximately 1 cubic metre).

Landscape ecology	Landscape ecology is the science of studying and improving relationships between ecological processes in the environment and particular ecosystems. This is done within a variety of landscape scas, development spatial patterns, and organizational vels of research and policy.

As a highly interdisciplinary science in systems ecology, landscape ecology integrates biophysical and analytical approaches with humanistic and holistic perspectives across the natural sciences and social sciences. |
| Lithosphere | The lithosphere is the rigid outermost shell of a rocky planet. On Earth, it comprises the crust and the portion of the upper mantle that behaves elastically on time scales of thousands of years or greater. Earth's lithosphere

In the Earth the lithosphere includes the crust and the uppermost mantle, which constitute the hard and rigid outer layer of the Earth. |
| Radiant energy | Radiant energy is the energy of electromagnetic waves. The quantity of radiant energy may be calculated by integrating radiant flux (or power) with spect to time and, like all forms of energy, its SI unit is the joule. The term is used particularly when radiation is emitted by a source into the surrounding environment. |
| Solar energy | Solar energy, radiant light and heat from the sun, has been harnessed by humans since ancient times using a range of ever-evolving technologies. Solar radiation, along with secondary solar-powered resources such as wind and wave power, hydroelectricity and biomass, account for most of the available renewable energy on earth. Only a minuscule fraction of the available solar energy is used. |
| Thermal energy | Thermal energy is the part of the total inrnal energy of a thermodynamic sysm or sample of matr that results in the sysm's mperature. The inrnal energy, also ofn called the thermodynamic energy, includes other forms of energy in a thermodynamic sysm in addition to thermal energy, namely forms of pontial energy, such as the chemical energy stored in its molecular structure and electronic configuration, inrmolecular inractions, and the nuclear energy that binds the sub-atomic particles of matr.

Microscopically, the thermal energy is the kinetic energy of a sysm's constituent particles, which may be atoms, molecules, electrons, or particles in plasmas. |

Chapter 3. Ecosystems and Energy

Closed system	The term closed system has different meanings in different contexts. In thermodynami, a closed system can exchange energy (as heat or work), but not matter, with its surroundings. In contrast, an isolated system cannot exchange any of heat, work, or matter with the surroundings, while an open system can exchange all of heat, work and matter.
Kinetic energy	The kinetic energy of an object is the energy which it possesses due to its motion. It is defined as the work needed to accelerate a body of a given mass from rest to its stated velocity. Having gained this energy during its acceleration, the body maintains this kinetic energy unless its speed changes.
Open system	An open system is a system which continuously interacts with its environment. An open system should be contrasted with the concept of an isolated system which exchanges neither energy, matter,nor information with its environment. The concept of an 'open system' was formalized within a framework that enabled one to interrelate the theory of the organism, thermodynamics, and evolutionary theory.
Thermodynamics	ImgProperty databaseimg Thermodynamics is the branch of physical science concerned with heat and its relation to other forms of energy and work. It defines macroscopic variables (such as temperature, entropy, and pressure) that describe average properties of material bodies and radiation, and explains how they are related and by what laws they change with time. Thermodynamics does not describe the microscopic constituents of matter, and its laws can be derived from statistical mechanics.
Entropy	In classical statistical mechanics, the entropy function earlier introduced by Clausius is changed to statistical entropy using probability theory. The statistical entropy perspective was introduced in 1870 with the work of the Austrian physicist Ludwig Boltzmann. The macroscopic state of the system is defined by a distribution on the microstates that are accessible to a system in the course of its thermal fluctuations.
First law of thermodynamics	ImgProperty databaseimg The first law of thermodynamics is a version of the law of conservation of energy, specialized for thermodynamical systems. It is usually formulated by stating that the change in the internal energy of a closed system is equal to the amount of heat supplied to the system, minus the amount of work performed by the system on its surroundings. The law of conservation of energy can be stated: The energy of an isolated system is constant.

Chapter 3. Ecosystems and Energy

Laws of thermodynamics	ImgProperty databaseimg The four laws of thermodynamics define fundamental physical quantities (temperature, energy, and entropy) that characterize thermodynamic systems. The laws describe how these quantities behave under various circumstances, and forbid certain phenomena (such as perpetual motion). The four laws of thermodynamics are:•Zeroth law of thermodynamics: If two systems are in thermal equilibrium with a third system, they must be in thermal equilibrium with each other.
Second law of thermodynamics	The second law of thermodynamics is an expression of the tendency that over time, differences in temperature, pressure, and chemical potential equilibrate in an isolated physical system. From the state of thermodynamic equilibrium, the law deduced the principle of the increase of entropy and explains the phenomenon of irreversibility in nature. The second law declares the impossibility of machines that generate usable energy from the abundant internal energy of nature by processes called perpetual motion of the second kind.
Cellular respiration	Cellular respiration is the set of the metabolic reactions and processes that take place in the cells of organisms to convert biochemical energy from nutrients into adenosine triphosphate (ATP), and then release waste products. The reactions involved in respiration are catabolic reactions that involve the redox reaction (oxidation of one molecule and the reduction of another). Respiration is one of the key ways a cell gains useful energy to fuel cellular changes.
Chlorophyll	Chlorophyll is a green pigment found in almost all plants, algae, and cyanobacteria. Its name is derived from the Greek words χλωρος, chloros ('green') and φ?λλον, phyllon ('leaf'). Chlorophyll is an extremely important biomolecule, critical in photosynthesis, which allows plants to obtain energy from light.
Food web	A food web depicts feeding connections (what eats what) in an ecological community. Ecologists can broadly lump all life forms into one of two categories called trophic levels: 1) the autotrophs, and 2) the heterotrophs. To maintain their bodies, grow, develop, and to reproduce, autotrophs produce organic matter from inorganic substances, including both minerals and gases such as carbon dioxide.
Hydrothermal vent	A hydrothermal vent is a fissure in a planet's surface from which geothermally heated water issues. Hydrothermal vents are commonly found near volcanically active places, areas where tectonic plates are moving apart, ocean basins, and hotspots. Hydrothermal vents exist because the earth is both geologically active and has large amounts of water on its surface and within its crust.

Chapter 3. Ecosystems and Energy

Photosynthesis	Photosynthesis is a chemical process that converts carbon dioxide into organic compounds, especially sugars, using the energy from sunlight. Photosynthesis occurs in plants, algae, and many species of bacteria, but not in archaea. Photosynthetic organisms are called photoautotrophs, since they can create their own food.
Sunlight	Sunlight, in the broad sense, is the total frequency spectrum of electromagnetic radiation given off by the Sun. On Earth, sunlight is filtered through the Earth's atmosphere, and solar radiation is obvious as daylight when the Sun is above the horizon.
	When the direct solar radiation is not blocked by clouds, it is experienced as sunshine, a combination of bright light and radiant heat.
Autotroph	An autotroph, is an organism that produces complex organic compounds (such as carbohydrates, fats, and proteins) from simple inorganic molecules using energy from light (by photosynthesis) or inorganic chemical reactions (chemosynthesis). They are the producers in a food chain, such as plants on land or algae in water. They are able to make their own food and can fix carbon.
Chemosynthesis	In biochemistry, chemosynthesis is the biological conversion of one or more carbon molecules (usually carbon dioxide or methane) and nutrients into organic matter using the oxidation of inorganic molecules (e.g. hydrogen gas, hydrogen sulfide) or methane as a source of energy, rather than sunlight, as in photosynthesis. Chemoautotrophs, organisms that obtain carbon through chemosynthesis, are phylogenetically diverse, but groups that include conspicuous or biogeochemically-important taxa include the sulfur-oxidizing gamma and epsilon proteobacteria, the Aquificaeles, the Methanogenic archaea and the neutrophilic iron-oxidizing bacteria.
	Many microorganisms in dark regions of the oceans also use chemosynthesis to produce biomass from single carbon molecules.
Energy flow	In ecology, energy flow, also called the calorific flow, rrs to the flow of energy through a food chain. In an ecosystem, ecologists seek to quantify the relative importance of different component species and feeding relationships.
	A general energy flow scenario follows:•Solar energy is fixed by the photoautotrophs, called primary producers, like green plants.
Heterotroph	A heterotroph is an organism that cannot fix carbon and uses organic carbon for growth.

This contrasts with autotrophs, such as plants and algae, which can use energy from sunlight (photoautotrophs) or inorganic compounds (lithoautotrophs) to produce organic compounds such as carbohydrates, fats, and proteins from inorganic carbon dioxide. These reduced carbon compounds can be used as an energy source by the autotroph and provide the energy in food consumed by heterotrophs.

Decomposers

Decomposers are organisms that break down dead or decaying organisms, and in doing so carry out the natural process of decomposition. Like herbivores and predators, decomposers are heterotrophic, meaning that they use organic substrates to get their energy, carbon and nutrients for growth and development. Decomposers can break down cells of other organisms using biochemical reactions that convert the prey tissue into metabolically useful chemical products, without need for internal digestion.

Detritivore

Detritivores, also known as detritophages or detritus feeders or detritus eaters or saprophages, are heterotrophs that obtain nutrients by consuming detritus (decomposing organic matter). By doing so, they contribute to decomposition and the nutrient cycles. They should be distinguished from other decomposers, such as many species of bacteria, fungi and protists, unable to ingest discrete lumps of matter, instead live by absorbing and metabolising on a molecular scale.

Food chain

A food chain is somewhat a linear sequence of links in a food web starting from a trophic species that eats no other species in the web and ends at a trophic species that is eaten by no other species in the web. A food chain differs from a food web, because the complex polyphagous network of feeding relations are aggregated into trophic species and the chain only follows linear monophagous pathways. A common metric used to quantify food web trophic structure is food chain length.

Carbon cycle

The carbon cycle is the biogeochemical cycle by which carbon is exchanged among the biosphere, pedosphere, geosphere, hydrosphere, and atmosphere of the Earth. It is one of the most important cycles of the earth and allows for carbon to be recycled and reused throughout the biosphere and all of its organisms.

The carbon cycle was initially discovered by Joseph Priestley and Antoine Lavoisier, and popularized by Humphry Davy.

Path

In mathematics, a path in a topological space X is a continuous map f from the unit interval I = [0,1] to Xf : I → X.

The initial point of the path is f(0) and the terminal point is f(1). One often speaks of a 'path from x to y' where x and y are the initial and terminal points of the path. Note that a path is not just a subset of X which 'looks like' a curve, it also includes a parameterization.

Krill	Krill are small crustaceans of the order Euphausiacea, and are found in all the world's oceans. The name krill comes from the Norwegian word, meaning 'young fry of fish', which is also often attributed to other species of fish.
	Krill are considered an important trophic level connection - near the bottom of the food chain - because they feed on phytoplankton and to a lesser extent zooplankton, converting these into a form suitable for many larger animals for whom krill makes up the largest part of their diet.
Southern Ocean	The Southern Ocean comprises the southernmost waters of the World Southern Ocean, generally taken to be south of 60°S latitude and encircling Antarctica. As such, it is regarded as the fourth-largest of the five principal oceanic divisions (after the Pacific, Atlantic, and Indian Southern Oceans, but larger than the Arctic Southern Ocean). This ocean zone is where cold, northward flowing waters from the Antarctic mix with warmer subantarctic waters.
	Geographers disagree on the Southern Ocean's northern boundary or even its existence, with many considering the waters part of the Pacific, Atlantic, and Indian Southern Oceans instead.
SQUID	A SQUID is a very sensitive magnetometer used to measure extremely subtle magnetic fields, based on superconducting loops containing Josephson junctions.
	SQUIDs are sensitive enough to measure fields as low as 5 aT ($5{\times}10^{-18}$ T) within a few days of averaged measurements. Their noise levels are as low as 3 fT$\cdot$Hz$^{-1/2}$.
Biomass	Biomass, in ecology, is the mass of living biological organisms in a given area or ecosystem at a given time. Biomass can refer to species biomass, which is the mass of one or more species, or to community biomass, which is the mass of all species in the community. It can include microorganisms, plants or animals.
Ecological pyramid	An ecological pyramid is a graphical rresentation designed to show the biomass or biomass productivity at each trophic level in a given ecosystem.
	Biomass is the amount of living or organic matter present in an organism. Biomass pyramids show how much biomass is present in the organisms at each trophic level, while productivity pyramids show the production or turnover in biomass.
Climate change	Climate change is a significant and lasting change in the statistical distribution of weather patterns over periods ranging from decades to millions of years. It may be a change in average weather conditions or the distribution of events around that average (e.g., more or fewer extreme weather events). Climate change may be limited to a specific region or may our across the whole Earth.

Chapter 3. Ecosystems and Energy

1. The term _____ has different meanings in different contexts.

    In thermodynami, a _____ can exchange energy (as heat or work), but not matter, with its surroundings. In contrast, an isolated system cannot exchange any of heat, work, or matter with the surroundings, while an open system can exchange all of heat, work and matter.

    a. Closed system
    b. Computational neuroscience
    c. Control reconfiguration
    d. Control theory

2. A _____, is a coastal ecosystem in the upper coastal intertidal zone between land and open salt water or brackish water that is regularly flooded by the tides. It is dominated by dense stands of salt-tolerant plants such as herbs, grasses, or low shrubs. These plants are terrestrial in origin and are essential to the stability of the _____ in trapping and binding sediments.

    a. Coastal zone
    b. coastal
    c. Salt marsh
    d. Oldhamia

3. _____ is the scientific study of the relations that living organisms have with respect to each other and their natural environment. Variables of interest to ecologists include the composition, distribution, amount (biomass), number, and changing states of organisms within and among ecosystems. Ecosystems are hierarchical systems that are organized into a graded series of regularly interacting and semi-independent parts (e.g., species) that aggregate into higher orders of complex integrated wholes (e.g., communities).

    a. Ecologist
    b. Ecology
    c. Elicitor
    d. Engorgement

4. In chemistry, _____ is the potential of a chemical substan to undergo a transformation through a chemical reaction or, to transform other chemical substans.Template:Fusion Breaking or making of chemical bonds involves energy, which may be either absorbed or evolved from a chemical system. Energy that can be released (or absorbed) because of a reaction between a set of chemical substans is equal to the differen between the energy content of the products and the reactants. This change in energy is change in internal energy of a chemical reaction.

    a. Chemical library
    b. Chemical reaction
    c. Chemical similarity
    d. Chemical energy

5. The _____ comprises the southernmost waters of the World _____, generally taken to be south of 60°S latitude and encircling Antarctica. As such, it is regarded as the fourth-largest of the five principal oceanic divisions (after the Pacific, Atlantic, and Indian _____s, but larger than the Arctic _____). This ocean zone is where cold, northward flowing waters from the Antarctic mix with warmer subantarctic waters.

Geographers disagree on the _____'s northern boundary or even its existence, with many considering the waters part of the Pacific, Atlantic, and Indian _____s instead.

a. Juglone
b. Perfect space
c. Plateau
d. Southern Ocean

1. a

2. c

3. b

4. d

5. d

You can take the complete Chapter Practice Test

for Chapter 3. Ecosystems and Energy
on all key terms, persons, places, and concepts.

Online 99 Cents

http://www.epub89.6.20924.3.cram101.com/

Use www.Cram101.com for all your study needs

including Cram101's online interactive problem solving labs in

chemistry, statistics, mathematics, and more.

Chapter 4. Ecosystems and the Physical Environment

———————————| Hubbard Brook Experimental Forest

———————————| Biogeochemical cycle

———————————| Carbon cycle

———————————| Cellular respiration

———————————| Limestone

———————————| Carbon

———————————| Subduction

———————————| Nitrogen cycle

———————————| Nitrogen fixation

———————————| Nitrogen

———————————| Ammonification

———————————| Dead zone

———————————| Nitrification

———————————| Phosphorus cycle

———————————| Smog

———————————| Groundwater

———————————| Phosphorus

———————————| Sulfur cycle

———————————| Transpiration

CHAPTER OUTLINE: KEY TERMS, PEOPLE, PLACES, CONCEPTS

	Aerosol
	Albedo
	Glacier
	Ice sheet
	Insolation
	Mesosphere
	Stratosphere
	Thermosphere
	Troposphere
	Ozone layer
	Atmospheric convection
	Atmospheric circulation
	Coriolis effect
	Indian Ocean
	Southern Ocean
	Trade wind
	Westerlies
	Gulf Stream
	Greenland ice sheet

Chapter 4. Ecosystems and the Physical Environment

CHAPTER OUTLINE: KEY TERMS, PEOPLE, PLACES, CONCEPTS

______ Hurricane

______ Upwelling

______ Precipitation

______ Rain shadow

______ Sahara

______ Cyclone

______ Tornado

______ Typhoon

______ Tropical cyclone

______ Asthenosphere

______ Divergent boundary

______ Lithosphere

______ Mississippi River Delta

______ Plate tectonics

______ Earthquake

______ Himalayas

______ Mid-Atlantic Ridge

______ Seismic wave

______ Mangrove

	Moment magnitude scale
	Polar easterlies
	Prevailing winds
	Tsunami
	Lava
	Magma

CHAPTER HIGHLIGHTS & NOTES: KEY TERMS, PEOPLE, PLACES, CONCEPTS

Hubbard Brook Experimental Forest	Hubbard Brook Experimental Forest is an area of land in the White Mountains of New Hampshire that functions as an outdoor laboratory for ecological studies. It was initially established in 1955 by the United States Forest Service for the study of the relationship between forest cover and water quality and supply.
	In 1955 the first tract was dedicated, in the Hubbard Brook watershed, just west of the village of West Thornton, New Hampshire.
Biogeochemical cycle	In ecology and Earth science, a biogeochemical cycle is a pathway by which a chemical element or molecule moves through both biotic (biosphere) and abiotic (lithosphere, atmosphere, and hydrosphere) compartments of Earth. A cycle is a series of change which comes back to the starting point and which can be repeated.
	The term 'biogeochemical' tells us that biological; geological and chemical factors are all involved.
Carbon cycle	The carbon cycle is the biogeochemical cycle by which carbon is exchanged among the biosphere, pedosphere, geosphere, hydrosphere, and atmosphere of the Earth. It is one of the most important cycles of the earth and allows for carbon to be recycled and reused throughout the biosphere and all of its organisms.

Chapter 4. Ecosystems and the Physical Environment

Cellular respiration	Cellular respiration is the set of the metabolic reactions and processes that take place in the cells of organisms to convert biochemical energy from nutrients into adenosine triphosphate (ATP), and then release waste products. The reactions involved in respiration are catabolic reactions that involve the redox reaction (oxidation of one molecule and the reduction of another). Respiration is one of the key ways a cell gains useful energy to fuel cellular changes.
Limestone	Limestone is a sedimentary rock composed largely of the minerals calcite and aragonite, which are different crystal forms of calcium carbonate ($CaCO_3$). Many limestones are composed from skeletal fragments of marine organisms such as coral or foraminifera. Limestone makes up about 10% of the total volume of all sedimentary rocks.
Carbon	Carbon is the chemical element with symbol C and atomic number 6. As a member of group 14 on the periodic table, it is nonmetallic and tetravalent-making four electrons available to form covalent chemical bonds. There are three naturally occurring isotopes, with ^{12}C and ^{13}C being stable, while ^{14}C is radioactive, decaying with a half-life of about 5,730 years. Carbon is one of the few elements known since antiquity.
Subduction	In geology, subduction is the process that takes place at convergent boundaries by which one tectonic plate moves under another tectonic plate, sinking into the Earth's mantle, as the plates converge. These 3D regions of mantle downwellings are known as 'Subduction Zones'. A subduction zone is an area on Earth where two tectonic plates move towards one another and one slides under the other.
Nitrogen cycle	The nitrogen cycle is the process by which nitrogen is converted between its various chemical forms. This transformation can be carried out via both biological and non-biological processes. Important processes in the nitrogen cycle include fixation, mineralization, nitrification, and denitrification.
Nitrogen fixation	Nitrogen fixation is a process, biological, abiotic, or synthetic by which nitrogen (N_2) in the atmosphere is converted into ammonia (NH_3). Atmospheric nitrogen or elemental nitrogen (N_2) is relatively inert: it does not easily react with other chemicals to form new compounds. Fixation processes free up the nitrogen atoms from their diatomic form (N_2) to be used in other ways.
Nitrogen	Nitrogen is a chemical element with symbol N and atomic number 7. Elemental nitrogen is a colorless, odorless, tasteless, and mostly inert diatomic gas at standard conditions, constituting 78.09% by volume of Earth's atmosphere. The element nitrogen was discovered as a separable component of air, by Scottish physician Daniel Rutherford, in 1772. It belongs to the pnictogen family.

Chapter 4. Ecosystems and the Physical Environment

Ammonification	The nitrogen cycle is the process by which nitrogen is converted between its various chemical forms. This transformation can be carried out through both biological and physical processes. Important processes in the nitrogen cycle include fixation, ammonification, nitrification, and denitrification. Ammonification or Mineralization is performed by bacteria to convert the ammonia to ammonium. Nitrification can then occur to convert the ammonium to nitrite and nitrate. Nitrate can be returned to the euphotic zone by vertical mixing and upwelling where it can be taken up by phytoplankton to continue the cycle. N_2 can be returned to the atmosphere through denitrification.
Dead zone	Dead zones are hypoxic (low-oxygen) areas in the world's oceans, the observed incidences of which have been increasing since oceanographers began noting them in the 1970s. These occur near inhabited coastlines, where aquatic life is most concentrated. (The vast middle portions of the oceans which naturally have little life are not considered 'dead zones'). The term can also be applied to the identical phenomenon in large lakes.
Nitrification	Nitrification is the biological oxidation of ammonia with oxygen into nitrite followed by the oxidation of these nitrites into nitrates. Degradation of ammonia to nitrite is usually the rate limiting step of nitrification. Nitrification is an important step in the nitrogen cycle in soil.
Phosphorus cycle	The phosphorus cycle is the biogeochemical cycle that describes the movement of phosphorus through the lithosphere, hydrosphere, and biosphere. Unlike many other biogeochemical cycles, the atmosphere does not play a significant role in the movement of phosphorus, because phosphorus and phosphorus-based compounds are usually solids at the typical ranges of temperature and pressure found on Earth. The production of phosphine gas occurs only in specialized, local conditions.
Smog	Smog is a type of air pollution; the word 'smog' was coined in the early 20th century as a portmanteau of the words smoke and fog to refer to smoky fog. The word was then intended to refer to what was sometimes known as pea soup fog, a familiar and serious problem in London from the 19th century to the mid 20th century. This kind of smog is caused by the burning of large amounts of coal within a city; this smog contains soot particulates from smoke, sulfur dioxide and other components.
Groundwater	Groundwater is water located beneath the ground surface in soil pore spaces and in the fractures of rock formations. A unit of rock or an unconsolidated deposit is called an aquifer when it can yield a usable quantity of water. The depth at which soil pore spaces or fractures and voids in rock become completely saturated with water is called the water table.
Phosphorus	Phosphorus is a chemical element with symbol P and atomic number 15.

A multivalent nonmetal of the nitrogen group, phosphorus as a mineral is almost always present in its maximally oxidised state, as inorganic phosphate rocks. Elemental phosphorus exists in two major forms-white phosphorus and red phosphorus-but due to its high reactivity, phosphorus is never found as a free element on Earth.

The first form of elemental phosphorus to be produced (white phosphorus, in 1669) emits a faint glow upon exposure to oxygen - hence its name given from Greek mythology, meaning 'light-bearer', referring to the 'Morning Star', the planet Venus.

Sulfur cycle	The sulfur cycle is the collection of processes by which sulfur moves to and from minerals (including the waterways) and living systems. Such biogeochemical cycles are important in geology because they affect many minerals. Biogeochemical cycles are also important for life because sulfur is an essential element, being a constituent of many proteins and cofactors.
Transpiration	Transpiration is a process similar to evaporation. It is a part of the water cycle, and it is the loss of water vapor from parts of plants (similar to sweating), especially in leaves but also in stems, flowers and roots. Leaf surfaces are dotted with openings which are collectively called stomata, and in most plants they are more numerous on the undersides of the foliage.
Aerosol	Technically, an aerosol is a colloid suspension of fine solid particles or liquid droplets in a gas. Examples are clouds, and air pollution such as smog and smoke. In general conversation, aerosol usually refers to an aerosol spray can or the output of such a can.
Albedo	Albedo or reflection coefficient, derived from Latin albedo 'whiteness' (or reflected sunlight), in turn from albus 'white', is the diffuse reflectivity or reflecting power of a surface. It is defined as the ratio of reflected radiation from the surface to incident radiation upon it. Being a dimensionless fraction, it may also be expressed as a percentage, and is measured on a scale from zero for no reflecting power of a perfectly black surface, to 1 for perfect reflection of a white surface.
Glacier	A glacier is a large persistent body of ice that forms where the accumulation of snow exceeds its ablation (melting and sublimation) over many years, often centuries. At least 0.1 km² in area and 50 m thick, but often much larger, a glacier slowly deforms and flows due to stresses induced by its weight. Crevasses, seracs, and other distinguishing features of a glacier are due to its flow.
Ice sheet	An ice sheet a mass of glacier ice that covers surrounding terrain and greater than 50,000 km^2 (19,000 sq mi), thus also known as continental glacier. The only current ice sheets are in Antarctica and Greenland; during the last glacial period at Last Glacial Maximum (LGM) the Laurentide ice sheet covered much of North America, the Weichselian ice sheet covered northern Europe and the Patagonian Ice Sheet covered southern South America.

	Ice sheets are bigger than ice shelves or alpine glaciers. Masses of ice covering less than $50,000$ km^2 are termed an ice cap.
Insolation	Insolation is a measure of solar radiation energy received on a given surface area and recorded during a given time. It is also called solar irradiation and expressed as 'hourly irradiation' if recorded during an hour or 'daily irradiation' if recorded during a day. The unit recommended by the World Meteorological Organization is megajoules per square metre (MJ/m^2) or joules per square millimetre (J/mm^2) .
Mesosphere	The mesosphere refers to the mantle in the region between the asthenosphere and the outer core. The upper boundary is defined as the sharp increase in seismic wave velocities and density at a depth of 660 km. As depth increases, pressure builds and forces atoms into a denser, more rigid structure; thus the difference between mesosphere and asthenosphere is likely due to density and rigidity differences, that is, physical factors, and not to any difference in chemical composition.
Stratosphere	The stratosphere is the second major layer of Earth's atmosphere, just above the troposphere, and below the mesosphere. It is stratified in temperature, with warmer layers higher up and cooler layers farther down. This is in contrast to the troposphere near the Earth's surface, which is cooler higher up and warmer farther down.
Thermosphere	The thermosphere is the layer of the Earth's atmosphere directly above the mesosphere and directly below the exosphere. Within this layer, ultraviolet radiation causes ionization. The International Space Station has a stable orbit within the middle of the thermosphere, between 320 and 380 kilometres (200 and 240 mi).
Troposphere	The troposphere is the lowest portion of Earth's atmosphere. It contains approximately 75% of the atmosphere's mass and 99% of its water vapor and aerosols.
	The average depth of the troposphere is approximately 17 km (11 mi) in the middle latitudes.
Ozone layer	The ozone layer is a layer in Earth's atmosphere which contains relatively high concentrations of ozone (O_3). This layer absorbs 97-99% of the Sun's high frequency ultraviet light, which potentially damages the life forms on Earth. It is mainly located in the lower portion of the stratosphere from approximately 20 to 30 kilometres (12 to 19 mi) above Earth, though the thickness varies seasonally and geographically.
Atmospheric convection	Atmospheric convection is the result of a parcel-environment instability, or temperature difference, layer in the atmosphere. It is often responsible for adverse weather throughout the world.

Chapter 4. Ecosystems and the Physical Environment

Overview

There are a few general archetypes of atmospheric instability that correspond to convection and lack thereof.

Atmospheric circulation

Atmospheric circulation is the large-scale movement of air, and the means (together with the smaller ocean circulation) by which thermal energy is distributed on the surfe of the Earth.

The large-scale structure of the atmospheric circulation varies from year to year, but the basic climatological structure remains fairly constant. Individual weather systems - mid-latitude depressions, or tropical convective cells - occur 'randomly', and it is cepted that weather cannot be predicted beyond a fairly short limit: perhaps a month in theory, or (currently) about ten days in prtice.

Coriolis effect

In physics, the Coriolis effect is a deflection of moving objects when they are viewed in a rotating referen frame. In a referen frame with clockwise rotation, the deflection is to the left of the motion of the object; in one with counter-clockwise rotation, the deflection is to the right. The mathematical expression for the Coriolis for appeared in an 1835 paper by French scientist Gaspard-Gustave Coriolis, in connection with the theory of water wheels, and also in the tidal equations of Pierre-Simon Lapla in 1778. And even earlier, Italian scientists Giovanni Battista Riccioli and his assistant Fransco Maria Grimaldi described the effect in connection with artillery in the 1651 Almagestum Novum, writing that rotation of the Earth should cause a cannon ball fired to the north to deflect to the east.

Indian Ocean

The Indian Ocean is the third largest of the world's oceanic divisions, covering approximately 20% of the water on the Earth's surface. It is bounded by Asia-including India, after which the ocean is named-on the north, on the west by Africa, on the east by Australia, and on the south by the Southern Indian Ocean.

As one component of the World Indian Ocean, the Indian Ocean is delineated from the Atlantic Indian Ocean by the 20° east meridian running south from Cape Agulhas, and from the Pacific Indian Ocean by the meridian of 146°55' east.

Southern Ocean

The Southern Ocean comprises the southernmost waters of the World Southern Ocean, generally taken to be south of 60°S latitude and encircling Antarctica. As such, it is regarded as the fourth-largest of the five principal oceanic divisions (after the Pacific, Atlantic, and Indian Southern Oceans, but larger than the Arctic Southern Ocean). This ocean zone is where cold, northward flowing waters from the Antarctic mix with warmer subantarctic waters.

Trade wind	The trade winds (also called trades) are the prevailing pattern of easterly surface winds found in the tropics, within the lower portion of the Earth's atmosphere, in the lower section of the troposphere near the Earth's equator. The trade winds blow predominantly from the northeast in the Northern Hemisphere and from the southeast in the Southern Hemisphere, strengthening during the winter and when the Arctic oscillation is in its warm phase. Historically, the trade winds have been used by captains of sailing ships to cross the world's oceans for centuries, and enabled European empire expansion into the Americas and trade routes to become established across the Atlantic and Pacific oceans.
Westerlies	The Westerlies, anti-trades, or Prevailing Westerlies, are the prevailing winds in the middle latitudes between 30 and 60 degrees latitude, blowing from the high pressure area in the horse latitudes towards the poles. These prevailing winds blow from the west to the east, and steer extratropical cyclones in this general manner. Tropical cyclones which cross the subtropical ridge axis into the Westerlies recurve due to the increased westerly flow.
Gulf Stream	The Gulf Stream, together with its northern extension towards Europe, the North Atlantic Drift, is a powerful, warm, and swift Atlantic ocean current that originates at the tip of Florida, and follows the eastern coastlines of the United States and Newfoundland before crossing the Atlantic Ocean. The process of western intensification causes the Gulf Stream to be a northward accelerating current off the east coast of North America. At about , it splits in two, with the northern stream crossing to northern Europe and the southern stream recirculating off West Africa. The Gulf Stream influences the climate of the east coast of North America from Florida to Newfoundland, and the west coast of Europe. Although there has been recent debate, there is consensus that the climate of Western Europe and Northern Europe is warmer than it would otherwise be due to the North Atlantic drift, one of the branches from the tail of the Gulf Stream.
Greenland ice sheet	The Greenland Ice Sheet is a vast body of ice covering 1,710,000 square kilometres (660,235 sq mi), roughly 80% of the surface of Greenland. It is the second largest ice body in the world, after the Antarctic Ice Sheet. The ice sheet is almost 2,400 kilometres (1,500 mi) long in a north-south direction, and its greatest width is 1,100 kilometres (680 mi) at a latitude of 77°N, near its northern margin.
Hurricane	Hurricane! (episode: 1616 (308)) is a Nova episode that aired on November 7, 1989 on PBS. The episode describes the fury of a hurricane and the history of hurricane forecasting. The episode features footage of Hurricane Camille of 1969 and Hurricane Gilbert of 1988 and behind the scenes footage at the National Hurricane Center as forecasters tracked Hurricane Gilbert from its formation to its landfall in northern Mexico. Notable meteorologists, Hugh Willoughby, Bob Sheets (then director of the National Hurricane Center) and Jeff Masters were shown in the episode.

Chapter 4. Ecosystems and the Physical Environment

Upwelling	Upwelling is an oceanographic phenomenon that involves wind-driven motion of dense, cooler, and usually nutrient-rich water towards the ocean surface, replacing the warmer, usually nutrient-depleted surface water. The increased availability in upwelling regions results in high levels of primary productivity and thus fishery production. Approximately 25% of the total global marine fish catches come from five upwellings that occupy only 5% of the total ocean area.
Precipitation	Precipitation is the formation of a solid in a solution or inside another solid during a chemical reaction or by diffusion in a solid. When the reaction occurs in a liquid, the solid formed is called the Precipitate, or when compacted by a centrifuge, a pellet. The liquid remaining above the solid is in either case called the supernate or supernatant.
Rain shadow	A rain shadow is a dry area on the lee side of a mountainous area. The mountains block the passage of rain-producing weather systems, casting a 'shadow' of dryness behind them. As shown by the diagram to the right, the warm moist air is 'pulled' by the prevailing winds over a mountain.
Sahara	The Sahara is the world's hottest desert, the third largest desert after Antarctica and the Arctic. At over 9,400,000 square kilometres (3,600,000 sq mi), it covers most of North Africa, making it almost as large as China or the United States. The Sahara stretches from the Red Sea, including parts of the Mediterranean coasts, to the outskirts of the Atlantic Ocean.
Cyclone	In meteorology, a cyclone is an area of closed, circular fluid motion rotating in the same direction as the Earth. This is usually characterized by inward spiraling winds that rotate counterclockwise in the Northern Hemisphere and clockwise in the Southern Hemisphere of the Earth. Most large-scale cyclonic circulations are centered on areas of low atmospheric pressure.
Tornado	A tornado is a violent, dangerous, rotating column of air that is in contact with both the surface of the earth and a cumulonimbus cloud or, in rare cases, the base of a cumulus cloud. They are often referred to as a twister or a cyclone, although the word cyclone is used in meteorology in a wider sense, to name any closed low pressure circulation. Tornadoes come in many shapes and sizes, but are typically in the form of a visible condensation funnel, whose narrow end touches the earth and is often encircled by a cloud of debris and dust.
Typhoon	A typhoon is a mature tropical cyclone that develops in the northwestern part of the Pacific Ocean between 180° and 100°E. This region is referred to as the northwest Pacific basin. For organizational purposes, the northern Pacific Ocean is divided into three regions: the eastern (North America to 140°W), central (140°W to 180°), and western (180° to 100°E). Identical phenomena in the eastern north Pacific are called hurricanes, with tropical cyclones moving into the western Pacific re-designated as typhoons.

Tropical cyclone	A tropical cyclone is a storm system characterized by a low-pressure center and numerous thunderstorms that produce strong winds and heavy rain. Tropical cyclones strengthen when water evaporated from the ocean is released as the saturated air rises, resulting in condensation of water vapor contained in the moist air. They are fueled by a different heat mechanism than other cyclonic windstorms such as nor'easters, European windstorms, and polar lows.
Asthenosphere	The asthenosphere is the highly viscous mechanically weak ductilely-deforming region of the upper mantle of the Earth. It lies below the lithosphere, at depths between 100 and 200 km (~ 62 and 124 miles) below the surface, but perhaps extending as deep as 700 km (~ 435 miles). Characteristics The asthenosphere is a portion of the upper mantle just below the lithosphere that is involved in plate tectonic movements and isostatic adjustments.
Divergent boundary	In plate tectonics, a divergent boundary is a linear feature that exists between two tectonic plates that are moving away from each other. Divergent boundaries within continents initially produce rifts which produce rift valleys. Most active divergent plate boundaries occur between oceanic plates and exist as mid-oceanic ridges.
Lithosphere	The lithosphere is the rigid outermost shell of a rocky planet. On Earth, it comprises the crust and the portion of the upper mantle that behaves elastically on time scales of thousands of years or greater. Earth's lithosphere In the Earth the lithosphere includes the crust and the uppermost mantle, which constitute the hard and rigid outer layer of the Earth.
Mississippi River Delta	The Mississippi River Delta is the modern area of land (the river delta) built up by alluvium deposited by the Mississippi River as it slows down and enters the Gulf of Mexico. The deltaic process has, over the past 5,000 years, caused the coastline of south Louisiana to advance gulfward from 15 to 50 miles (24 to 80 km). It is a biologically significant region, comprising 3 million acres (12,000 km²) of coastal wetlands and 40% of the salt marsh in the contiguous United States.
Plate tectonics	Plate tectonics is a scientific theory which describes the large scale motions of Earth's lithosphere. The theory builds on the older concepts of continental drift, developed during the first decades of the 20th century (one of the most famous advocates was Alfred Wegener), and was accepted by the majority of the geoscientific community when the concepts of seafloor spreading were developed in the late 1950s and early 1960s.

Chapter 4. Ecosystems and the Physical Environment

Earthquake	An earthquake is the result of a sudden release of energy in the Earth's crust that creates seismic waves. The seismicity or seismic activity of an area refers to the frequency, type and size of earthquakes experienced over a period of time. Earthquakes are measured using observations from seismometers.
Himalayas	The Himalayas, is a mountain range immediately at the north of the Indian subcontinent. By extension, it is also the name of a massive mountain system that includes the Karakoram, the Hindu Kush, and other, lesser, ranges that extend out from the Pamir Knot.
	Together, the Himalayan mountain system is the world's highest, and home to the world's highest peaks, the Eight-thousanders, which include Mount Everest and K2. To comprehend the enormous scale of this mountain range, consider that Aconcagua, in the Andes, at 6,962 metres (22,841 ft) is the highest peak outside Asia, whereas the Himalayan system includes over 100 mountains exceeding 7,200 m (23,600 ft).
Mid-Atlantic Ridge	The Mid-Atlantic Ridge is a mid-ocean ridge, a divergent tectonic plate boundary located along the floor of the Atlantic Ocean, and part of the longest mountain range in the world. It separates the Eurasian Plate and North American Plate in the North Atlantic, and the African Plate from the South American Plate in the South Atlantic. The Ridge extends from a junction with the Gakkel Ridge (Mid-Arctic Ridge) northeast of Greenland southward to the Bouvet Triple Junction in the South Atlantic.
Seismic wave	Seismic waves are waves of energy that travel through the earth, for example as a result of an earthquake, explosion, or some other process that imparts low-frequency acoustic energy. Many other natural and anthropogenic sources create low amplitude waves commonly referred to as ambient vibrations. Seismic waves are studied by seismologists and geophysicists.
Mangrove	Mangroves are various kinds of trees up to medium height and shrubs that grow in saline coastal sediment habitats in the tropics and subtropics - mainly between latitudes 25° N and 25° S. The remaining mangrove forest areas of the world in 2000 was 53,190 square miles (137,760 km²) spanning 118 countries and territories. The word is used in at least three senses: (1) most broadly to refer to the habitat and entire plant assemblage or mangal, for which the terms mangrove forest biome, mangrove swamp and mangrove forest are also used, (2) to refer to all trees and large shrubs in the mangrove swamp, and (3) narrowly to refer to the mangrove family of plants, the Rhizophoraceae, or even more specifically just to mangrove trees of the genus Rhizophora. The term 'mangrove' comes to English from Spanish (perhaps by way of Portuguese), and is of Caribbean origin, likely Taíno.
Moment magnitude scale	The moment magnitude scale is used by seismologists to measure the size of earthquakes in terms of the energy released.

The magnitude is based on the seismic moment of the earthquake, which is equal to the rigidity of the Earth multiplied by the average amount of slip on the fault and the size of the area that slipped. The scale was developed in the 1970s to succeed the 1930s-era Richter magnitude scale (M_L).

Polar easterlies	The polar easterlies are the dry, cold prevailing winds that blow from the high-pressure areas of the polar highs at the north and south poles towards low-pressure areas within the Westerlies at high latitudes. Cold air subsides at the pole creating the high pressure, forcing an equatorward outflow of air; that outflow is then deflected westward by the Coriolis effect. Unlike the westerlies in the middle latitudes, the polar easterlies are often weak and irregular.
Prevailing winds	Prevailing winds are winds that blow predominantly from a single general direction over a particular point on Earth's surface. The dominant winds are the trends in direction of wind with the highest speed over a particular point on the Earth's surface. A region's prevailing and dominant winds are often affected by global patterns of movement in the Earth's atmosphere.
Tsunami	A tsunami, and at one time referred to as a tidal wave, is a series of water waves caused by the displacement of a large volume of a body of water, usually an ocean, though it can occur in large lakes. Tsunamis are a frequent occurrence in Japan; approximately 195 events have been recorded. Owing to the immense volumes of water and the high energy involved, tsunamis can devastate coastal regions.
Lava	Lava refers both to molten rock expelled by a volcano during an eruption and the resulting rock after solidification and cooling. This molten rock is formed in the interior of some planets, including Earth, and some of their satellites. When first erupted from a volcanic vent, lava is a liquid at temperatures from 700 to 1,200 °C (1,292 to 2,192 °F).
Magma	Magma is a mixture of molten or semi molten rock, volatiles and solids that is found beneath the surface of the Earth, and is expected to exist on other terrestrial planets. Besides molten rock, magma may also contain suspended crystals and dissolved gas and sometimes also gas bubbles. Magma often collects in magma chambers that may feed a volcano or turn into a pluton.

Chapter 4. Ecosystems and the Physical Environment

1. _____ is the chemical element with symbol C and atomic number 6. As a member of group 14 on the periodic table, it is nonmetallic and tetravalent-making four electrons available to form covalent chemical bonds. There are three naturally occurring isotopes, with ^{12}C and ^{13}C being stable, while ^{14}C is radioactive, decaying with a half-life of about 5,730 years. _____ is one of the few elements known since antiquity.

   a. nitrogen
   b. Juglone
   c. Carbon
   d. Citric acid cycle

2. _____ is the set of the metabolic reactions and processes that take place in the cells of organisms to convert biochemical energy from nutrients into adenosine triphosphate (ATP), and then release waste products. The reactions involved in respiration are catabolic reactions that involve the redox reaction (oxidation of one molecule and the reduction of another). Respiration is one of the key ways a cell gains useful energy to fuel cellular changes.

   a. Beta oxidation
   b. Cellular respiration
   c. Blood oxygen level
   d. Citric acid cycle

3. In ecology and Earth science, a _____ is a pathway by which a chemical element or molecule moves through both biotic (biosphere) and abiotic (lithosphere, atmosphere, and hydrosphere) compartments of Earth. A cycle is a series of change which comes back to the starting point and which can be repeated.

   The term 'biogeochemical' tells us that biological; geological and chemical factors are all involved.

   a. Biogeochemistry
   b. Biogeochemical cycle
   c. Carbon cycle
   d. Carbon-13

4. The _____ is the second major layer of Earth's atmosphere, just above the troposphere, and below the mesosphere. It is stratified in temperature, with warmer layers higher up and cooler layers farther down. This is in contrast to the troposphere near the Earth's surface, which is cooler higher up and warmer farther down.

   a. Trajectory
   b. Tropical Atlantic Variability
   c. Stratosphere
   d. Weather window

5. . The _____s (also called trades) are the prevailing pattern of easterly surface winds found in the tropics, within the lower portion of the Earth's atmosphere, in the lower section of the troposphere near the Earth's equator.

The _____s blow predominantly from the northeast in the Northern Hemisphere and from the southeast in the Southern Hemisphere, strengthening during the winter and when the Arctic oscillation is in its warm phase. Historically, the _____s have been used by captains of sailing ships to cross the world's oceans for centuries, and enabled European empire expansion into the Americas and trade routes to become established across the Atlantic and Pacific oceans.

a. Trade wind
b. Jet stream
c. Juglone
d. Reactive centrifugal force

1. c
2. b
3. b
4. c
5. a

You can take the complete Chapter Practice Test

for Chapter 4. Ecosystems and the Physical Environment
on all key terms, persons, places, and concepts.

Online 99 Cents

http://www.epub89.6.20924.4.cram101.com/

Use www.Cram101.com for all your study needs

including Cram101's online interactive problem solving labs in

chemistry, statistics, mathematics, and more.

Chapter 5. Ecosystems and Living Organisms

CHAPTER OUTLINE: KEY TERMS, PEOPLE, PLACES, CONCEPTS

- Endangered Species Act
- Adaptation
- Charles Darwin
- Natural selection
- Reproductive success
- Domain
- Population ecology
- Birth rate
- Population density
- Biotic potential
- Carrying capacity
- Great Smoky Mountains National Park
- Ecological niche
- Ecosystem
- Interspecific competition
- Intraspecific competition
- Coevolution
- Symbiosis
- Symbiodinium

_____ Commensalism

_____ Epiphyte

_____ Predation

_____ Insecticide

_____ Keystone species

_____ Keystone

_____ Coral reef

_____ Ecotone

_____ Species richness

_____ Ecosystem services

_____ Resilience

_____ Lake Victoria

_____ Nile perch

_____ Ozone depletion

_____ Stratosphere

_____ Climax community

_____ Ecological succession

_____ Primary succession

_____ Colony collapse disorder

Chapter 5. Ecosystems and Living Organisms

CHAPTER OUTLINE: KEY TERMS, PEOPLE, PLACES, CONCEPTS

	Climate change

CHAPTER HIGHLIGHTS & NOTES: KEY TERMS, PEOPLE, PLACES, CONCEPTS

Endangered Species Act	The Endangered Species Act of 1973 (Endangered Species Act; 7 U.S.C. § 136, 16 U.S.C. § 1531 et seq). is one of the dozens of United States environmental laws passed in the 1970s. Signed into law by President Richard Nixon on December 28, 1973, it was designed to protect critically imperiled species from extinction as a 'consequence of economic growth and development untempered by adequate concern and conservation.' The Act is administered by two federal agencies, the United States Fish and Wildlife Service (FWS) and the National Oceanic and Atmospheric Administration (NOAA).
Adaptation	An adaptation in biology is a trait with a current functional role in the life history of an organism that is maintained and evolved by means of natural selection. An adaptation refers to both the current state of being adapted and to the dynamic evolutionary process that leads to the adaptation. Adaptations contribute to the fitness and survival of individuals.
Charles Darwin	Charles Darwin, FRS (12 February 1809 - 19 April 1882) was an English naturalist. He established that all species of life have descended over time from common ancestors, and proposed the scientific theory that this branching pattern of evolution resulted from a process that he called natural selection, in which the struggle for existence has a similar effect to the artificial selection involved in selective breeding. Charles Darwin published his theory of evolution with compelling evidence in his 1859 book On the Origin of Species, overcoming scientific rejection of earlier concepts of transmutation of species.
Natural selection	Natural selection is the gradual, non-random, process by which biological traits become either more or less common in a population as a function of differential reproduction of their bearers. It is a key mechanism of evolution. Variation exists within all populations of organisms.

Chapter 5. Ecosystems and Living Organisms

Reproductive success	Reproductive success is defined as the passing of genes onto the next generation in a way that they too can pass on those genes. In practice, this is often a tally of the number of offspring produced by an individual. A more correct definition, which incorporates inclusive fitness, is the relative production of fertile offspring by a genotype.
Domain	In mathematical analysis, a domain is any connected open subset of a finite-dimensional vector space. This is a different concept than the domain of a function, though it is often used for that purpose, for example in partial differential equations and Sobolev spaces.
	Various degrees of smoothness of the boundary of the domain are required for various properties of functions defined on the domain to hold, such as integral theorems (Green's theorem, Stokes theorem), properties of Sobolev spaces, and to define measures on the boundary and spaces of traces (spaces of smooth functions defined on the boundary).
Population ecology	Population ecology is a major sub-field of ecology that deals with the dynamics of species populations and how these populations interact with the environment. It is the study of how the population sizes of species living together in groups change over time and space.
	The development of population ecology owes much to demography and actuarial life tables.
Birth rate	The birth rate is typically the rate of births in a population over time. The rate of births in a population is calculated in several ways: live births from a universal registration system for births, deaths, and marriages; population counts from a census, and estimation through specialized demographic techniques. The birth rate are used to calculate population growth.
Population density	Population density is a measurement of population per unit area or unit volume. It is frequently applied to living organisms, and particularly to humans. It is a key geographic term.
Biotic potential	Biotic potential is the maximum reproductive capacity of a population if resources are unlimited. Full expression of the biotic potential of an organism is restricted by environmental resistance, any condition that inhibits the increase in number of the population. It is generally only reached when environmental conditions are very favorable.
Carrying capacity	The carrying capacity of a biological species in an environment is the maximum population size of the species that the environment can sustain indefinitely, given the food, habitat, water and other necessities available in the environment. In population biology, carrying capacity is defined as the environment's maximal load, which is different from the concept of population equilibrium.

Chapter 5. Ecosystems and Living Organisms

Great Smoky Mountains National Park	Great Smoky Mountains National Park is a United States National Park and UNESCO World Heritage Site that straddles the ridgeline of the Great Smoky Mountains, part of the Blue Ridge Mountains, which are a division of the larger Appalachian Mountain chain. The border between Tennessee and North Carolina runs northeast to southwest through the centerline of the park. It is the most visited national park in the United States.
Ecological niche	In ecology, a niche is a term describing the relational position of a species or population in its ecosystem to each other; e.g. a dolphin could pottially be in another ecological niche from one that travels in a differt pod if the members of these pods utilize significantly differt food resources and foraging methods. A shorthand definition of niche is how an organism makes a living. The ecological niche describes how an organism or population responds to the distribution of resources and competitors (e.g., by growing wh resources are abundant, and wh predators, parasites and pathogs are scarce) and how it in turn alters those same factors (e.g., limiting access to resources by other organisms, acting as a food source for predators and a consumer of prey).
Ecosystem	An ecosystem is a community of living organisms (plants, animals and microbes) in conjunction with the nonliving components of their environment (things like air, water and mineral soil), interacting as a system. These components are regarded as linked together through nutrient cycles and energy flows. As ecosystems are defined by the network of interactions among organisms, and between organisms and their environment, they can come in any size but usually encompass specific, limited spaces (although some scientists say that the entire planet is an ecosystem).
Interspecific competition	Interspecific competition, in ecology, is a form of competition in which individuals of different species compete for the same resource in an ecosystem (e.g. food or living space). The other form of competition is intraspecific competition, which involves organisms of the same species. If a tree species in a dense forest grows taller than surrounding tree species, it is able to absorb more of the incoming sunlight.
Intraspecific competition	Intraspecific competition is a particular form of competition in which members of the same species vie for the same resource in an ecosystem (e.g. food, light, nutrients, space). This can be contrasted with interspecific competition, in which different species compete. For example, two trees of the same species growing close together will compete for light, water and nutrients in the soil.

Chapter 5. Ecosystems and Living Organisms

Coevolution	In biology, coevolution is 'the change of a biological object triggered by the change of a related object.' Coevolution can occur at many biological levels: it can be as microscopic as correlated mutations between amino acids in a protein, or as macroscopic as covarying traits between different species in an environment. Each party in a coevolutionary relationship exerts selective pressures on the other, thereby affecting each other's evolution. Coevolution of different species includes the evolution of a host species and its parasites (host-parasite coevolution), and examples of mutualism evolving through time.
Symbiosis	The biological term Symbiosis was adopted for chemistry by Jøergensen in 1964, who applied it to the process by which, say, a hard ligand on a metal predisposes the metal to receive another hard ligand rather than a soft ligand. In fact, two superficially antithetical phenomena occur: symbiosis and antisymbiosis. This is found principally with soft metals.
Symbiodinium	The genus Symbiodinium encompasses the largest and most prevalent group of endosymbiotic dinoflagellates known to science. These unicellular algae commonly reside in the endoderm of tropical cnidarians such as corals, sea anemones, and jellyfish, where they translocate products of photosynthesis to the host and in turn receive inorganic nutrients (e.g. CO_2, NH_4^+) (Fig. 1). They are also harbored by various species of sponges, flatworms, mollusks (e.g. giant clams), foraminifera (soritids), and some ciliates.
Commensalism	In ecology, commensalism is a class of relationship between two organisms where one organism benefits but the other is neutral (there is no harm or benefit). There are two other types of association: mutualism (where both organisms benefit) and parasitism (one organism benefits and the other one is harmed). Originally, the term was used to describe the use of waste food by second animals, like the carcass eaters that follow hunting animals, but wait until they have finished their meal.
Epiphyte	An epiphyte is a plant that grows upon another plant (such as a tree) non-parasitically or sometimes upon some other object (such as a building or a telegraph wire), derives its moisture and nutrients from the air and rain and sometimes from debris accumulating around it. Epiphytes are usually found in the temperate zone (e.g., many mosses, liverworts, lichens and algae) or in the tropics (e.g., many ferns, cacti, orchids, and bromeliads). Epiphyte is one of the subdivisions of the Raunkiær system.
Predation	In ecology, predation describes a biological interaction where a predator (an organism that is hunting) feeds on its prey (the organism that is attacked). Predators may or may not kill their prey prior to feeding on them, but the act of predation always results in the death of its prey and the eventual absorption of the prey's tissue through consumption.

Insecticide	An insecticide is a pesticide used against insects. They include ovicides and larvicides used against the eggs and larvae of insects respectively. Insecticides are used in agriculture, medicine, industry and the household.
Keystone species	A keystone species is a species that has a disproportionately large effect on its environment relative to its abundance. Such species play a critical role in maintaining the structure of an ecological community, affecting many other organisms in an ecosystem and helping to determine the types and numbers of various other species in the community. The role that a keystone species plays in its ecosystem is analogous to the role of a keystone in an arch.
Keystone	Keystone refers to a type of limestone, or coral rag, quarried in the Florida Keys, in particular from Windley Key fossil quarry, which is now a State Park of Florida. The limestone is Pleistocene in age, and the rock primarily consists of scleractinian coral, such as Elkhorn coral and Brain coral. The Hurricane Monument, commemorating victims of the Labor Day Hurricane of 1935, and located at mile marker 82 on US Route 1 near Islamorada, is constructed of keystone, as is the David W. Dyer Federal Building and United States Courthouse.
Coral reef	Coral reefs are underwater structures made from calcium carbonate secreted by corals. Corals are colonies of tiny living animals found in marine waters that contain few nutrients. Most coral reefs are built from stony corals, which in turn consist of polyps that cluster in groups.
Ecotone	An ecotone is a transition area between two biomes but different patches of the landscape, such as forest and grassland. It may be narrow or wide, and it may be local (the zone between a field and forest) or regional (the transition between forest and grassland ecosystems). An ecotone may appear on the ground as a gradual blending of the two communities across a broad area, or it may manifest itself as a sharp boundary line.
Species richness	Species richness is the number of different species in a given area. It is represented in equation form as S. Species richness is the fundamental unit in which to assess the homogeneity of an environment. Typically, species richness is used in conservation studies to determine the sensitivity of ecosystems and their resident species. The actual number of species calculated alone is largely an arbitrary number. These studies, therefore, often develop a rubric or measure for valuing the species richness number(s) or adopt one from previous studies on similar ecosystems.

Chapter 5. Ecosystems and Living Organisms

Ecosystem services	Humankind benefits from a multitude of resources and processes that are supplied by natural ecosystems. Collectively, these benefits are known as ecosystem services and include products like clean drinking water and processes such as the decomposition of wastes. While scientists and environmentalists have discussed ecosystem services for decades, these services were popularized and their definitions formalized by the United Nations 2004 Millennium Ecosystem Assessment (MA), a four-year study involving more than 1,300 scientists worldwide.
Resilience	Resilience is the ability of a material to absorb energy when it is deformed elastically, and release that energy upon unloading. The modulus of resilience is defined as the maximum energy that can be absorbed per unit volume without creating a permanent distortion. It can be calculated by integrating the stress-strain curve from zero to the elastic limit.
Lake Victoria	Lake Victoria is one of the African Great Lakes. The lake was named after Queen Victoria of the United Kingdom, by John Hanning Speke, the first European to discover this lake. With a surface area of 68,800 square kilometres (26,600 sq mi), Lake Victoria is Africa's largest lake by area, and it is the largest tropical lake in the world.
Nile perch	The Nile perch is a species of freshwater fish in family Latidae of order Perciformes. The introduction of this species to Lake Victoria is one of the most commonly cited examples of the negative effects invasive alien species can have on ecosystems. The Nile perch was introduced to Lake Victoria in East Africa in the 1950s, and has since been fished commercially. It is attributed with causing the extinction or near-extinction of several hundred native species, but as Nile perch stocks decrease due to commercial fishing, at least some of them are making a comeback.
Ozone depletion	Ozone depletion describes two distinct but related phenomena observed since the late 1970s: a steady decline of about 4% per decade in the total volume of ozone in Earth's stratosphere (the ozone layer), and a much larger springtime decrease in stratospheric ozone over Earth's polar regions. The latter phenomenon is referred to as the ozone hole. In addition to these well-known stratospheric phenomena, there are also springtime polar tropospheric ozone depletion events.
Stratosphere	The stratosphere is the second major layer of Earth's atmosphere, just above the troposphere, and below the mesosphere. It is stratified in temperature, with warmer layers higher up and cooler layers farther down. This is in contrast to the troposphere near the Earth's surface, which is cooler higher up and warmer farther down.
Climax community	In ecology, a climax community, is a biological community of plants and animals which, through the process of ecological succession -- the development of vegetation in an area over time -- has reached a steady state.

This equilibrium occurs because the climax community is composed of species best adapted to average conditions in that area. The term is sometimes also applied in soil development.

Ecological succession	Ecological succession, is the phenomenon or process by which an ecological community undergoes more or less orderly and predictable changes following disturbance or initial colonization of new habitat. Succession was among the first theories advanced in ecology and the study of succession remains at the core of ecological science. Succession may be initiated either by formation of new, unoccupied habitat (e.g., a lava flow or a severe landslide) or by some form of disturbance (e.g. fire, severe windthrow, logging) of an existing community.
Primary succession	Primary succession is one of two types of biological and ecological succession of plant life, occurring in an environment in which new substrate devoid of vegetation and usually lacking soil, such as a lava flow or area left from retreated glacier, is deposited. In other words, it is the gradual growth of an ecosystem over a longer period of time. In contrast, secondary succession occurs on substrate that previously supported vegetation before an ecological disturbance such as forest fire, tsunami, flood, destroyed the plant life.
Colony collapse disorder	Colony collapse disorder is a phenomenon in which worker bees from a beehive or European honey bee colony abruptly disappear. While such disappearances have occurred throughout the history of apiculture, the term colony collapse disorder was first applied to a drastic rise in the number of disappearances of Western honey bee colonies in North America in late 2006. Colony collapse is significant economically because many agricultural crops worldwide are pollinated by bees; and ecologically, because of the major role that bees play in the reproduction of plant communities in the wild. European beekeepers observed similar phenomena in Belgium, France, the Netherlands, Greece, Italy, Portugal, and Spain, and initial reports have also come in from Switzerland and Germany, albeit to a lesser degree while the Northern Ireland Assembly received reports of a decline greater than 50%.
Climate change	Climate change is a significant and lasting change in the statistical distribution of weather patterns over periods ranging from decades to millions of years. It may be a change in average weather conditions or the distribution of events around that average (e.g., more or fewer extreme weather events). Climate change may be limited to a specific region or may our across the whole Earth.

Chapter 5. Ecosystems and Living Organisms

1. _____ is a United States National Park and UNESCO World Heritage Site that straddles the ridgeline of the Great Smoky Mountains, part of the Blue Ridge Mountains, which are a division of the larger Appalachian Mountain chain. The border between Tennessee and North Carolina runs northeast to southwest through the centerline of the park. It is the most visited national park in the United States.

   a. Grizzly Creek Redwoods State Park
   b. Gwaii Haanas National Park Reserve and Haida Heritage Site
   c. Hartwick Pines State Park
   d. Great Smoky Mountains National Park

2. The _____ is the second major layer of Earth's atmosphere, just above the troposphere, and below the mesosphere. It is stratified in temperature, with warmer layers higher up and cooler layers farther down. This is in contrast to the troposphere near the Earth's surface, which is cooler higher up and warmer farther down.

   a. Trajectory
   b. Tropical Atlantic Variability
   c. Vapor pressure
   d. Stratosphere

3. An _____ in biology is a trait with a current functional role in the life history of an organism that is maintained and evolved by means of natural selection. An _____ refers to both the current state of being adapted and to the dynamic evolutionary process that leads to the _____. _____s contribute to the fitness and survival of individuals.

   a. Adaptation
   b. Odyssey
   c. Endangered Species Act
   d. United Nations Framework Convention on Climate Change

4. _____ is defined as the passing of genes onto the next generation in a way that they too can pass on those genes. In practice, this is often a tally of the number of offspring produced by an individual. A more correct definition, which incorporates inclusive fitness, is the relative production of fertile offspring by a genotype.

   a. Juglone
   b. Reproductive success
   c. Krakatoa
   d. Diesel engine

5. . _____ is a particular form of competition in which members of the same species vie for the same resource in an ecosystem (e.g. food, light, nutrients, space). This can be contrasted with interspecific competition, in which different species compete.

   For example, two trees of the same species growing close together will compete for light, water and nutrients in the soil.

   a. Intraspecific competition

Chapter 5. Ecosystems and Living Organisms

b. Odyssey

c. Endangered Species Act

d. Ecological trap

1. d

2. d

3. a

4. b

5. a

You can take the complete Chapter Practice Test

for Chapter 5. Ecosystems and Living Organisms
on all key terms, persons, places, and concepts.

Online 99 Cents

http://www.epub89.6.20924.5.cram101.com/

Use www.Cram101.com for all your study needs

including Cram101's online interactive problem solving labs in

chemistry, statistics, mathematics, and more.

_____ | Grassland

_____ | Wildfire

_____ | Chaparral

_____ | Alpine tundra

_____ | Biome

_____ | Tundra

_____ | Albedo

_____ | Arctic tundra

_____ | Permafrost

_____ | Taiga

_____ | Monoculture

_____ | Leaching

_____ | Temperate deciduous forest

_____ | Mediterranean sea

_____ | Mediterranean climate

_____ | Soil conservation

_____ | Desertification

_____ | Epiphyte

_____ | Tropics

Chapter 6. Major Ecosystems of the World

———————— Aquatic ecosystem

———————— Benthos

———————— Food web

———————— Freshwater ecosystem

———————— Nekton

———————— Phytoplankton

———————— River continuum concept

———————— Salinity

———————— Zooplankton

———————— Floodplain

———————— Littoral zone

———————— Salt marsh

———————— Tributary

———————— Algal bloom

———————— Eutrophication

———————— Limnetic zone

———————— Thermocline

———————— Ecosystem services

———————— Wetland

Chapter 6. Major Ecosystems of the World

CHAPTER OUTLINE: KEY TERMS, PEOPLE, PLACES, CONCEPTS

_____ | Estuary

_____ | Intertidal zone

_____ | Marine ecosystem

_____ | Coral reef

_____ | Fringing reef

_____ | Great Barrier Reef

_____ | Kelp forest

_____ | Symbiodinium

_____ | Atoll

_____ | Coral bleaching

_____ | Marine snow

_____ | Stewardship

Chapter 6. Major Ecosystems of the World

Grassland	Grasslands are areas where the vegetation is dominated by grasses (Poaceae) and other herbaceous (non-woody) plants (forbs). However, sedge (Cyperaceae) and rush (Juncaceae) families can also be found. Grasslands occur naturally on all continents except Antarctica. In temperate latitudes, such as northwestern Europe and the Great Plains and California in North America, native grasslands are dominated by perennial bunch grass species, whereas in warmer climates annual species form a greater component of the vegetation.
Wildfire	A wildfire is any uncontrolled fire in combustible vegetation that occurs in the countryside or a wilderness area. Other names such as brush fire, bushfire, forest fire, desert fire, grass fire, hill fire, peat fire, vegetation fire, and veldfire may be used to describe the same phenomenon depending on the type of vegetation being burned. A wildfire differs from other fires by its extensive size, the speed at which it can spread out from its original source, its potential to change direction unexpectedly, and its ability to jump gaps such as roads, rivers and fire breaks.
Chaparral	Chaparral is a shrubland or heathland plant community found primarily in the U.S. state of California and in the northern portion of the Baja California peninsula, Mexico. It is shaped by a Mediterranean climate (mild, wet winters and hot dry summers) and wildfire, having summer drought-tolerant plants with hard sclerophyllous evergreen leaves, as contrasted with the associated soft leaved, drought deciduous, scrub community of Coastal sage scrub, found below the chaparral biome. Chaparral covers 5% of the state of California, and associated Mediterranean scrubland an additional 3.5%.
Alpine tundra	Alpine tundra is a type of tundra that does not contain trees because it is at high altitude. Alpine tundra is distinguished from arctic tundra, because alpine soils are generally better drained than arctic soils. Alpine tundra transitions to subalpine forests below the tree line; stunted forests occurring at the forest-tundra ecotone are known as Krummholz.
Biome	Biomes are climatically and geographically defined as similar climatic conditions on the Earth, such as communities of plants, animals, and soil organisms, and are often referred to as ecosystems. Some parts of the earth have more or less the same kind of abiotic and biotic factors spread over a large area, creating a typical ecosystem over that area. Such major ecosystems are termed as biomes.
Tundra	In physical geography, tundra is a biome where the tree growth is hindered by low temperatures and short growing seasons. The term tundra comes through Russian тундра from the Kildin Sami word tundâr 'uplands,' 'treeless mountain tract.' There are three types of tundra: Arctic tundra, alpine tundra, and Antarctic tundra. In tundra, the vegetation is composed of dwarf shrubs, sedges and grasses, mosses, and lichens.
Albedo	Albedo or reflection coefficient, derived from Latin albedo 'whiteness' (or reflected sunlight), in turn from albus 'white', is the diffuse reflectivity or reflecting power of a surface.

	It is defined as the ratio of reflected radiation from the surface to incident radiation upon it. Being a dimensionless fraction, it may also be expressed as a percentage, and is measured on a scale from zero for no reflecting power of a perfectly black surface, to 1 for perfect reflection of a white surface.
Arctic tundra	In physical geography, tundra is a biome where the tree growth is hindered by low temperatures and short growing seasons. The term tundra comes through Russian тундра from the Kildin Sami word tundâr 'uplands', 'treeless mountain tract'. There are three types of tundra: Arctic tundra, alpine tundra, and Antarctic tundra. Arctic tundra occurs in the far Northern Hemisphere, north of the taiga belt. The word 'tundra' usually refers only to the areas where the subsoil is permafrost, or permanently frozen soil. Permafrost tundra includes vast areas of northern Russia and Canada.
Permafrost	In geology, permafrost is soil at or below the freezing point of water 0 °C (32 °F) for two or more years. Ice is not always present, as may be in the case of nonporous bedrock, but it frequently occurs and it may be in amounts exceeding the potential hydraulic saturation of the ground material. Most permafrost is located in high latitudes (i.e. land close to the North and South poles), but alpine permafrost may exist at high altitudes in much lower latitudes.
Taiga	Taiga, is a biome characterized by coniferous forests. Taiga is the world's largest terrestrial biome. In North America it covers most of inland Canada and Alaska as well as parts of the extreme northern continental United States and is known as the Northwoods.
Monoculture	Monoculture is the agricultural practice of producing or growing one single crop over a wide area. It is also known as a way of farming practice of growing large stands of a single species. It is widely used in modern industrial agriculture and its implementation has allowed for large harvests from minimal labor.
Leaching	Leaching Many Biological organic and inorganic substances occur in a mixture of different components in a solid. In order to separate the desired solute constituent or remove an undesirable solute component from the solid phase, the solid is brought into contact with a liquid. The solid and liquid are in contact and the solute or solutes can diffuse from the solid into the solvent, resulting in separation of the components originally in the solid.
Temperate deciduous forest	A temperate deciduous forest, more precisely termed temperate broadleaf forest or temperate broadleaved forest, is a biome found in the eastern and western United States, Canada, central Mexico, southern South America, Europe, West Asia, China, Japan, North Korea, South Korea and parts of Russia.

Chapter 6. Major Ecosystems of the World

A temperate deciduous forest consists of trees that lose their leaves every year. Examples include oak, maple, beech, and elm.

Mediterranean sea	In oceanography, a mediterranean sea is a mostly enclosed sea that has limited exchange of water with outer oceans and where the water circulation is dominated by salinity and temperature differences rather than winds. The mediterranean seas of the Atlantic Ocean •The Mediterranean Sea (or the Eurafrican Mediterranean Sea or the European Mediterranean Sea): including the Black Sea, the Sea of Azov, the Aegean Sea, the Adriatic Sea, the Ligurian Sea, the Balearic Sea, the Tyrrhenian Sea, the Ionian Sea, and the Sea of Marmara.•The Arctic Ocean (or the Arctic Mediterranean Sea, considered an ocean by many)•The American Mediterranean Sea: the combination of the Gulf of Mexico and the Caribbean Sea.•The Baltic Sea•Baffin BayThe mediterranean seas of the Indian Ocean •The Persian Gulf•The Red SeaThe mediterranean sea between the Indian and Pacific Oceans •The Australasian Mediterranean Sea: the sea enclosed by the Sunda Islands and the Philippines, including the Banda Sea, the Sulu Sea, the Sulawesi Sea, the Java Sea, etc.Types of mediterranean seas There are two types of mediterranean seaConcentration basin •A concentration basin has a higher salinity than the outer ocean due to evaporation, and its water exchange consists of inflow of the fresher oceanic water in the upper layer and outflow of the saltier mediterranean water in the lower layer of the connecting channel.
Mediterranean climate	A Mediterranean climate is the climate typical of most of the lands in the Mediterranean Basin as part of subtropical climate. Worldwide, this is where the largest area of this climate type is found. Beyond the Mediterranean area, this climatic type prevails in much of California, in parts of Western and South Australia, in southwestern South Africa, in isolated sections of Central Asia, and in parts of central Chile.
Soil conservation	Soil conservation is a set of management strategies for prevention of soil being eroded from the Earth's surface or becoming chemically altered by overuse, acidification, salinization or other chemical soil contamination. It is a component of environmental soil ience. Decisions regarding appropriate crop rotation, cover crops, and planted windbreaks are central to the ability of surface soils to retain their integrity, both with respect to erosive forces and chemical change from nutrient depletion.
Desertification	Desertification is the degradation of land in any drylands. Caused by a variety of factors, such as climate change and human activities, desertification is one of the most significant global environmental problems.

Epiphyte	An epiphyte is a plant that grows upon another plant (such as a tree) non-parasitically or sometimes upon some other object (such as a building or a telegraph wire), derives its moisture and nutrients from the air and rain and sometimes from debris accumulating around it. Epiphytes are usually found in the temperate zone (e.g., many mosses, liverworts, lichens and algae) or in the tropics (e.g., many ferns, cacti, orchids, and bromeliads). Epiphyte is one of the subdivisions of the Raunkiær system.
Tropics	The tropics is a region of the Earth surrounding the Equator. It is limited in latitude by the Tropic of Cancer in the northern hemisphere at approximately 23° 26′ 16″ (or 23.4378°) N and the Tropic of Capricorn in the southern hemisphere at 23° 26′ 16″ (or 23.4378°) S; these latitudes correspond to the axial tilt of the Earth. The tropics are also referred to as the tropical zone and the torrid zone .
Aquatic ecosystem	An aquatic ecosystem is an ecosystem in a body of water. Communities of organisms that are dependent on each other and on their environment live in aquatic ecosystems. The two main types of aquatic ecosystems are marine ecosystems and freshwater ecosystems.
Benthos	Benthos is the community of organisms which live on, in, or near the seabed, also known as the benthic zone. This community lives in or near marine sedimentary environments, from tidal pools along the foreshore, out to the continental shelf, and then down to the abyssal depths. Many organisms adapted to deep-water pressure cannot survive in the upper parts of the water column.
Food web	A food web depicts feeding connections (what eats what) in an ecological community. Ecologists can broadly lump all life forms into one of two categories called trophic levels: 1) the autotrophs, and 2) the heterotrophs. To maintain their bodies, grow, develop, and to reproduce, autotrophs produce organic matter from inorganic substances, including both minerals and gases such as carbon dioxide.
Freshwater ecosystem	Freshwater ecosystems are a subset of Earth's aquatic ecosystems. They include lakes and ponds, rivers, streams and springs, and wetlands. They can be contrasted with marine ecosystems, which have a larger salt content.
Nekton	Nekton refers to the aggregate of actively swimming aquatic organisms in a body of water (usually oceans or lakes) able to move independently of water currents. Nekton are contrasted with plankton which refers to the aggregate of passively floating, drifting, or somewhat motile organisms occurring in a body of water, primarily comprising tiny algae and bacteria, small eggs and larvae of marine organisms, and protozoa and other minute predators.

Chapter 6. Major Ecosystems of the World

Phytoplankton	Phytoplankton are the autotrophic component of the plankton community. Most phytoplankton are too small to be individually seen with the unaided eye. However, when present in high enough numbers, they may appear as a green discoloration of the water due to the presence of chlorophyll within their cells (although the actual color may vary with the species of phytoplankton present due to varying levels of chlorophyll or the presence of accessory pigments such as phycobiliproteins, xanthophylls, etc.).
River continuum concept	The River Continuum Concept is a model for classifying and describing flowing water, in addition to the classification of individual sections of waters after the occurrence of indicator organisms. The theory is based on the concept of dynamic equilibrium in which streamforms balance between physical parameters, such as width, depth, velocity, and sediment load, also taking into account biological factors. It offers the introduction to map out pure living communities, but also an explanation for their sequence in individual sections of water.
Salinity	Salinity is the saltiness or dissolved salt content of a body of water. It is a general term used to describe the levels of different salts such as sodium chloride, magnesium and calcium sulfates, and bicarbonates. Salinity in Australian English and North American English may also refer to the salt content of soil .
Zooplankton	Zooplankton are heterotrophic (sometimes detritivorous) plankton. Plankton are organisms drifting in oceans, seas, and bodies of fresh water. Zooplankton is a categorisation spanning a range of organism sizes including small protozoans and large metazoans. It includes holoplanktonic organisms whose complete life cycle lies within the plankton, as well as meroplanktonic organisms that spend part of their lives in the plankton before graduating to either the nekton or a sessile, benthic existence.
Floodplain	A floodplain, is a flat or nearly flat land adjacent a stream or river that stretches from the banks of its channel to the base of the enclosing valley walls and experiences flooding during periods of high discharge. It includes the floodway, which consists of the stream channel and adjacent areas that carry flood flows, and the flood fringe, which are areas covered by the flood, but which do not experience a strong current. In other words, a floodplain is an area near a river or a stream which floods easily.
Littoral zone	The littoral zone is that part of a sea, lake or river that is close to the shore. In coastal environments the littoral zone extends from the high water mark, which is rarely inundated, to shoreline areas that are permanently submerged. It always includes this intertidal zone and is often used to mean the same as the intertidal zone.
Salt marsh	A salt marsh, is a coastal ecosystem in the upper coastal intertidal zone between land and open salt water or brackish water that is regularly flooded by the tides.

It is dominated by dense stands of salt-tolerant plants such as herbs, grasses, or low shrubs. These plants are terrestrial in origin and are essential to the stability of the salt marsh in trapping and binding sediments.

Tributary	A tributary is a stream or river that flows into a main stem (or parent) river or a lake. A tributary does not flow directly into a sea or ocean. Tributaries and the mainstem river serve to drain the surrounding drainage basin of its surface water and groundwater by leading the water out into an ocean or sea.
Algal bloom	An algal bloom is a rapid increase or accumulation in the population of algae in an aquatic system. Algal blooms may occur in freshwater as well as marine environments. Typically, only one or a small number of phytoplankton species are involved, and some blooms may be recognized by discoloration of the water resulting from the high density of pigmented cells.
Eutrophication	Eutrophication, is the ecosystem response to the addition of artificial or natural substances, such as nitrates and phosphates, through fertilizers or sewage, to an aquatic system. One example is the 'bloom' or great increase of phytoplankton in a water body as a response to increased levels of nutrients. Negative environmental effects include hypoxia, the depletion of oxygen in the water, which induces reductions in specific fish and other animal populations.
Limnetic zone	The limnetic zone is the well-lit, open surface waters in a lake, away from the shore. The vegetation of the littoral zone surrounds this expanse of open water and it is above the profundal zone. It can be defined as the lighted surface waters in the area where the lake bottom is too deep and unlit to support rooted aquatic plants.
Thermocline	A thermocline is a thin but distinct layer in a large body of fluid (e.g. water, such as an ocean or lake, or air, such as an atmosphere), in which temperature changes more rapidly with depth than it does in the layers above or below. In the ocean, the thermocline may be thought of as an invisible blanket which separates the upper mixed layer from the calm deep water below. Depending largely on season, latitude and turbulent mixing by wind, thermoclines may be a semi-permanent feature of the body of water in which they occur, or they may form temporarily in response to phenomena such as the radiative heating/cooling of surface water during the day/night.
Ecosystem services	Humankind benefits from a multitude of resources and processes that are supplied by natural ecosystems. Collectively, these benefits are known as ecosystem services and include products like clean drinking water and processes such as the decomposition of wastes.

Chapter 6. Major Ecosystems of the World

Wetland	A wetland is a land area that is saturated with water, either permanently or seasonally, such that it takes on characteristics that distinguish it as a distinct ecosystem. The primary factor that distinguishes wetlands is the characteristic vegetation that is adapted to its unique soil conditions: Wetlands are made up primarily of hydric soil, which supports aquatic plants. The water found in wetlands can be saltwater, freshwater, or brackish.
Estuary	An estuary is a partly enclosed coastal body of water with one or more rivers or streams flowing into it, and with a free connection to the open sea. Estuaries form a transition zone between river environments and ocean environments and are subject to both marine influences, such as tides, waves, and the influx of saline water; and riverine influences, such as flows of fresh water and sediment. The inflow of both seawater and freshwater provide high levels of nutrients in both the water column and sediment, making estuaries among the most productive natural habitats in the world.
Intertidal zone	The intertidal zone is the area that is above water at low tide and under water at high tide (for example, the area between tide marks). This area can include many different types of habitats, with many types of animals like starfish, sea urchins, and some species of coral. The well known area also includes steep rocky cliffs, sandy beaches, or wetlands (e.g., vast mudflats).
Marine ecosystem	Marine ecosystems are among the largest of Earth's aquatic ecosystems. They include oceans, salt marsh and intertidal ecology, estuaries and lagoons, mangroves and coral reefs, the deep sea and the sea floor. They can be contrasted with freshwater ecosystems, which have a lower salt content. Marine waters cover two-thirds of the surface of the Earth. Such places are considered ecosystems because the plant life supports the animal life and vice-versa.
Coral reef	Coral reefs are underwater structures made from calcium carbonate secreted by corals. Corals are colonies of tiny living animals found in marine waters that contain few nutrients. Most coral reefs are built from stony corals, which in turn consist of polyps that cluster in groups.
Fringing reef	A fringing reef is one of the three main types of coral reefs recognized by most coral reef scientists. It is distinguished from the other two main types (barrier reefs and atolls) in that it has either an entirely shallow backreef zone (lagoon) or none at all. If a fringing reef grows directly from the shoreline the reef flat extends right to the beach and there is no backreef.
Great Barrier Reef	The Great Barrier Reef is the world's largest reef system composed of over 2,900 individual reefs and 900 islands stretching for over 2,600 kilometres (1,600 mi) over an area of approximately 344,400 square kilometres (133,000 sq mi). The reef is located in the Coral Sea, off the coast of Queensland in north-east Australia.

Kelp forest	Kelp forests are underwater areas with a high density of kelp. They are recognized as one of the most productive and dynamic ecosystems on Earth. Smaller areas of anchored kelp are called kelp beds.
Symbiodinium	The genus Symbiodinium encompasses the largest and most prevalent group of endosymbiotic dinoflagellates known to science. These unicellular algae commonly reside in the endoderm of tropical cnidarians such as corals, sea anemones, and jellyfish, where they translocate products of photosynthesis to the host and in turn receive inorganic nutrients (e.g. CO_2, NH_4^+) (Fig. 1). They are also harbored by various species of sponges, flatworms, mollusks (e.g. giant clams), foraminifera (soritids), and some ciliates.
Atoll	An atoll is a coral island (or islands) that encircles a lagoon partially or completely. Usage The word atoll comes from the Dhivehi (an Indo-Aryan language spoken on the Maldive Islands) word atholhu [OED]. Its first recorded use in English was in 1625 as atollon - Charles Darwin recognized its indigenous origin and coined, in his The Structure and Distribution of Coral Reefs, the definition of atolls as '..circular groups of coral islets [...] and [the word] is synonymous with 'lagoon-island'.' (1842, p. 2).
Coral bleaching	Coral bleaching is the loss of intracellular endosymbionts (Symbiodinium, also known as zooxanthellae) through either expulsion or loss of algal pigmentation. The corals that form the structure of the great reef ecosystems of tropical seas depend upon a symbiotic relationship with unicellular flagellate protozoa that are photosynthetic and live within their tissues. Zooxanthellae give coral its coloration, with the specific color depending on the particular clade.
Marine snow	In the deep ocean, marine snow is a continuous shower of mostly organic detritus falling from the upper layers of the water column. It is a significant means of exporting energy from the light-rich photic zone to the aphotic zone below. The term was first coined by the explorer William Beebe as he observed it from his bathysphere.
Stewardship	Stewardship is an ethic that embodies responsible planning and management of resources. The concept of stewardship has been applied in diverse realms, including with respect to environment, economics, health, property, information, and religion, and is linked to the concept of sustainability. Historically, stewardship was the responsibility given to household servants to bring food and drinks to a castle dining hall.

Chapter 6. Major Ecosystems of the World

1. A _____, is a coastal ecosystem in the upper coastal intertidal zone between land and open salt water or brackish water that is regularly flooded by the tides. It is dominated by dense stands of salt-tolerant plants such as herbs, grasses, or low shrubs. These plants are terrestrial in origin and are essential to the stability of the _____ in trapping and binding sediments.

   a. Coastal zone
   b. Salt marsh
   c. Juglone
   d. Nekton

2. _____ or reflection coefficient, derived from Latin _____ 'whiteness' (or reflected sunlight), in turn from albus 'white', is the diffuse reflectivity or reflecting power of a surface. It is defined as the ratio of reflected radiation from the surface to incident radiation upon it. Being a dimensionless fraction, it may also be expressed as a percentage, and is measured on a scale from zero for no reflecting power of a perfectly black surface, to 1 for perfect reflection of a white surface.

   a. Albedo
   b. Antarctic Cold Reversal
   c. Arid
   d. Aridity index

3. A _____ depicts feeding connections (what eats what) in an ecological community. Ecologists can broadly lump all life forms into one of two categories called trophic levels: 1) the autotrophs, and 2) the heterotrophs. To maintain their bodies, grow, develop, and to reproduce, autotrophs produce organic matter from inorganic substances, including both minerals and gases such as carbon dioxide.

   a. Food web
   b. Chronospecies
   c. Clonograptus
   d. Litothallus

4. . In physical geography, tundra is a biome where the tree growth is hindered by low temperatures and short growing seasons. The term tundra comes through Russian тундра from the Kildin Sami word tundâr 'uplands', 'treeless mountain tract'. There are three types of tundra: _____, alpine tundra, and Ant_____.

   _____ occurs in the far Northern Hemisphere, north of the taiga belt. The word 'tundra' usually refers only to the areas where the subsoil is permafrost, or permanently frozen soil. Permafrost tundra includes vast areas of northern Russia and Canada.

   a. Odyssey
   b. Antarctic Cold Reversal
   c. Arid

5. A _____, is a flat or nearly flat land adjacent a stream or river that stretches from the banks of its channel to the base of the enclosing valley walls and experiences flooding during periods of high discharge. It includes the floodway, which consists of the stream channel and adjacent areas that carry flood flows, and the flood fringe, which are areas covered by the flood, but which do not experience a strong current. In other words, a _____ is an area near a river or a stream which floods easily.

a. Floodplain
b. Fold mountain
c. Forebulge
d. Frost heaving

1. b
2. a
3. a
4. d
5. a

You can take the complete Chapter Practice Test

for Chapter 6. Major Ecosystems of the World
on all key terms, persons, places, and concepts.

Online 99 Cents

http://www.epub89.6.20924.6.cram101.com/

Use www.Cram101.com for all your study needs

including Cram101's online interactive problem solving labs in

chemistry, statistics, mathematics, and more.

CHAPTER OUTLINE: KEY TERMS, PEOPLE, PLACES, CONCEPTS

	Malnutrition
	Infectious diseases
	Lyme disease
	Dengue fever
	Malaria
	Smallpox
	Tuberculosis
	Bioaccumulation
	Heavy metal
	Hormone
	Polychlorinated biphenyl
	Acute toxicity
	Chronic toxicity
	Food Quality Protection Act
	Toxicology
	Health effect
	Hormesis
	Chemical hazard
	Ecotoxicology

_____ Environmental Health Perspectives

_____ Environmental toxicology

_____ Love Canal

_____ Zero population growth

_____ Algal bloom

_____ Food web

_____ Red tide

_____ Risk assessment

_____ Cost-benefit analysis

_____ Nanotechnology

_____ Precautionary principle

_____ Heat wave

_____ Climate change

Malnutrition	Malnutrition is the condition that results from taking an unbalanced diet in which certain nutrients are lacking, in excess (too high an intake), or in the wrong proportions. A number of different nutrition disorders may arise, depending on which nutrients are under or overabundant in the diet. In most of the world, malnutrition is present in the form of undernutrition, which is caused by a diet lacking adequate calories and protein.
Infectious diseases	Infectious diseases, comprise clinically evident illness (i.e. transmissible diseases or communicable diseases comprise clinically evident illness (i.e. characteristic medical signs and/or symptoms of disease) resulting from the infection, presence and growth of pathogenic biological agents in an individual host organism. In certain cases, infectious diseases may be asymptomatic for much or even all of their course in a given host. In the latter case, the disease may only be defined as a 'disease' (which by definition means an illness) in hosts who secondarily become ill after contact with an asymptomatic carrier.
Lyme disease	Lyme disease, is an emerging infectious disease caused by at least three species of bacteria belonging to the genus Borrelia. Borrelia burgdorferi sensu stricto is the main cause of Lyme disease in the United States, whereas Borrelia afzelii and Borrelia garinii cause most European cases. he town of Lyme, Connecticut, USA, where a number of cases were identified in 1975. Although Allen Steere realized that Lyme disease was a tick-borne disease in 1978, the cause of the disease remained a mystery until 1981, when B. burgdorferi was identified by Willy Burgdorfer.
Dengue fever	Dengue fever also known as breakbone fever, is an infectious tropical disease caused by the dengue virus. Symptoms include fever, headache, muscle and joint pains, and a characteristic skin rash that is similar to measles. In a small proportion of cases the disease develops into the life-threatening dengue hemorrhagic fever, resulting in bleeding, low levels of blood platelets and blood plasma leakage, or into dengue shock syndrome, where dangerously low blood pressure occurs.
Malaria	Malaria is a mosquito-borne infectious disease of humans and other animals caused by protists (a type of microorganism) of the genus Plasmodium. It begins with a bite from an infected female mosquito (Anopheles Mosquito), which introduces the protists via its saliva into the circulatory system, and ultimately to the liver where they mature and reproduce. The disease causes symptoms that typically include fever and headache, which in severe cases can progress to coma or death.
Smallpox	Smallpox was an infectious disease unique to humans, caused by either of two virus variants, Variola major and Variola minor. The disease is also known by the Latin names Variola or Variola vera, which is a derivative of the Latin varius, meaning 'spotted', or varus, meaning 'pimple'.

Chapter 7. Human Health and Environmental Toxicology

Tuberculosis	Tuberculosis, MTB, or TB is a common, and in many cases lethal, infectious disease caused by various strains of mycobacteria, usually Mycobacterium tuberculosis. Tuberculosis typically attacks the lungs, but can also affect other parts of the body.
Bioaccumulation	Bioaccumulation refers to the accumulation of substances, such as pesticides, or other organic chemicals in an organism. Bioaccumulation occurs when an organism absorbs a toxic substance at a rate greater than that at which the substance is lost. Thus, the longer the biological half-life of the substance the greater the risk of chronic poisoning, even if environmental levels of the toxin are not very high.
Heavy metal	A heavy metal is a member of a loosely-defined subset of elements that exhibit metallic properties. It mainly includes the transition metals, some metalloids, lanthanides, and actinides. Many different definitions have been proposed--some based on density, some on atomic number or atomic weight, and some on chemical properties or toxicity.
Hormone	A hormone is a chemical released by a cell or a gland in one part of the body that sends out messages that affect cells in other parts of the organism. Only a small amount of hormone is required to alter cell metabolism. In essence, it is a chemical messenger that transports a signal from one cell to another.
Polychlorinated biphenyl	A polychlorinated biphenyl is any of the 209 configurations of organochlorides with 2 to 10 chlorine atoms attached to biphenyl, which is a molecule composed of two benzene rings. The chemical formula for a PCB is $C_{12}H_{10-x}Cl_x$. 130 of the 209 different PCB arrangements and orientations are used commercially.
Acute toxicity	Acute toxicity describes the adverse effects of a substance which result either from a single exposure or from multiple exposures in a short space of time (usually less than 24 hours). To be described as acute toxicity, the adverse effects should occur within 14 days of the administration of the substance.
	Acute toxicity is distinguished from chronic toxicity, which describes the adverse health effects from repeated exposures, often at lower levels, to a substance over a longer time period (months or years).
Chronic toxicity	Chronic toxicity is a property of a substance that has toxic effects on a living organism, when that organism is exposed to the substance continuously or repeatedly. Compared with acute toxicity.
	Two distinct situations need to be considered:•Prolonged exposure to a substance

Food Quality Protection Act	The Food Quality Protection Act or H.R.1627, was passed unanimously by Congress in 1996 and was signed into law by former U.S. President Bill Clinton on August 3, 1996. The Food Quality Protection Act standardized the way the Environmental Protection Agency (EPA) would manage the use of pesticides and amended the Federal Insecticide, Fungicide, and Rodenticide Act and the Federal Food Drug and Cosmetic Act. It mandated a health-based standard for pesticides used in foods, provided special protections for babies and infants, streamlined the approval of safe pesticides, established incentives for the creation of safer pesticides, and required that pesticide registrations remain current.
	One of the most prominent sections of the act, the specified protections for babies and infants, was the topic of the National Academy of Science's 1993 report, Pesticides in the Diets of Infants & Children.
Toxicology	Toxicology is a branch of biology, chemistry, and medicine concerned with the study of the adverse effects of chemicals on living organisms. It is the study of symptoms, mechanisms, treatments and detection of poisoning, especially the poisoning of people.
	Dioscorides, a Greek physician in the court of the Roman emperor Nero, made the first attempt to classify plants according to their toxic and therapeutic effect.
Health effect	Health effects are changes in health resulting from exposure to a source. Health effects are an important consideration in many areas, such as hygiene, pollution studies, occupational safety and health, nutrition and health sciences in general. Some of the major environmental sources of health effects are air pollution, water pollution, soil contamination, noise pollution and over-illumination.
Hormesis	Hormesis is the term for generally favorable biological responses to low exposures to toxins and other stressors. A pollutant or toxin showing hormesis thus has the opposite effect in small doses as in large doses. A related concept is Mithridatism, which refers to the willful exposure to toxins in an attempt to develop immunity against them.
Chemical hazard	A chemical hazard arises from contamination of an area with harmful or potentially harmful chemicals. Possible sources of chemical hazards include the burning of fossils, materials and chemicals used in construction and industry, pollution of the environment and water supply, chemical spillages, industrial accidents, and the deliberate release of toxic materials.
Ecotoxicology	Ecotoxicology is the study of the effects of toxic chemicals on biological organisms, especially at the population, community, ecosystem level. Ecotoxicology is a multidisciplinary field, which integrates toxicology and ecology.

Chapter 7. Human Health and Environmental Toxicology

Environmental Health Perspectives	Environmental Health Perspectives is a peer-reviewed open-access medical journal published monthly by the National Institute of Environmental Health Sciences. According to the Journal Citation Reports, the journal has a 2009 impact factor of 6.191.
Environmental toxicology	Environmental toxicology, is a multidisciplinary field of science concerned with the study of the harmful effects of various chemical, biological and physical agents on living organisms. Ecotoxicology is a subdiscipline of environmental toxicology concerned with studying the harmful effects of toxicants at the population and ecosystem levels. Rachel Carson is considered the mother of environmental toxicology, as she made it a distinct field within toxicology in 1962 with the publication of her book Silent Spring, which covered the effects of uncontrolled pesticide use.
Love Canal	Love Canal was a neighborhood in Niagara Falls, New York, located in the white collar LaSalle section of the city. It officially covers 36 square blocks in the far southeastern corner of the city, along 99th Street and Read Avenue. Two bodies of water define the northern and southern boundaries of the neighborhood: Bergholtz Creek to the north and the Niagara River one-quarter mile (400 m) to the south.
Zero population growth	Zero population growth is a condition of demographic balance where the number of people in a specified population neither grows nor declines, considered as a social aim. According to some, zero population growth is the ideal towards which countries and the whole world should aspire in the interests of accomplishing long-term environmental sustainability.
Algal bloom	An algal bloom is a rapid increase or accumulation in the population of algae in an aquatic system. Algal blooms may occur in freshwater as well as marine environments. Typically, only one or a small number of phytoplankton species are involved, and some blooms may be recognized by discoloration of the water resulting from the high density of pigmented cells.
Food web	A food web depicts feeding connections (what eats what) in an ecological community. Ecologists can broadly lump all life forms into one of two categories called trophic levels: 1) the autotrophs, and 2) the heterotrophs. To maintain their bodies, grow, develop, and to reproduce, autotrophs produce organic matter from inorganic substances, including both minerals and gases such as carbon dioxide.
Red tide	Red tide is a common name for a phenomenon also known as an algal bloom (large concentrations of aquatic microorganisms), an event in which estuarine, marine, or fresh water algae accumulate rapidly in the water column and results in discoloration of the surface water. It is usually found in coastal areas.

Chapter 7. Human Health and Environmental Toxicology

Risk assessment	Risk assessment is a step in a risk management procedure. Risk assessment is the determination of quantitative or qualitative value of risk related to a concrete situation and a recognized threat (also called hazard). Quantitative risk assessment requires calculations of two components of risk (R):, the magnitude of the potential loss (L), and the probability (p) that the loss will occur.
Cost-benefit analysis	Cost-benefit analysis sometimes called benefit-cost analysis (BCA), is a systematic process for calculating and comparing benefits and costs of a project, decision or government policy (hereafter, 'project'). Cost benefit analysis has two purposes:•To determine if it is a sound investment/decision (justification/feasibility),•To provide a basis for comparing projects. It involves comparing the total expected cost of each option against the total expected benefits, to see whether the benefits outweigh the costs, and by how much Cost benefit analysis is related to, but distinct from cost-effectiveness analysis.
Nanotechnology	Nanotechnology is the study of manipulating matter on an atomic and molecular scale. Generally, nanotechnology deals with developing materials, devices, or other structures possessing at least one dimension sized from 1 to 100 nanometres. Quantum mechanical effects are important at this quantum-realm scale.
Precautionary principle	The precautionary principle, states that if an action or policy has a suspected risk of causing harm to the public or to the environment, in the absence of scientific consensus that the action or policy is harmful, the burden of proof that it is not harmful falls on those taking the action. This principle allows policy makers to make discretionary decisions in situations where there is the possibility of harm from taking a particular course or making a certain decision when extensive scientific knowledge on the matter is lacking. The principle implies that there is a social responsibility to protect the public from exposure to harm, when scientific investigation has found a plausible risk.
Heat wave	A heat wave is a prolonged period of excessively hot weather, which may be accompanied by high humidity. There is no universal definition of a heat wave; the term is relative to the usual weather in the area. Temperatures that people from a hotter climate consider normal can be termed a heat wave in a cooler area if they are outside the normal climate pattern for that area.
Climate change	Climate change is a significant and lasting change in the statistical distribution of weather patterns over periods ranging from decades to millions of years. It may be a change in average weather conditions or the distribution of events around that average (e.g., more or fewer extreme weather events). Climate change may be limited to a specific region or may our across the whole Earth.

Chapter 7. Human Health and Environmental Toxicology

1. A _____ is a member of a loosely-defined subset of elements that exhibit metallic properties. It mainly includes the transition metals, some metalloids, lanthanides, and actinides. Many different definitions have been proposed-- some based on density, some on atomic number or atomic weight, and some on chemical properties or toxicity.

   a. Herbicide
   b. Heavy metal
   c. Kombucha
   d. Maximum tolerated dose

2. _____ is a branch of biology, chemistry, and medicine concerned with the study of the adverse effects of chemicals on living organisms. It is the study of symptoms, mechanisms, treatments and detection of poisoning, especially the poisoning of people.

   Dioscorides, a Greek physician in the court of the Roman emperor Nero, made the first attempt to classify plants according to their toxic and therapeutic effect.

   a. Toxicology
   b. Coliform index
   c. Committee on Toxicity
   d. Cross-resistance

3. _____, is an emerging infectious disease caused by at least three species of bacteria belonging to the genus Borrelia. Borrelia burgdorferi sensu stricto is the main cause of _____ in the United States, whereas Borrelia afzelii and Borrelia garinii cause most European cases. he town of Lyme, Connecticut, USA, where a number of cases were identified in 1975. Although Allen Steere realized that _____ was a tick-borne disease in 1978, the cause of the disease remained a mystery until 1981, when B. burgdorferi was identified by Willy Burgdorfer.

   a. Lyme disease
   b. Gibbons v. Ogden
   c. Krakatoa
   d. Diesel engine

4. _____ is a significant and lasting change in the statistical distribution of weather patterns over periods ranging from decades to millions of years. It may be a change in average weather conditions or the distribution of events around that average (e.g., more or fewer extreme weather events). _____ may be limited to a specific region or may our across the whole Earth.

   a. Climate oscillation
   b. Climate change
   c. CLIWOC
   d. Cretaceous Thermal Maximum

5. _____ sometimes called benefit-cost analysis (BCA), is a systematic process for calculating and comparing benefits and costs of a project, decision or government policy (hereafter, 'project'). Cost benefit analysis has two purposes:•To determine if it is a sound investment/decision (justification/feasibility),•To provide a basis for comparing projects. It involves comparing the total expected cost of each option against the total expected benefits, to see whether the benefits outweigh the costs, and by how much

Cost benefit analysis is related to, but distinct from cost-effectiveness analysis.

a. taxes
b. Juglone
c. Cost-benefit analysis
d. Saint John, New Brunswick harbour cleanup

---

1. b
2. a
3. a
4. b
5. c

You can take the complete Chapter Practice Test

for Chapter 7. Human Health and Environmental Toxicology
on all key terms, persons, places, and concepts.

Online 99 Cents

http://www.epub89.6.20924.7.cram101.com/

Use www.Cram101.com for all your study needs

including Cram101's online interactive problem solving labs in

chemistry, statistics, mathematics, and more.

Chapter 8. The Human Population

CHAPTER OUTLINE: KEY TERMS, PEOPLE, PLACES, CONCEPTS

_______________ Demographic

_______________ Demography

_______________ Carrying capacity

_______________ Cholera

_______________ Red tide

_______________ Birth rate

_______________ Purchasing power parity

_______________ Population growth

_______________ Demographic transition

_______________ Fertility

_______________ Total fertility rate

_______________ Population decline

_______________ Food security

_______________ Quality of life

_______________ Famine

_______________ MDGs

_______________ Malaria

Demographic	Demographics are statistical characteristics of a population. These types of data are used widely in public opinion polling and marketing. Commonly examined demographics include gender, age, ethnicity, knowledge of languages, disabilities, mobility, home ownership, employment status, and even location.
Demography	Demography is the statistical study of human populations and sub-populations. It can be a very general science that can be applied to any kind of dynamic human population, that is, one that changes over time or space . It encompasses the study of the size, structure, and distribution of these populations, and spatial and/or temporal changes in them in response to birth, migration, aging and death.
Carrying capacity	The carrying capacity of a biological species in an environment is the maximum population size of the species that the environment can sustain indefinitely, given the food, habitat, water and other necessities available in the environment. In population biology, carrying capacity is defined as the environment's maximal load, which is different from the concept of population equilibrium. For the human population, more complex variables such as sanitation and medical care are sometimes considered as part of the necessary establishment.
Cholera	Cholera is an infection of the small intestine that is caused by the bacterium Vibrio cholerae. The main symptoms are profuse watery diarrhea and vomiting. Transmission is primarily through consuming contaminated drinking water or food.
Red tide	Red tide is a common name for a phenomenon also known as an algal bloom (large concentrations of aquatic microorganisms), an event in which estuarine, marine, or fresh water algae accumulate rapidly in the water column and results in discoloration of the surface water. It is usually found in coastal areas. These algae, known as phytoplankton, are single-celled protists, plant-like organisms that can form dense, visible patches near the water's surface.
Birth rate	The birth rate is typically the rate of births in a population over time. The rate of births in a population is calculated in several ways: live births from a universal registration system for births, deaths, and marriages; population counts from a census, and estimation through specialized demographic techniques. The birth rate are used to calculate population growth.
Purchasing power parity	Purchasing power parity is an economic theory and a technique used to determine the relative value of currencies, estimating the amount of adjustment needed on the exchange rate between countries in order for the exchange to be equivalent to each currency's purchasing power.

Chapter 8. The Human Population

It asks how much money would be needed to purchase the same goods and services in two countries, and uses that to calculate an implicit foreign exchange rate. Using that purchasing power parity rate, an amount of money thus has the same purchasing power in different countries.

Population growth	Population growth is the change in a population over time, and can be quantified as the change in the number of individuals of any species in a population using 'per unit time' for measurement. Population growth is determined by four factors, births (B), deaths (D), immigrants (I), and emigrants (E). Using a formula expressed as $\Delta P \equiv (B-D)+(I-E)$ In other words, the population growth of a period can be calculated in two parts, natural growth of population (B-D) and mechanical growth of population (I-E), in which mechanical growth of population is mainly affected by social factors, e.g. the advanced economies are growing faster while the backward economies are growing slowly even with negative growth.
Demographic transition	The demographic transition is the transition from high birth and death rates to low birth and death rates as a country develops from a pre-industrial to an industrialized economic system. The theory is based on an interpretation of demographic history developed in 1929 by the American demographer Warren Thompson (1887-1973). Thompson observed changes, or transitions, in birth and death rates in industrialized societies over the previous 200 years.
Fertility	Fertility is the natural human capability of producing offsprings. As a measure, 'fertility rate' is the number of children born per couple, person or population. Fertility differs from fecundity, which is defined as the potential for reproduction (influenced by gamete production, fertilisation and carrying a pregnancy to term).
Total fertility rate	The total fertility rate of a population is the average number of children that would be born to a woman over her lifetime if (1) she were to experience the exact current age-specific fertility rates (ASFRs) through her lifetime, and (2) she were to survive from birth through the end of her reproductive life. It is obtained by summing the single-year age-specific rates at a given time.
Population decline	Population decline can refer to the decline in population of any organism. It is a term usually used to describe any great reduction in a human population. It can be used to refer to long-term demographic trends, as in urban decay or rural flight, but it is also commonly employed to describe large reductions in population due to violence, disease, or other catastrophes.
Food security	Food security refers to the availability of food and one's access to it.

A household is considered food-secure when its occupants do not live in hunger or fear of starvation. According to the World Resources Institute, global per capita food production has been increasing substantially for the past several decades.

Quality of life	The term quality of life is used to evaluate the general well-being of individuals and societies. The term is used in a wide range of contexts, including the fields of international development, healthcare, and politics. Quality of life should not be confused with the concept of standard of living, which is based primarily on income.
Famine	A famine is a widespread scarcity of food, caused by several factors including crop failure, population unbalance, or government policies. This phenomenon is usually accompanied or followed by regional malnutrition, starvation, epidemic, and increased mortality. Nearly every continent in the world has experienced a period of famine throughout history.
MDGs	The Millennium Development Goals (MDGs) are eight international development goals that were officially established following the Millennium Summit of the United Nations in 2000, following the adoption of the United Nations Millennium Declaration. All 193 United Nations member states and at least 23 international organizations have agreed to achieve these goals by the year 2015. The goals are:•Eradicating extreme poverty and hunger,•Achieving universal primary education,•Promoting gender equality and empowering women,•Reducing child mortality rates,•Improving maternal health,•Combating HIV/AIDS, malaria, and other diseases,•Ensuring environmental sustainability, and•Developing a global partnership for development Each of the goals has specific stated targets and dates for achieving those targets. To accelerate progress, the G8 Finance Ministers agreed in June 2005 to provide enough funds to the World Bank, the International Monetary Fund (IMF), and the African Development Bank (AfDB) to cancel an additional $40 to $55 billion in debt owed by members of the Heavily Indebted Poor Countries (HIPC) to allow impoverished countries to re-channel the resources saved from the forgiven debt to social programs for improving health and education and for alleviating poverty.
Malaria	Malaria is a mosquito-borne infectious disease of humans and other animals caused by protists (a type of microorganism) of the genus Plasmodium. It begins with a bite from an infected female mosquito (Anopheles Mosquito), which introduces the protists via its saliva into the circulatory system, and ultimately to the liver where they mature and reproduce. The disease causes symptoms that typically include fever and headache, which in severe cases can progress to coma or death.

Chapter 8. The Human Population

1. The _____ of a biological species in an environment is the maximum population size of the species that the environment can sustain indefinitely, given the food, habitat, water and other necessities available in the environment. In population biology, _____ is defined as the environment's maximal load, which is different from the concept of population equilibrium.

   For the human population, more complex variables such as sanitation and medical care are sometimes considered as part of the necessary establishment.

   a. Juglone
   b. Carrying capacity
   c. Human geography
   d. Natural resource management

2. _____s are statistical characteristics of a population. These types of data are used widely in public opinion polling and marketing. Commonly examined _____s include gender, age, ethnicity, knowledge of languages, disabilities, mobility, home ownership, employment status, and even location.

   a. Demographic
   b. Gibbons v. Ogden
   c. Krakatoa
   d. Diesel engine

3. The _____ is the transition from high birth and death rates to low birth and death rates as a country develops from a pre-industrial to an industrialized economic system. The theory is based on an interpretation of demographic history developed in 1929 by the American demographer Warren Thompson (1887-1973). Thompson observed changes, or transitions, in birth and death rates in industrialized societies over the previous 200 years.

   a. Demographic transition
   b. Juglone
   c. Gibbons v. Ogden
   d. Natural resource management

4. _____ is an infection of the small intestine that is caused by the bacterium Vibrio cholerae. The main symptoms are profuse watery diarrhea and vomiting. Transmission is primarily through consuming contaminated drinking water or food.

   a. Cholera
   b. Juglone
   c. Gibbons v. Ogden
   d. Natural resource management

5. . A _____ is a widespread scarcity of food, caused by several factors including crop failure, population unbalance, or government policies. This phenomenon is usually accompanied or followed by regional malnutrition, starvation, epidemic, and increased mortality. Nearly every continent in the world has experienced a period of _____ throughout history.

a. Juglone
b. Spaceship Earth
c. Famine
d. Stewardship

1. b
2. a
3. a
4. a
5. c

You can take the complete Chapter Practice Test

for Chapter 8. The Human Population
on all key terms, persons, places, and concepts.

Online 99 Cents

http://www.epub89.6.20924.8.cram101.com/

Use www.Cram101.com for all your study needs

including Cram101's online interactive problem solving labs in

chemistry, statistics, mathematics, and more.

Chapter 9. The Urban Environment

CHAPTER OUTLINE: KEY TERMS, PEOPLE, PLACES, CONCEPTS

_____ Urbanization

_____ Megacity

_____ Population density

_____ Ecosystem

_____ Urban ecology

_____ Urban heat island

_____ Urban runoff

_____ Noise pollution

_____ Urban sprawl

_____ Smart growth

_____ Sustainable city

_____ Sustainable

Chapter 9. The Urban Environment

Urbanization	Urbanization, urbanisation or urban drift is the physical growth of urban areas as a result of rural migration and even suburban concentration into cities, particularly the very largest ones. The United Nations projected that half of the world's population would live in urban areas at the end of 2008. By 2050 it is predicted that 64.1% and 85.9% of the developing and developed world respectively will be urbanised. Urbanization is closely linked to modernisation, industrialisation, and the sociological process of rationalisation.
Megacity	A megacity is usually defined as a metropolitan area with a total population in excess of 10 million people. Some definitions also set a minimum level for population density (at least 2,000 persons/square km). A megacity can be a single metropolitan area or two or more metropolitan areas that converge.
Population density	Population density is a measurement of population per unit area or unit volume. It is frequently applied to living organisms, and particularly to humans. It is a key geographic term.
Ecosystem	An ecosystem is a community of living organisms (plants, animals and microbes) in conjunction with the nonliving components of their environment (things like air, water and mineral soil), interacting as a system. These components are regarded as linked together through nutrient cycles and energy flows. As ecosystems are defined by the network of interactions among organisms, and between organisms and their environment, they can come in any size but usually encompass specific, limited spaces (although some scientists say that the entire planet is an ecosystem).
Urban ecology	Urban ecology is a subfield of ecology which deals with the interaction between organisms in an urban or urbanized community, and their interaction with that community. Urban ecologists study the trees, rivers, wildlife and open spaces found in cities to understand the extent of those resources and the way they are affected by pollution, over-development and other pressures. Analysis of urban settings in the context of ecosystem ecology (looking at the cycling of matter and the flow of energy through the ecosystem) may ultimately help us to design healthier, better managed communities, by understanding what threats the urban environment brings to humans.
Urban heat island	An urban heat island is a metropolitan area which is significantly warmer than its surrounding rural areas. The phenomenon was first investigated and described by Luke Howard in the 1810s, although he was not the one to name the phenomenon. The temperature difference usually is larger at night than during the day, and is most apparent when winds are weak.
Urban runoff	Urban runoff is surface runoff of rainwater created by urbanization. This runoff is a major source of water pollution in many parts of the United States and other urban communities worldwide.

Overview

Impervious surfaces (roads, parking lots and sidewalks) are constructed during land development.

Noise pollution

Noise pollution is excessive, displeasing human, animal, or machine-created environmental noise that disrupts the activity or balance of human or animal life. The word noise may be from the Latin word nauseas, metaphorically meaning disgust or discomfort.

The source of most outdoor noise worldwide is mainly construction and transportation systems, including motor vehicle noise, aircraft noise, and rail noise.

Urban sprawl

Urban sprawl, is a multifaceted concept, which includes the spreading outwards of a city and its suburbs to its outskirts to low-density and auto-dependent development on rural land, high segregation of es (e.g. stores and residential), and vario design features that encourage car dependency.

Discsions and debates about sprawl are often obfcated by the ambiguity associated with the phrase. For example, some commentators measure sprawl only with the average number of residential units per acre in a given area.

Smart growth

Smart growth is an urban planning and transportation theory that concentrates growth in compact walkable urban centers to avoid sprawl and advocates compact, transit-oriented, walkable, bicycle-friendly land use, including neighborhood schools, complete streets, and mixed-use development with a range of housing choices. The term 'smart growth' is particularly used in North America. In Europe and particularly the UK, the terms 'Compact City' or 'urban intensification' have often been used to describe similar concepts, which have influenced Government planning policies in the UK, the Netherlands and several other European countries.

Sustainable city

A sustainable city is a city designed with consideration of environmental impact, inhabited by people dedicated to minimization of required inputs of energy, water and food, and waste output of heat, air pollution - CO_2, methane, and water pollution. Richard Register first coined the term 'ecocity' in his 1987 book, Ecocity Berkeley: building cities for a healthy future. Other leading figures who envisioned the sustainable city are architect Paul F Downton, who later founded the company Ecopolis Pty Ltd, and authors Timothy Beatley and Steffen Lehmann, who have written extensively on the subject.

Sustainable

Sustainability is the capacity to endure. In ecology the word describes how biological systems remain diverse and productive over time.

Chapter 9. The Urban Environment

1. An _____ is a metropolitan area which is significantly warmer than its surrounding rural areas. The phenomenon was first investigated and described by Luke Howard in the 1810s, although he was not the one to name the phenomenon. The temperature difference usually is larger at night than during the day, and is most apparent when winds are weak.

   a. Urban thermal plume
   b. Urban heat island
   c. Provisional Administrative Line
   d. Rank-size distribution

2. A _____ is usually defined as a metropolitan area with a total population in excess of 10 million people. Some definitions also set a minimum level for population density (at least 2,000 persons/square km). A _____ can be a single metropolitan area or two or more metropolitan areas that converge.

   a. Famine
   b. Juglone
   c. Gibbons v. Ogden
   d. Megacity

3. _____, urbanisation or urban drift is the physical growth of urban areas as a result of rural migration and even suburban concentration into cities, particularly the very largest ones. The United Nations projected that half of the world's population would live in urban areas at the end of 2008. By 2050 it is predicted that 64.1% and 85.9% of the developing and developed world respectively will be urbanised.

   _____ is closely linked to modernisation, industrialisation, and the sociological process of rationalisation.

   a. Alfonso Jordan
   b. Urbanization
   c. Rowland Hill
   d. Richard Russell Waldron

4. _____ is surface runoff of rainwater created by urbanization. This runoff is a major source of water pollution in many parts of the United States and other urban communities worldwide.

   Overview

   Impervious surfaces (roads, parking lots and sidewalks) are constructed during land development.

   a. Agricultural wastewater treatment
   b. Aquatic biomonitoring
   c. Urban runoff
   d. Erosion control

5. . _____ is a measurement of population per unit area or unit volume.

It is frequently applied to living organisms, and particularly to humans. It is a key geographic term.

a. Poquoson
b. Population density
c. Provisional Administrative Line
d. Rank-size distribution

1. b
2. d
3. b
4. c
5. b

You can take the complete Chapter Practice Test

for Chapter 9. The Urban Environment
on all key terms, persons, places, and concepts.

Online 99 Cents

http://www.epub89.6.20924.9.cram101.com/

Use www.Cram101.com for all your study needs

including Cram101's online interactive problem solving labs in

chemistry, statistics, mathematics, and more.

Chapter 10. Energy Consumption

CHAPTER OUTLINE: KEY TERMS, PEOPLE, PLACES, CONCEPTS

_____ Energy conservation

_____ Natural gas

_____ Cogeneration

_____ Quality of life

_____ Current

_____ Electrolysis

_____ Fuel cell

_____ Plug-in hybrid

_____ Thermal energy

_____ Storage

_____ Energy policy

_____ Superconducting magnetic energy storage

_____ Carbon sequestration

Chapter 10. Energy Consumption

Energy conservation	Energy conservation refers to efforts made to reduce energy consumption. Energy conservation can be achieved through increased efficient energy use, in conjunction with dreased energy consumption and/or reduced consumption from conventional energy sources. An energy conservation act was passed in 2001.
Natural gas	Natural gas is a naturally occurring hydrocarbon gas mixture consisting primarily of methane, with other hydrocarbons, carbon dioxide, nitrogen and hydrogen sulfide. Natural gas is an important energy source to provide heating and electricity. It is also used as fuel for vehicles and as a chemical feedstock in the manufacture of plastics and other commercially important organic chemicals.
Cogeneration	Cogeneration is the use of a heat engine or a power station to simultaneously generate both electricity and useful heat. All thermal power plants emit a certain amount of heat during electricity generation. This can be released into the natural environment through cooling towers, flue gas, or by other means. By contrast, cogeneration captures some or all of the by-product heat for heating purposes, either very close to the plant, or-especially in Scandinavia and eastern Europe-as hot water for district heating with temperatures ranging from approximately 80 to 130 °C.
Quality of life	The term quality of life is used to evaluate the general well-being of individuals and societies. The term is used in a wide range of contexts, including the fields of international development, healthcare, and politics. Quality of life should not be confused with the concept of standard of living, which is based primarily on income.
Current	In mathematics, more particularly in functional analysis, differential topology, and geometric measure theory, a k-current in the sense of Georges de Rham is a functional on the space of compactly supported differential k-forms, on a smooth manifold M. Formally currents behave like Schwartz distributions on a space of differential forms. In a geometric setting, they can represent integration over a submanifold, generalizing the Dirac delta function, or more generally even directional derivatives of delta functions (multipoles) spread out along subsets of M. Let $\Omega_c^m(\mathbb{R}^n)$ denote the space of smooth m-forms with compact support on $\mathbb{R}^n$. A current is a linear functional on $\Omega_c^m(\mathbb{R}^n)$ which is continuous in the sense of distributions.
Electrolysis	In chemistry and manufacturing, electrolysis is a method of using a direct electric current (DC) to drive an otherwise non-spontaneous chemical reaction. Electrolysis is commercially highly important as a stage in the separation of elements from naturally occurring sources such as ores using an electrolytic cell.

Fuel cell	A fuel cell is a device that converts the chemical energy from a fuel into electricity through a chemical reaction with oxygen or another oxidizing agent. Hydrogen is the most common fuel, but hydrocarbons such as natural gas and alcohols like methanol are sometimes used. Fuel cells are different from batteries in that they require a constant source of fuel and oxygen to run, but they can produce electricity continually for as long as these inputs are supplied.
Plug-in hybrid	A plug-in hybrid is a hybrid vehicle which utilizes rechargeable batteries, or another energy storage device, that can be restored to full charge by connecting a plug to an external electric power source (usually a normal electric wall socket). A plug-in hybrid shares the characteristics of both a conventional hybrid electric vehicle, having an electric motor and an internal combustion engine (ICE); and of an all-electric vehicle, having a plug to connect to the electrical grid. Most plug-in hybrids on the road today are passenger cars, but there are also plug-in hybrid versions of commercial vehicles and vans, utility trucks, buses, trains, motorcycles, scooters, and military vehicles.
Thermal energy	Thermal energy is the part of the total inrnal energy of a thermodynamic sysm or sample of matr that results in the sysm's mperature. The inrnal energy, also ofn called the thermodynamic energy, includes other forms of energy in a thermodynamic sysm in addition to thermal energy, namely forms of pontial energy, such as the chemical energy stored in its molecular structure and electronic configuration, inrmolecular inractions, and the nuclear energy that binds the sub-atomic particles of matr.
	Microscopically, the thermal energy is the kinetic energy of a sysm's constituent particles, which may be atoms, molecules, electrons, or particles in plasmas.
Storage	Storage in human memory is one of three core process of memory, along with Recall and Encoding. It refers to the retention of information, which has been achieved through the encoding process, in the brain for a prolonged period of time until it is accessed through recall. Modern memory psychology differentiates the two distinct type of memory storage: short-term memory and long-term memory.
Energy policy	Energy policy is the manner in which a given entity (often governmental) has decided to address issues of energy development including energy production, distribution and consumption. The attributes of energy policy may include legislation, international treaties, incentives to investment, guidelines for energy conservation, taxation and other public policy techniques. Measures used to produce an energy policy
	A national energy policy comprises a set of measures involving that country's laws, treaties and agency directives.

Chapter 10. Energy Consumption

Superconducting magnetic energy storage	Superconducting Magnetic Energy Storage systems store energy in the magnetic field created by the flow of direct current in a superconducting coil which has been cryogenically cooled to a temperature below its superconducting critical temperature.
	A typical superconducting magnetic energy storage system includes three parts: superconducting coil, power conditioning system and cryogenically cooled refrigerator. Once the superconducting coil is charged, the current will not decay and the magnetic energy can be stored indefinitely.
Carbon sequestration	Carbon sequestration is the capture of carbon dioxide (CO_2) and may refer specifically to:•'The process of removing carbon from the atmosphere and depositing it in a reservoir.' When carried out deliberately, this may also be referred to as carbon dioxide removal, which is a form of geoengineering.•The process of carbon capture and storage, where carbon dioxide is removed from flue gases, such as on power stations, before being stored in underground reservoirs.•Natural biogeochemical cycling of carbon between the atmosphere and reservoirs, such as by chemical weathering of rocks.
	Carbon sequestration describes long-term storage of carbon dioxide or other forms of carbon to either mitigate or defer global warming. It has been proposed as a way to slow the atmospheric and marine accumulation of greenhouse gases, which are released by burning fossil fuels.
	Carbon dioxide is naturally captured from the atmosphere through biological, chemical or physical processes.

1. . In mathematics, more particularly in functional analysis, differential topology, and geometric measure theory, a k-_____ in the sense of Georges de Rham is a functional on the space of compactly supported differential k-forms, on a smooth manifold M. Formally _____s behave like Schwartz distributions on a space of differential forms. In a geometric setting, they can represent integration over a submanifold, generalizing the Dirac delta function, or more generally even directional derivatives of delta functions (multipoles) spread out along subsets of M.

Let $\Omega_c^m(\mathbb{R}^n)$ denote the space of smooth m-forms with compact support on $\mathbb{R}^n$. A _____ is a linear functional on $\Omega_c^m(\mathbb{R}^n)$ which is continuous in the sense of distributions.

a. Spin geometry
b. Disc theorem
c. Current

Chapter 10. Energy Consumption

2. _____ is the use of a heat engine or a power station to simultaneously generate both electricity and useful heat.

All thermal power plants emit a certain amount of heat during electricity generation. This can be released into the natural environment through cooling towers, flue gas, or by other means. By contrast, _____ captures some or all of the by-product heat for heating purposes, either very close to the plant, or-especially in Scandinavia and eastern Europe-as hot water for district heating with temperatures ranging from approximately 80 to 130 °C.

a. Combined heat and power
b. Juglone
c. Cogeneration
d. Krakatoa

3. _____ refers to efforts made to reduce energy consumption. _____ can be achieved through increased efficient energy use, in conjunction with dreased energy consumption and/or reduced consumption from conventional energy sources. An _____ act was passed in 2001.

a. Energy conservation
b. Environmental impact of wind power
c. Odyssey
d. Endangered Species Act

4. _____ is the part of the total inrnal energy of a thermodynamic sysm or sample of matr that results in the sysm's mperature. The inrnal energy, also ofn called the thermodynamic energy, includes other forms of energy in a thermodynamic sysm in addition to _____, namely forms of pontial energy, such as the chemical energy stored in its molecular structure and electronic configuration, inrmolecular inractions, and the nuclear energy that binds the sub-atomic particles of matr.

Microscopically, the _____ is the kinetic energy of a sysm's constituent particles, which may be atoms, molecules, electrons, or particles in plasmas.

a. Thermal energy
b. Hofmann voltameter
c. Hybrid moored balloon
d. Hydreliox

5. . _____ is a naturally occurring hydrocarbon gas mixture consisting primarily of methane, with other hydrocarbons, carbon dioxide, nitrogen and hydrogen sulfide. _____ is an important energy source to provide heating and electricity. It is also used as fuel for vehicles and as a chemical feedstock in the manufacture of plastics and other commercially important organic chemicals.

a. compressed natural gas
b. Natural gas
c. Gibbons v. Ogden

1. c
2. c
3. a
4. a
5. b

You can take the complete Chapter Practice Test

for Chapter 10. Energy Consumption
on all key terms, persons, places, and concepts.

Online 99 Cents

http://www.epub89.6.20924.10.cram101.com/

Use www.Cram101.com for all your study needs

including Cram101's online interactive problem solving labs in

chemistry, statistics, mathematics, and more.

Chapter 11. Fossil Fuels

CHAPTER OUTLINE: KEY TERMS, PEOPLE, PLACES, CONCEPTS

Fossil fuel

Oil spill

Carbon cycle

Natural gas

Bituminous coal

Lignite

Effects of global warming

Surface mining

Acid mine drainage

Clean coal

Resource recovery

Scrubber

Carbon capture and storage

Cogeneration

Methane

Liquefied natural gas

Great Salt Lake

Peak oil

Prestige oil spill

Chapter 11. Fossil Fuels

	Tundra
	Asphalt
	Kerogen
	Oil sands
	Oil shale
	Coal gasification
	Coal liquefaction
	Clathrate hydrate

CHAPTER HIGHLIGHTS & NOTES: KEY TERMS, PEOPLE, PLACES, CONCEPTS

Fossil fuel	Fossil fuels are fuels formed by natural processes such as anaerobic decomposition of buried dead organisms. The age of the organisms and their resulting fossil fuels is typically millions of years, and sometimes exceeds 650 million years. Fossil fuels contain high percentages of carbon and include coal, petroleum, and natural gas.
Oil spill	An oil spill is the release of a liquid petroleum hydrocarbon into the environment, especially marine areas, due to human activity, and is a form of pollution. The term is mtly used to describe marine oil spills, where oil is released into the ocean or coastal waters. Oil spills may be due to releases of crude oil from tankers, offshore platforms, drilling rigs and wells, as well as spills of refined petroleum products (such as gasoline, diesel) and their by-products, heavier fuels used by large ships such as bunker fuel, or the spill of any oily refuse or waste oil.
Carbon cycle	The carbon cycle is the biogeochemical cycle by which carbon is exchanged among the biosphere, pedosphere, geosphere, hydrosphere, and atmosphere of the Earth. It is one of the most important cycles of the earth and allows for carbon to be recycled and reused throughout the biosphere and all of its organisms.

Chapter 11. Fossil Fuels

Natural gas	Natural gas is a naturally occurring hydrocarbon gas mixture consisting primarily of methane, with other hydrocarbons, carbon dioxide, nitrogen and hydrogen sulfide. Natural gas is an important energy source to provide heating and electricity. It is also used as fuel for vehicles and as a chemical feedstock in the manufacture of plastics and other commercially important organic chemicals.
Bituminous coal	Bituminous coal is a relatively soft coal containing a tarlike substance called bitumen. It is of higher quality than lignite coal but of poorer quality than anthracite. It was usually formed as a result of high pressure on lignite.
Lignite	Lignite, often referred to as brown coal, or Rosebud coal by Northern Pacific Railroad, is a soft brown fuel with characteristics that put it somewhere between coal and peat. It is considered the lowest rank of coal; it is mined in Greece, Germany, Poland, Serbia, Russia, the United States, India, Australia and many other parts of Europe and it is used almost exclusively as a fuel for steam-electric power generation. Up to 50% of Greece's electricity and 24.6% of Germany's comes from lignite power plants.
Effects of global warming	The effects of global warming are the ecological and social changes caused by the rise in global temperatures. Evidence of climate change includes the instrumental temperature record, rising sea levels, and decreased snow cover in the Northern Hemisphere. Most of the observed increase in global average temperatures since the mid-20th century is very likely due to the observed increase in human greenhouse gas concentrations.
Surface mining	Surface mining is a type of mining in which soil and rock overlying the mineral deposit (the overburden) are removed. It is the opposite of underground mining, in which the overlying rock is left in place, and the mineral removed through shafts or tunnels. Surface mining began in the mid-sixteenth century and is practiced throughout the world, although the majority of surface mining occurs in North America. It gained popularity throughout the 20th century, and is now the predominant form of mining in coal beds such as those in Appalachia and America's Midwest.
Acid mine drainage	Acid mine drainage or acid rock drainage (ARD), refers to the outflow of acidic water from (usually abandoned) metal mines or coal mines. However, other areas where the earth has been disturbed (e.g. construction sites, subdivisions, transportation corridors, etc). may also contribute acid rock drainage to the environment.
Clean coal	Historically used to refer to technologies for reducing emissions of ash, sulfur, and heavy metals from coal combustion; the term is now commonly used to refer to carbon capture and storage (S) technology.

Chapter 11. Fossil Fuels

	Clean coal is an umbrella term used primarily to describe technologies that may reduce emissions of carbon dioxide (CO_2) and other greenhouse gas that arise from the burning of coal for electrical power. Typically, clean coal is used by coal companies in reference to carbon capture and storage, which pumps and stores CO_2 emissions underground, and to plants using an Integrated gasification combined cycle which gasifies coal to reduce CO_2 emissions.
Resource recovery	Resource recovery is the selective extraction of disposed materials for a specific next use, such as recycling, composting or energy generation. The aim of the resource recovery is to extract the maximum practical benefits from products, delay the consumption of virgin natural resources, and to generate the minimum amount of waste. Resource recovery differs from the management of waste by using life cycle analysis (LCA) to offer alternatives to landfill disposal of discarded materials.
Scrubber	'Scrubber' systems are a diverse group of air pollution control devices that can be used to remove some particulates and/or gases from industrial exhaust streams. Traditionally, the term 'scrubber' has referred to pollution control devices that use liquid to wash unwanted pollutants from a gas stream. Recently, the term is also used to describe systems that inject a dry reagent or slurry into a dirty exhaust stream to 'wash out' acid gases.
Carbon capture and storage	Carbon capture and storage is the process of capturing waste carbon dioxide (CO_2) from large point sources, such as fossil fuel power plants, transporting it to a storage site, and depositing it where it will not enter the atmosphere, normally an underground geological formation. The aim is to prevent the release of large quantities of CO_2 into the atmosphere (from fossil fuel use in power generation and other industries). It is a potential means of mitigating the contribution of fossil fuel emissions to global warming and ocean acidification.
Cogeneration	Cogeneration is the use of a heat engine or a power station to simultaneously generate both electricity and useful heat. All thermal power plants emit a certain amount of heat during electricity generation. This can be released into the natural environment through cooling towers, flue gas, or by other means. By contrast, cogeneration captures some or all of the by-product heat for heating purposes, either very close to the plant, or-especially in Scandinavia and eastern Europe-as hot water for district heating with temperatures ranging from approximately 80 to 130 °C.
Methane	Appendix: extraterrestrial methane Methane has been detected or is believed to exist in several locations of the solar system. In most cases, it is believed to have been created by abiotic processes. Possible exceptions are Mars and Titan.

Chapter 11. Fossil Fuels

Liquefied natural gas	Liquefied natural gas is natural gas (predominantly methane, CH_4) that has been converted to liquid form for ease of storage or transport.
	Liquefied natural gas takes up about 1/600th the volume of natural gas in the gaseous state. It is odorless, colorless, non-toxic and non-corrosive.
Great Salt Lake	The Great Salt Lake, located in the northern part of the U.S. state of Utah, is the largest salt water lake in the western hemisphere, and the fourth-largest terminal lake in the world. In an average year the lake covers an area of around 1,700 square miles (4,400 km^2), but the lake's size fluctuates substantially due to its shallowness. For instance, in 1963 it reached its lowest recorded level at 950 square miles (2,460 km²), but in 1988 the surface area was at the historic high of 3,300 square miles (8,500 km^2).
Peak oil	Peak oil is the int in time when the maximum rate of global petroleum extraction is reached, after which the rate of production enters terminal decline. This concept is based on the observed production rates of individual oil wells, projected reserves and the combined production rate of a field of related oil wells. In order to understand physical Peak oil, the growing effort for production must be considered.
Prestige oil spill	The Prestige oil spill was an oil spill off the coast of Galicia caused by the sinking of an oil tanker in 2002. The spill polluted thousands of kilometers of coastline and more than one thousand beaches on the Spanish and French coast, as well as causing great harm to the local fishing industry. The spill is the largest environmental disaster in Spain's history. The Event The Prestige was a Greek-operated, single-hulled oil tanker, officially registered in the Bahamas, but with a Liberian-registered single-purpose corporation as the owner.
Tundra	In physical geography, tundra is a biome where the tree growth is hindered by low temperatures and short growing seasons. The term tundra comes through Russian тундра from the Kildin Sami word tundâr 'uplands,' 'treeless mountain tract.' There are three types of tundra: Arctic tundra, alpine tundra, and Antarctic tundra. In tundra, the vegetation is composed of dwarf shrubs, sedges and grasses, mosses, and lichens.
Asphalt	Asphalt or or, also known as bitumen, is a sticky, black and highly viscous liquid or semi-solid form of petroleum. It may be found in natural deposits or may be a refined product; it is a substance classed as a pitch. Until the 20th century, the term asphaltum was also used.
Kerogen	Kerogen is a mixture of organic chemical compounds that make up a portion of the organic matter in sedimentary rocks.

Chapter 11. Fossil Fuels

	It is insoluble in normal organic solvents because of the huge molecular weight (upwards of 1,000 daltons) of its component compounds. The soluble portion is known as bitumen.
Oil sands	Bituminous sands, colloquially known as oil sands, are a type of unconventional petroleum deposit. The sands contain naturally occurring mixtures of sand, clay, water, and a dense and extremely viscous form of petroleum technically referred to as bitumen (or colloquially 'tar' due to its similar appearance, odour, and colour). Oil sands are found in large amounts in many countries throughout the world, but are found in extremely large quantities in Canada and Venezuela.
Oil shale	Oil shale, an organic-rich fine-grained sedimentary rock, contains significant amounts of kerogen (a solid mixture of organic chemical compounds) from which liquid hydrocarbons called shale oil can be produced. Shale oil is a substitute for conventional crude oil; however, extracting shale oil from oil shale is more costly than the production of conventional crude oil both financially and in terms of its environmental impact. Deposits of oil shale occur around the world, including major deposits in the United States of America. Estimates of global deposits range from 2.8 trillion to 3.3 trillion barrels (450×10^9 to 520×10^9 m^3) of recoverable oil.
Coal gasification	Coal gasification is the process of producing coal gas, a type of syngas-a mixture of carbon monoxide (CO), hydrogen (H_2), carbon dioxide (CO_2) and water vapour (H_2O)-from coal. Coal gas, which is a combustible gas, was traditionally used as a source of energy for municipal lighting and heat before the advent of industrial-scale production of natural gas, while the hydrogen obtained from gasification can be used for various purposes such as making ammonia, powering a hydrogen economy, or upgrading fossil fuels. Alternatively, the coal gas (also known as 'town gas') can be converted into transportation fuels such as gasoline and diesel through additional treatment via the Fischer-Tropsch process.
Coal liquefaction	Coal liquefaction is the process of producing synthetic liquid fuels from coal. The liquefaction processes are classified as direct conversion to liquids processes and indirect conversion to liquids processeses. Direct processes are carbonization and hydrogenation.
Clathrate hydrate	Clathrate hydrates are crystalline water-based solids physically resembling ice, in which small non polar molecules (typically gases) or polar molecules with large hydrophobic moieties are trapped inside 'cages' of hydrogen bonded water molecules. In other words, clathrate hydrates are clathrate compounds in which the host molecule is water and the guest molecule is typically a gas or liquid.

Chapter 11. Fossil Fuels

1. _____ is the selective extraction of disposed materials for a specific next use, such as recycling, composting or energy generation. The aim of the _____ is to extract the maximum practical benefits from products, delay the consumption of virgin natural resources, and to generate the minimum amount of waste. _____ differs from the management of waste by using life cycle analysis (LCA) to offer alternatives to landfill disposal of discarded materials.

   a. Rio Declaration on Environment and Development
   b. The Science of Survival
   c. Self-sufficiency
   d. Resource recovery

2. _____ is the int in time when the maximum rate of global petroleum extraction is reached, after which the rate of production enters terminal decline. This concept is based on the observed production rates of individual oil wells, projected reserves and the combined production rate of a field of related oil wells. In order to understand physical _____, the growing effort for production must be considered.

   a. Peak uranium
   b. Peak water
   c. Peak oil
   d. Polluter pays principle

3. The _____ are the ecological and social changes caused by the rise in global temperatures. Evidence of climate change includes the instrumental temperature record, rising sea levels, and decreased snow cover in the Northern Hemisphere. Most of the observed increase in global average temperatures since the mid-20th century is very likely due to the observed increase in human greenhouse gas concentrations.

   a. Effects of global warming
   b. Effects of global warming on Australia
   c. Ocean acidification
   d. Open Polar Sea

4. In physical geography, _____ is a biome where the tree growth is hindered by low temperatures and short growing seasons. The term _____ comes through Russian тундра from the Kildin Sami word tundâr 'uplands,' 'treeless mountain tract.' There are three types of _____: Arctic _____, alpine _____, and Antarctic _____. In _____, the vegetation is composed of dwarf shrubs, sedges and grasses, mosses, and lichens.

   a. steppe
   b. Sputnik program
   c. Taiga
   d. Tundra

5. . The _____ is the biogeochemical cycle by which carbon is exchanged among the biosphere, pedosphere, geosphere, hydrosphere, and atmosphere of the Earth. It is one of the most important cycles of the earth and allows for carbon to be recycled and reused throughout the biosphere and all of its organisms.

Chapter 11. Fossil Fuels

The _____ was initially discovered by Joseph Priestley and Antoine Lavoisier, and popularized by Humphry Davy.

a. Carbon-to-nitrogen ratio
b. Cation-exchange capacity
c. Carbon cycle
d. Glomalin

ANSWER KEY
Chapter 11. Fossil Fuels

---

1. d
2. c
3. a
4. d
5. c

You can take the complete Chapter Practice Test

for Chapter 11. Fossil Fuels
on all key terms, persons, places, and concepts.

Online 99 Cents

http://www.epub89.6.20924.11.cram101.com/

Use www.Cram101.com for all your study needs

including Cram101's online interactive problem solving labs in

chemistry, statistics, mathematics, and more.

CHAPTER OUTLINE: KEY TERMS, PEOPLE, PLACES, CONCEPTS

_____ Hydropower

_____ Renewable energy

_____ Wind energy

_____ Energy technology

_____ Solar cooker

_____ Mojave Desert

_____ Photovoltaics

_____ Solar cell

_____ Biodiesel

_____ Biogas

_____ Biomass

_____ Ethanol

_____ Methanol

_____ Crop residue

_____ Wind turbine

_____ Earthquake

_____ Schistosomiasis

_____ Three Gorges Dam

_____ Wave energy

Ocean thermal energy conversion

Geothermal energy

Geothermal electricity

Tidal energy

Atomic mass

Atomic number

Atom

Deuterium

Isotope

Nuclear fission

Nuclear fusion

Nuclear fuel cycle

Nuclear reactor

Radioactive decay

Tritium

Uranium

Condenser

Steam generator

Spent nuclear fuel

CHAPTER OUTLINE: KEY TERMS, PEOPLE, PLACES, CONCEPTS

_____ | Radioactive waste

_____ | Megatons to Megawatts Program

_____ | Nuclear weapon

_____ | Plutonium

_____ | Dry cask storage

_____ | Vitrification

_____ | Plasma

CHAPTER HIGHLIGHTS & NOTES: KEY TERMS, PEOPLE, PLACES, CONCEPTS

Hydropower	Hydropower, hydraulic power or water power is power that is derived from the force or energy of moving water, which may be harnessed for useful purposes. Prior to the development of electric power, hydropower was used for irrigation, and operation of various machines, such as watermills, textile machines, sawmills, dock cranes, and domestic lifts.
	Another method used a trompe to produce compressed air from falling water, which could then be used to power other machinery at a distance from the water.
Renewable energy	Renewable energy is energy that comes from natural resources such as sunlight, wind, rain, tides, waves and geothermal heat, which are renewable because they are naturally replenished at a constant rate. About 16% of global final energy consumption comes from renewables, with 10% coming from traditional biomass, which is mainly used for heating, and 3.4% from hydroelectricity. New renewables (small hydro, modern biomass, wind, solar, geothermal, and biofuels) accounted for another 3% and are growing very rapidly.
Wind energy	Wind energy is the kinetic energy of the air in motion. Total wind energy flowing through an imaginary area A during the time t is:
	$E = A$.

Chapter 12. Renewable Energy and Nuclear Power

Energy technology	Energy technology is an interdisciplinary engineering science having to do with the efficient, safe, environmentally friendly and economical extraction, conversion, transportation, storage and use of energy, targeted towards yielding high efficiency whilst skirting side effects on humans, nature and the environment.
	For people, energy is an overwhelming need and as a scarce resource it has been an underlying cause of political conflicts and wars. The gathering and use of energy resources can be harmful to local ecosystems and may have global outcomes.
Solar cooker	A solar cooker, is a device which uses the energy of sunlight to heat food or drink to cook it or sterilize it. High-tech versions, for example electric ovens powered by solar cells, are possible, and have some advantages such as being able to work in diffuse light. However at present they are very unusual because they are expensive.
Mojave Desert	The Mojave Desert occupies a significant portion of southeastern California and smaller parts of central California, southern Nevada, southwestern Utah and northwestern Arizona, in the United States. Named after the Mohave tribe of Native Americans, it displays typical basin and range topography.
	The Mojave Desert's boundaries are generally defined by the presence of Yucca brevifolia (Joshua trees); considered an indicator species for this desert.
Photovoltaics	Photovoltaics is a method of generating electrical power by converting solar radiation into direct current electricity using semiconductors that exhibit the photovoltaic effect. Photovoltaic power generation employs solar panels composed of a number of solar cells containing a photovoltaic material. Materials presently used for photovoltaics include monocrystalline silicon, polycrystalline silicon, amorphous silicon, cadmium telluride, and copper indium gallium selenide/sulfide.
Solar cell	A solar cell is a solid state electrical device that converts the energy of light directly into electricity by the photovoltaic effect.
	Assemblies of cells used to make solar modules which are used to capture energy from sunlight, are known as solar panels. The energy generated from these solar modules, referred to as solar power, is an example of solar energy.
Biodiesel	Biodiesel refers to a vegetable oil- or animal fat-based diesel fuel consisting of long-chain alkyl (methyl, propyl or ethyl) esters. Biodiesel is typically made by chemically reacting lipids (e.g., vegetable oil, animal fat (tallow)) with an alcohol producing fatty acid esters.

Biogas	Biogas typically refers to a gas produced by the biological breakdown of organic matter in the absence of oxygen. Organic waste such as dead plant and animal material, animal feces, and kitchen waste can be converted into a gaseous fuel called biogas. Biogas originates from biogenic material and is a type of biofuel.
Biomass	Biomass, in ecology, is the mass of living biological organisms in a given area or ecosystem at a given time. Biomass can refer to species biomass, which is the mass of one or more species, or to community biomass, which is the mass of all species in the community. It can include microorganisms, plants or animals.
Ethanol	Ethanol, pure alcohol, grain alcohol, or drinking alcohol, is a volatile, flammable, colorless liquid. It is a psychoactive drug and one of the oldest recreational drugs. Best known as the type of alcohol found in alcoholic beverages, it is also used in thermometers, as a solvent, and as a fuel.
Methanol	Methanol, wood alcohol, wood naphtha or wood spirits, is a chemical with the formula CH_3OH. Methanol acquired the name 'wood alcohol' because it was once produced chiefly as a byproduct of the destructive distillation of wood. Modern methanol is produced in a catalytic industrial process directly from carbon monoxide, carbon dioxide, and hydrogen.
Crop residue	There are two types of agricultural crop residues: Field residues are materials left in an agricultural field or orchard after the crop has been harvested. These residues include stalks and stubble (stems), leaves, and seed pods. Good management of field residues can increase efficiency of irrigation and control of erosion. Process residues are those materials left after the processing of the crop into a usable resource. These residues include husks, seeds, bagasse, and roots. They can be used as animal fodder and soil amendment, fertilizers and in manufacturing.
Wind turbine	A wind turbine is a device that converts kinetic energy from the wind, also called wind energy, into mechanical energy; a process known as wind power. If the mechanical energy is used to produce electricity, the device may be called wind turbine or wind power plant. If the mechanical energy is used to drive machinery, such as for grinding grain or pumping water, the device is called a windmill or wind pump.
Earthquake	An earthquake is the result of a sudden release of energy in the Earth's crust that creates seismic waves. The seismicity or seismic activity of an area refers to the frequency, type and size of earthquakes experienced over a period of time. Earthquakes are measured using observations from seismometers.

Chapter 12. Renewable Energy and Nuclear Power

Schistosomiasis	Schistosomiasis is a parasitic disease caused by several species of tremotodes('clatyhelminth' infection) ('flukes'), a parasitic worm of the genus Schistosoma. Although it has a low mortality rate, schistosomiasis often is a chronic illness that can damage internal organs and, in children, impair growth and cognitive development. The urinary form of schistosomiasis is associated with increased risks for bladder cancer in adults.
Three Gorges Dam	The Three Gorges Dam is a hydroelectric dam that spans the Yangtze River by the town of Sandouping, located in the Yiling District of Yichang, in Hubei province, China. The Three Gorges Dam is the world's largest power station in terms of installed capacity (21,000 MW) but is second to Itaipu Dam with regard to the generation of electricity annually. The dam body was completed in 2006. Except for a ship lift, the originally planned components of the project were completed on October 30, 2008, when the 26th turbine in the shore plant began commercial operation.
Wave energy	Wave energy is the transport of energy by ocean surface waves, and the capture of that energy to do useful work - for example, electricity generation, water desalination, or the pumping of water (into reservoirs). Machinery able to exploit wave power is generally known as a wave energy converter (WEC). Wave power is distinct from the diurnal flux of tidal power and the steady gyre of ocean currents.
Ocean thermal energy conversion	Ocean thermal energy conversion uses the difference between cooler deep and warmer shallow or surface ocean waters to run a heat engine and produce useful work, usually in the form of electricity. A heat engine gives greater efficiency and power when run with a large temperature difference. In the oceans the temperature difference between surface and deep water is greatest in the tropics, although still a modest 20°C to 25°C. It is therefore in the tropics that Ocean thermal energy conversion offers the greatest possibilities.
Geothermal energy	Geothermal energy is thermal energy generated and stored in the Earth. Thermal energy is the energy that determines the temperature of matter. Earth's geothermal energy originates from the original formation of the planet (20%) and from radioactive decay of minerals (80%).
Geothermal electricity	
Tidal energy	Tidal power, also called tidal energy, is a form of hydropower that converts the energy of tides into useful forms of power - mainly electricity.

	Although not yet widely used, tidal power has potential for future electricity generation. Tides are more predictable than wind energy and solar power.
Atomic mass	The atomic mass is the mass of a specific isotope, most often expressed in unified atomic mass units. The atomic mass is the total mass of protons, neutrons and electrons in a single atom. The atomic mass is sometimes incorrectly used as a synonym of relative atomic mass, average atomic mass and atomic weight; these differ subtly from the atomic mass.
Atomic number	In chemistry d physics, the atomic number is the number of protons found in the nucleus of atom d therefore identical to the charge number of the nucleus. It is conventionally represented by the symbol Z. The atomic number uniquely identifies a chemical element. In atom of neutral charge, the atomic number is also equal to the number of electrons.
Atom	In the mathematical field of order theory, given two elements a and b of a partially ordered set, one says that b covers a, and writes a <: b or b :> a, if a < b and there is no element c such that a < c < b. In other words, b covers a if b is greater than a and minimal with this property, or equivalently if a is smaller than b and maximal with this property. In a partially ordered set with least element 0, an atom is an element that covers 0, i.e. an element that is minimal among the non-zero elements.
Deuterium	Deuterium, is one of two stable isotopes of hydrogen. It has a natural abundance in Earth's oceans of about one atom in 6,420 of hydrogen (~156.25 ppm on an atom basis). Deuterium accounts for approximately 0.0156% (or on a mass basis: 0.0312%) of all naturally occurring hydrogen in Earth's oceans, while the most common isotope (hydrogen-1 or protium) accounts for more than 99.98%.
Isotope	Isotopes are variants of a particular chemical element. While all isotopes of a given element share the same number of protons, each isotope differs from the others in its number of neutrons. The term isotope is formed from the Greek roots isos and topos .
Nuclear fission	In nuclear physics and nuclear chemistry, nuclear fission refers to either a nuclear reaction or a radioactive decay process in which the nucleus of an atom splits into smaller parts (lighter nuclei), often producing free neutrons and photons (in the form of gamma rays), and releasing a very large amount of energy, even by the energetic standards of radioactive decay. The two nuclei produced are most often of comparable but slightly different sizes, typically with a mass ratio of products of about 3 to 2, for common fissile isotopes.

Chapter 12. Renewable Energy and Nuclear Power

Nuclear fusion	Nuclear fusion is the process by which two or more atomic nuclei join together, or 'fuse', to form a single heavier nucleus. This is usually accompanied by the release or absorption of large quantities of energy. Fusion is the process that powers active stars, the hydrogen bomb and some experimental devices examining fusion power for electrical generation.
Nuclear fuel cycle	The nuclear fuel cycle, is the progression of nuclear fuel through a series of differing stages. It consists of steps in the front end, which are the preparation of the fuel, steps in the service period in which the fuel is used during reactor operation, and steps in the back end, which are necessary to safely manage, contain, and either reprocess or dispose of spent nuclear fuel. If spent fuel is not reprocessed, the fuel cycle is referred to as an open fuel cycle (or a once-through fuel cycle); if the spent fuel is reprocessed, it is referred to as a closed fuel cycle.
Nuclear reactor	A nuclear reactor is a device to initiate and control a sustained nuclear chain reaction. Most commonly they are used for generating electricity and for the propulsion of ships. Usually heat from nuclear fission is passed to a working fluid (water or gas), which runs through turbines that power either ship's propellers or generators.
Radioactive decay	Radioactive decay is the process by which an atomic nucleus of an unstable atom loses energy by emitting ionizing particles (ionizing radiation) A decay, or loss of energy, results when an atom with one type of nucleus, called the parent radionuclide, transforms to an atom with a nucleus in a different state, or to a different nucleus containing different numbers of nucleons.
Tritium	Tritium is a radioactive isotope of hydrogen. The nucleus of tritium contains one proton and two neutrons, whereas the nucleus of protium (by far the most abundant hydrogen isotope) contains one proton and no neutrons. Naturally occurring tritium is extremely rare on Earth, where trace amounts are formed by the interaction of the atmosphere with cosmic rays.
Uranium	Uranium is a silvery-white metallic chemical element in the actinide series of the periodic table, with atomic number 92. It is assigned the chemical symbol U. A uranium atom has 92 protons and 92 electrons, of which 6 are valence electrons. The uranium nucleus binds between 141 and 146 neutrons, establishing six isotopes (U-233 through U-238), the most common of which are uranium-238 (146 neutrons) and uranium-235 (143 neutrons). All isotopes are unstable and uranium is weakly radioactive.
Condenser	In systems involving heat transfer, a condenser is a device or unit used to condense a substance from its gaseous to its liquid state, typically by cooling it. In so doing, the latent heat is given up by the substance, and will transfer to the condenser coolant.

Steam generator	A steam generator is a form of low water-content boiler, similar to a flash steam boiler. The usual construction is as a spiral coil of water-tube, arranged as a single, or monotube, coil. Circulation is once-through and pumped under pressure, as a forced-circulation boiler.
Spent nuclear fuel	Spent nuclear fuel, occasionally called used nuclear fuel, is nuclear fuel that has been irradiated in a nuclear reactor (usually at a nuclear power plant). It is no longer useful in sustaining a nuclear reaction in an ordinary thermal reactor.
	Spent low enriched uranium nuclear fuel is an example of a nanomaterial.
Radioactive waste	Radioactive wastes are wastes that contain radioactive material. Radioactive wastes are usually by-products of nuclear power generation and other applications of nuclear fission or nuclear technology, such as research and medicine. Radioactive waste is hazardous to most forms of life and the environment, and is regulated by government agencies in order to protect human health and the environment.
Megatons to Megawatts Program	The Megatons to Megawatts Program is the name given to the program that implemented the 1993 United States-Russia nonproliferation agreement to convert high-enriched uranium (HEU) taken from dismantled Russian nuclear weapons into low-enriched-uranium (LEU) for nuclear fuel. Extent of program since 1995
	From 1995 through September 2010, 400 metric tons of highly-enriched uranium from Russian nuclear warheads have been recycled into low-enriched-uranium fuel for U.S. nuclear power plants. The first plant to receive fuel containing uranium under this program was the Cooper Nuclear Station in 1998. This program has eliminated the equivalent of 16,000 nuclear warheads.
Nuclear weapon	A nuclear weapon is an explosive device that derives its destructive force from nuclear reactions, either fission or a combination of fission and fusion. Both reactions release vast quantities of energy from relatively small amounts of matter. The first fission ('atomic') bomb test released the same amount of energy as approximately 20,000 tons of TNT. The first thermonuclear ('hydrogen') bomb test released the same amount of energy as approximately 10,000,000 tons of TNT.
Plutonium	Plutonium is a transuranic radioactive chemical element with the chemical symbol Pu and atomic number 94. It is an actinide metal of silvery-white appearance that tarnishes when exposed to air, forming a dull coating when oxidized. The element normally exhibits six allotropes and four oxidation states. It reacts with carbon, halogens, nitrogen and silicon.
Dry cask storage	Dry cask storage is a method of storing high-level radioactive waste, such as spent nuclear fuel that has already been cooled in the spent fuel pool for at least one year..

Chapter 12. Renewable Energy and Nuclear Power

	These casks are typically steel cylinders that are either welded or bolted closed. When inside, the fuel rods are surrounded by inert gas.
Vitrification	Vitrification is the transformation of a substance into a glass. Usually, it is achieved by rapidly cooling a liquid through the glass transition. Certain chemical reactions also result in glasses.
Plasma	In physics and chemistry, plasma is a state of matter similar to gas in which a certain portion of the particles are ionized. Heating a gas may ionize its molecules or atoms (reduce or increase the number of electrons in them), thus turning it into a plasma, which contains charged particles: positive ions and negative electrons or ions. Ionization can be induced by other means, such as strong electromagnetic field alied with a laser or microwave generator, and is accompanied by the dissociation of molecular bonds, if present.

CHAPTER QUIZ: KEY TERMS, PEOPLE, PLACES, CONCEPTS

1. _____, hydraulic power or water power is power that is derived from the force or energy of moving water, which may be harnessed for useful purposes. Prior to the development of electric power, _____ was used for irrigation, and operation of various machines, such as watermills, textile machines, sawmills, dock cranes, and domestic lifts.

   Another method used a trompe to produce compressed air from falling water, which could then be used to power other machinery at a distance from the water.

   a. Hydropower
   b. Juglone
   c. Gibbons v. Ogden
   d. Krakatoa

2. a. Geothermal electricity
   b. Traveston Crossing Dam
   c. Vilarinho da Furna
   d. Wellington Weir

3. . _____ refers to a vegetable oil- or animal fat-based diesel fuel consisting of long-chain alkyl (methyl, propyl or ethyl) esters. _____ is typically made by chemically reacting lipids (e.g., vegetable oil, animal fat (tallow)) with an alcohol producing fatty acid esters.

_____ is meant to be used in standard diesel engines and is thus distinct from the vegetable and waste oils used to fuel converted diesel engines.

a. Juglone
b. Biodiesel
c. Gibbons v. Ogden
d. Krakatoa

4. A _____ is a device to initiate and control a sustained nuclear chain reaction. Most commonly they are used for generating electricity and for the propulsion of ships. Usually heat from nuclear fission is passed to a working fluid (water or gas), which runs through turbines that power either ship's propellers or generators.

a. Nuclear submarine
b. Nuclear reactor
c. Nuclear-free zone
d. Nucleate boiling

5. A _____ is an explosive device that derives its destructive force from nuclear reactions, either fission or a combination of fission and fusion. Both reactions release vast quantities of energy from relatively small amounts of matter. The first fission ('atomic') bomb test released the same amount of energy as approximately 20,000 tons of TNT. The first thermonuclear ('hydrogen') bomb test released the same amount of energy as approximately 10,000,000 tons of TNT.

a. Nuclear material
b. Nuclear weapon
c. Gibbons v. Ogden
d. Naval Nuclear Power Training Command

1. a
2. a
3. b
4. b
5. b

You can take the complete Chapter Practice Test

for Chapter 12. Renewable Energy and Nuclear Power
on all key terms, persons, places, and concepts.

Online 99 Cents

http://www.epub89.6.20924.12.cram101.com/

Use www.Cram101.com for all your study needs

including Cram101's online interactive problem solving labs in

chemistry, statistics, mathematics, and more.

Chapter 13. Water: A Limited Resource

CHAPTER OUTLINE: KEY TERMS, PEOPLE, PLACES, CONCEPTS

Heat capacity

Hydrogen bond

Drainage basin

Surface water

Wetland

Aquifer

Artesian aquifer

Groundwater

Water table

Floodplain

Mississippi River Delta

Drought

Irrigation

Saltwater intrusion

Sinkhole

Subsidence

Colorado River Compact

Distribution

Precipitation

Chapter 13. Water: A Limited Resource

CHAPTER OUTLINE: KEY TERMS, PEOPLE, PLACES, CONCEPTS

	Indus River
	Yellow River
	Climate change
	Aral Sea
	Glen Canyon Dam
	Water management
	Water right
	Endangered Species Act
	Fish ladder
	Distillation
	Drip irrigation
	Reverse osmosis
	Water conservation
	Conservation
	Geographic information system
	Hydropower

Chapter 13. Water: A Limited Resource

Heat capacity	ImgProperty databaseimg Heat capacity or thermal capacity, is the measurable physical quantity that characterizes the amount of heat required to change a substance's temperature by a given amount. In the International System of Units (SI), heat capacity is expressed in units of joule(s) (J) per kelvin (K). Derived quantities that specify heat capacity as an intensive property, i.e., independent of the size of a sample, are the molar heat capacity, which is the heat capacity per mole of a pure substance, and the specific heat capacity, often simply called specific heat, which is the heat capacity per unit mass of a material.
Hydrogen bond	A hydrogen bond is the attractive interaction of a hydrogen atom with an electronegative atom, such as nitrogen, oxygen or fluorine, that comes from another molecule or chemical group. The hydrogen must be covalently bonded to another electronegative atom to create the bond. These bonds can occur between molecules (intermolecularly), or within different parts of a single molecule (intramolecularly).
Drainage basin	A drainage basin is an extent or an area of land where surface water from rain and melting snow or ice converges to a single point, usually the exit of the basin, where the waters join another waterbody, such as a river, lake, reservoir, estuary, wetland, sea, or ocean. In closed drainage basins the water converges to a single point inside the basin, known as a sink, which may be a permanent lake, dry lake, or a point where surface water is lost underground. The drainage basin includes both the streams and rivers that convey the water as well as the land surfaces from which water drains into those channels, and is separated from adjacent basins by a drainage divide.
Surface water	Surface water is water collecting on the ground or in a stream, river, lake, wetland, or ocean; it is related to water collecting as groundwater or atmospheric water. Surface water is naturally replenished by precipitation and naturally lost through discharge to evaporation and sub-surface seepage into the ground. Although there are other sources of groundwater, such as connate water and magmatic water, precipitation is the major one and groundwater originated in this way is called meteoric water.
Wetland	A wetland is a land area that is saturated with water, either permanently or seasonally, such that it takes on characteristics that distinguish it as a distinct ecosystem. The primary factor that distinguishes wetlands is the characteristic vegetation that is adapted to its unique soil conditions: Wetlands are made up primarily of hydric soil, which supports aquatic plants.

Aquifer	An aquifer is a wet underground layer of water-bearing permeable rock or unconsolidated materials (gravel, sand, or silt) from which groundwater can be usefully extracted using a water well. The study of water flow in aquifers and the characterization of aquifers is called hydrogeology. Related terms include aquitard, which is a bed of low permeability along an aquifer, and aquiclude (or aquifuge), which is a solid, impermeable area underlying or overlying an aquifer.
Artesian aquifer	An artesian aquifer is a confined aquifer containing groundwater under positive pressure. This causes the water level in a well to rise to a point where hydrostatic equilibrium has been reached. This type of well is called an artesian well.
Groundwater	Groundwater is water located beneath the ground surface in soil pore spaces and in the fractures of rock formations. A unit of rock or an unconsolidated deposit is called an aquifer when it can yield a usable quantity of water. The depth at which soil pore spaces or fractures and voids in rock become completely saturated with water is called the water table.
Water table	The water table is the surface where the water pressure head is equal to the atmospheric pressure (where gauge pressure = 0). It may be conveniently visualized as the 'surface' of the subsurface materials that are saturated with groundwater in a given vicinity. However, saturated conditions may extend above the water table as surface tension holds water in some pores below atmospheric pressure.
Floodplain	A floodplain, is a flat or nearly flat land adjacent a stream or river that stretches from the banks of its channel to the base of the enclosing valley walls and experiences flooding during periods of high discharge. It includes the floodway, which consists of the stream channel and adjacent areas that carry flood flows, and the flood fringe, which are areas covered by the flood, but which do not experience a strong current. In other words, a floodplain is an area near a river or a stream which floods easily.
Mississippi River Delta	The Mississippi River Delta is the modern area of land (the river delta) built up by alluvium deposited by the Mississippi River as it slows down and enters the Gulf of Mexico. The deltaic process has, over the past 5,000 years, caused the coastline of south Louisiana to advance gulfward from 15 to 50 miles (24 to 80 km).
	It is a biologically significant region, comprising 3 million acres (12,000 km²) of coastal wetlands and 40% of the salt marsh in the contiguous United States.
Drought	A drought is an extended period of months or years when a region notes a deficiency in its water supply whether surface or underground water. Generally, this occurs when a region receives consistently below average precipitation.

Chapter 13. Water: A Limited Resource

Irrigation	Irrigation is the artificial application of water to the land or soil. It is used to assist in the growing of agricultural crops, maintenance of landscapes, and revegetation of disturbed soils in dry areas and during periods of inadequate rainfall. Additionally, irrigation also has a few other uses in crop production, which include protecting plants against frost, suppressing weed growing in grain fields and helping in preventing soil consolidation.
Saltwater intrusion	Saltwater intrusion is the movement of saline water into freshwater aquifers. Most often, it is caused by ground-water pumping from coastal wells, or from construction of navigation channels or oil field canals. The channels and canals provide conduits for salt water to be brought into fresh water marshes.
Sinkhole	A sinkhole, shake hole, swallow hole, swallet, doline or cenote, is a natural depression or hole in the Earth's surface caused by karst processes -- the chemical dissolution of carbonate rocks or suffosion processes for example in sandstone. Sinkholes may vary in size from 1 to 600 meters (3.3 to 2,000 ft) both in diameter and depth, and vary in form from soil-lined bowls to bedrock-edged chasms. Sinkholes may be formed gradually or suddenly, and are found worldwide.
Subsidence	Subsidence is the motion of a surface (usually, the Earth's surface) as it shifts downward relative to a datum such as sea-level. The opposite of subsidence is uplift, which results in an increase in elevation. Ground subsidence is of concern to geologists, geotechnical engineers and surveyors.
Colorado River Compact	The Colorado River Compact is a 1922 agreement among seven U.S. states in the basin of the Colorado River in the American Southwest governing the allocation of the water rights to the river's water among the parties of the interstate compact. The agreement was signed at a meeting at Bishop's Lodge, near Santa Fe, New Mexico, by representatives of the seven states the Colorado river and its tributaries pass through on the way to Mexico. The Colorado River is managed and operated under numerous compacts, federal laws, court decisions and decrees, contracts, and regulatory guidelines collectively known as 'The Law of the River.' Provisions The compact divides the river basin into two areas, the Upper Division (comprising Colorado, New Mexico, Utah and Wyoming) and the Lower Division (Nevada, Arizona and California).
Distribution	In differential geometry, a discipline within mathematics, a distribution is a subset of the tangent bundle of a manifold satisfying certain properties.
Precipitation	Precipitation is the formation of a solid in a solution or inside another solid during a chemical reaction or by diffusion in a solid.

	When the reaction occurs in a liquid, the solid formed is called the Precipitate, or when compacted by a centrifuge, a pellet. The liquid remaining above the solid is in either case called the supernate or supernatant.
Indus River	The Indus River is a major river which flows through Pakistan. It also has courses through western Tibet (in China) and Northern India. Originating in the Tibetan plateau in the vicinity of Lake Mansarovar, the river runs a course through the Ladakh region of Jammu and Kashmir, Gilgit, Baltistan and flows through Pakistan in a southerly direction along the entire length of Pakistan to merge into the Arabian Sea near the port city of Karachi in Sindh.
Yellow River	The Yellow River, formerly spelled Hwang Ho, is the second-longest river in China after the Yangtze and the sixth-longest in the world at the estimated length of 5,464 kilometers (3,395 mi). Originating in the Bayan Har Mountains in Qinghai Province in western China, it flows through nine provinces of China and empties into the Bohai Sea. The Yellow River basin has an east-west extent of 1900 km (1,180 mi) and a north-south extent of 1100 km (684 mi).
Climate change	Climate change is a significant and lasting change in the statistical distribution of weather patterns over periods ranging from decades to millions of years. It may be a change in average weather conditions or the distribution of events around that average (e.g., more or fewer extreme weather events). Climate change may be limited to a specific region or may our across the whole Earth.
Aral Sea	The Aral Sea was a lake lying between Kazakhstan (Aktobe and Kyzylorda provinces) in the north and Karakalpakstan, an autonomous region of Uzbekistan, in the south. The name roughly translates as 'Sea of Islands', referring to about 1,534 islands that once dotted its waters; in Old Turkic 'aral' means island and thicket. Formerly one of the four largest lakes in the world with an area of 68,000 square kilometres (26,300 sq mi), the Aral Sea has been steadily shrinking since the 1960s after the rivers that fed it were diverted by Soviet irrigation projects.
Glen Canyon Dam	Glen Canyon Dam is a concrete arch dam on the Colorado River in northern Arizona in the United States, just north of Page. The dam was built to provide hydroelectricity and flow regulation from the upper Colorado River Basin to the lower. Its reservoir is called Lake Powell, and is the second largest artificial lake in the country, extending upriver well into Utah.
Water management	Water management is the process of allocating water as a resource in a sustainable and efficient manor. This includes planning, developing, distributing and managing the optimum use of water resources. Water management planning has to regard all the competing demands for water and seeks to allocate water on an equitable basis to satisfy all uses and demands.

Chapter 13. Water: A Limited Resource

Water right	Water right in water law refers to the right of a user to use water from a water source, e.g., a river, stream, pond or source of groundwater. In areas with plentiful water and few users, such systems are generally not complicated or contentious. In other areas, especially arid areas where irrigation is practiced, such systems are often the source of conflict, both legal and physical.
Endangered Species Act	The Endangered Species Act of 1973 (Endangered Species Act; 7 U.S.C. § 136, 16 U.S.C. § 1531 et seq). is one of the dozens of United States environmental laws passed in the 1970s. Signed into law by President Richard Nixon on December 28, 1973, it was designed to protect critically imperiled species from extinction as a 'consequence of economic growth and development untempered by adequate concern and conservation.'
	The Act is administered by two federal agencies, the United States Fish and Wildlife Service (FWS) and the National Oceanic and Atmospheric Administration (NOAA).
Fish ladder	A fish ladder, fish pass or fish steps, is a structure on or around artificial barriers (such as dams and locks) to facilitate diadromous fishes' natural migration. Most fishways enable fish to pass around the barriers by swimming and leaping up a series of relatively low steps (hence the term ladder) into the waters on the other side. The velocity of water falling over the steps has to be great enough to attract the fish to the ladder, but it cannot be so great that it washes fish back downstream or exhausts them to the point of inability to continue their journey upriver.
Distillation	Distillation is a method of separating mixtures based on differences in volatilities of components in a boiling liquid mixture. Distillation is a unit operation, or a physical separation process, and not a chemical reaction.
	Commercially, distillation has a number of applications.
Drip irrigation	Drip irrigation, is an irrigation method which saves water and fertilizer by allowing water to drip slowly to the roots of plants, either onto the soil surface or directly onto the root zone, through a network of valves, pipes, tubing, and emitters. It is done with the help of narrow tubes which deliver water directly to the base of the plant.
	Heda irrigation has been used since ancient times when buried clay pots were filled with water, which would gradually seep into the grass. Modern drip irrigation began its development in Afghanistan in 1866 when researchers began experimenting with irrigation using clay pipe to create combination irrigation and drainage systems.
Reverse osmosis	Reverse osmosis is a filtration method that removes many types of large molecules and ions from solutions by applying pressure to the solution when it is on one side of a selective membrane.

The result is that the solute is retained on the pressurized side of the membrane and the pure solvent is allowed to pass to the other side. To be 'selective,' this membrane should not allow large molecules or ions through the pores (holes), but should allow smaller components of the solution (such as the solvent) to pass freely.

Water conservation	Water conservation refers to reducing the usage of water and recycling of waste water for different purposes such as cleaning, manufacturing, and agricultural irrigation. Water conservation can be defined as: 1.Any beneficial reduction in water loss, use or waste as well as the preservation of water quality. 2.A reduction in water use accomplished by implementation of water conservation or water efficiency measures; or, 3.Improved water management practices that reduce or enhance the beneficial use of water. A water conservation measure is an action, behavioral change, device, technology, or improved design or process implemented to reduce water loss, waste, or use.
Conservation	Conservation is an ethic of resour use, allocation, and protection. Its primary focus is upon maintaining the health of the natural world: its, fisheries, habitats, and biological diversity. Secondary focus is on materials conservation and energy conservation, which are seen as important to protect the natural world.
Geographic information system	A geographic information system is a system designed to capture, store, manipulate, analyze, manage, and present all types of geographically referenced data. The acronym is sometimes used to mean geographical information science or geospatial information studies; these latter terms refer to the academic discipline or career of working with geographic information systems. In the simplest terms, is the merging of cartography, statistical analysis, and database technology.
Hydropower	Hydropower, hydraulic power or water power is power that is derived from the force or energy of moving water, which may be harnessed for useful purposes. Prior to the development of electric power, hydropower was used for irrigation, and operation of various machines, such as watermills, textile machines, sawmills, dock cranes, and domestic lifts. Another method used a trompe to produce compressed air from falling water, which could then be used to power other machinery at a distance from the water.

1. A _____ is the attractive interaction of a hydrogen atom with an electronegative atom, such as nitrogen, oxygen or fluorine, that comes from another molecule or chemical group. The hydrogen must be covalently bonded to another electronegative atom to create the bond. These bonds can occur between molecules (intermolecularly), or within different parts of a single molecule (intramolecularly).

    a. Hydrogen bond
    b. J-aggregate
    c. Macrocycle
    d. Mechanical bond

2. ImgProperty databaseimg

    _____ or thermal capacity, is the measurable physical quantity that characterizes the amount of heat required to change a substance's temperature by a given amount. In the International System of Units (SI), _____ is expressed in units of joule(s) (J) per kelvin (K).

    Derived quantities that specify _____ as an intensive property, i.e., independent of the size of a sample, are the molar _____, which is the _____ per mole of a pure substance, and the specific _____, often simply called specific heat, which is the _____ per unit mass of a material.

    a. Heat capacity
    b. Condensation
    c. Condenser
    d. Thermal grease

3. A _____ is an extent or an area of land where surface water from rain and melting snow or ice converges to a single point, usually the exit of the basin, where the waters join another waterbody, such as a river, lake, reservoir, estuary, wetland, sea, or ocean. In closed _____s the water converges to a single point inside the basin, known as a sink, which may be a permanent lake, dry lake, or a point where surface water is lost underground. The _____ includes both the streams and rivers that convey the water as well as the land surfaces from which water drains into those channels, and is separated from adjacent basins by a drainage divide.

    a. Drainage divide
    b. Drainage system
    c. Drought
    d. Drainage basin

4. . _____, is an irrigation method which saves water and fertilizer by allowing water to drip slowly to the roots of plants, either onto the soil surface or directly onto the root zone, through a network of valves, pipes, tubing, and emitters.It is done with the help of narrow tubes which deliver water directly to the base of the plant.

    Heda irrigation has been used since ancient times when buried clay pots were filled with water, which would gradually seep into the grass.

Modern _____ began its development in Afghanistan in 1866 when researchers began experimenting with irrigation using clay pipe to create combination irrigation and drainage systems.

a. Juglone
b. Flocculation
c. Fluid extract
d. Drip irrigation

5. _____ is water collecting on the ground or in a stream, river, lake, wetland, or ocean; it is related to water collecting as groundwater or atmospheric water.

_____ is naturally replenished by precipitation and naturally lost through discharge to evaporation and sub-surface seepage into the ground. Although there are other sources of groundwater, such as connate water and magmatic water, precipitation is the major one and groundwater originated in this way is called meteoric water.

a. phreatic
b. Surface water
c. Parent rock
d. Key bed

1. a
2. a
3. d
4. d
5. b

You can take the complete Chapter Practice Test

for Chapter 13. Water: A Limited Resource
on all key terms, persons, places, and concepts.

Online 99 Cents

http://www.epub89.6.20924.13.cram101.com/

Use www.Cram101.com for all your study needs

including Cram101's online interactive problem solving labs in

chemistry, statistics, mathematics, and more.

Chapter 14. Soil Resources

CHAPTER OUTLINE: KEY TERMS, PEOPLE, PLACES, CONCEPTS

_____ Desertification

_____ Dust storm

_____ Glacier

_____ Humus

_____ Leaching

_____ Casting

_____ Soil texture

_____ Alfisols

_____ Podzol

_____ Mollisols

_____ Oxisol

_____ Dust Bowl

_____ Drought

_____ Soil conservation

_____ Contour plowing

_____ Crop rotation

_____ Windbreak

_____ Agroforestry

_____ Conservation Reserve Program

Chapter 14. Soil Resources

Desertification	Desertification is the degradation of land in any drylands. Caused by a variety of factors, such as climate change and human activities, desertification is one of the most significant global environmental problems. Considerable controversy exists over the proper definition of the term 'desertification' for which Helmut Geist (2005) has identified more than 100 formal definitions.
Dust storm	A dust storm is a meteorological phenomenon common in arid and semi-arid regions. Dust storms arise when a gust front or other strong wind blows loose sand and dirt from a dry surface. Particles are transported by saltation and suspension, a process that moves soil from one place and deposits it in another.
Glacier	A glacier is a large persistent body of ice that forms where the accumulation of snow exceeds its ablation (melting and sublimation) over many years, often centuries. At least 0.1 km² in area and 50 m thick, but often much larger, a glacier slowly deforms and flows due to stresses induced by its weight. Crevasses, seracs, and other distinguishing features of a glacier are due to its flow.
Humus	In soil science, humus refers to any organic matter that has reached a point of stability, where it will break down no further and might, if conditions do not change, remain as it is for centuries, if not millennia. In agriculture, humus is sometimes also used to describe mature compost, or natural compost extracted from a forest or other spontaneous source for use to amend soil. It is also used to describe a topsoil horizon that contains organic matter (humus type, humus form, humus profile).
Leaching	Leaching Many Biological organic and inorganic substances occur in a mixture of different components in a solid. In order to separate the desired solute constituent or remove an undesirable solute component from the solid phase, the solid is brought into contact with a liquid. The solid and liquid are in contact and the solute or solutes can diffuse from the solid into the solvent, resulting in separation of the components originally in the solid.
Casting	In metalworking, casting involves pouring liquid metal into a mold, which contains a hollow cavity of the desired shape, and then allowing it to cool and solidify. The solidified part is also known as a casting, which is ejected or broken out of the mold to complete the process. Casting is most often used for making complex shapes that would be difficult or uneconomical to make by other methods.
Soil texture	Soil texture is a qualitative classification tool used in both the field and laboratory to determine classes for agricultural soils based on their physical texture.

Chapter 14. Soil Resources

The classes are diinguished in the field by the 'textural feel' which can be further clarified by separating the relative proportions of sand, silt and clay using grading sieves: The Particle Size Diribution (PSD). The class is then used to determine crop suitability and to approximate the soils responses to environmental and management conditions such as drought or calcium (lime) requirements.

Alfisols	Alfisols are a soil order in USDA soil taxonomy. Alfisols form in semiarid to humid areas, typically under a hardwood forest cover. They have a clay-enriched subsoil and relatively high native fertility.
Podzol	In soil science, podzols (also known as podsols or Spodosols) are the typical soils of coniferous, or boreal forests. They are also the typical soils of eucalypt forests and heathlands in southern Australia. The name is Russian for 'under ash' (под/pod=under, зола/zola=ash) and likely refers to the common experience of Russian peasants of plowing up an apparent under-layer of ash (leached or E horizon) during first plowing of a virgin soil of this type.
Mollisols	Mollisols are a soil order in USDA soil taxonomy. Mollisols form in semi-arid to semi-humid areas, typically under a grassland cover. They are most commonly found in the mid-latitudes, namely in North America, mostly east of the Rocky Mountains, in South America in Argentina (Pampas) and Brazil, and in Asia in Mongolia and the Russian Steppes.
Oxisol	Oxisols are an order in USDA soil taxonomy, best known for their occurrence in tropical rain forest, 15-25 degrees north and south of the Equator. Some oxisols have been previously classified as laterite soils. Formation The main processes of soil formation of oxisols are weathering, humification and pedoturbation due to animals.
Dust Bowl	The Dust Bowl, was a period of severe dust storms causing major ecological and agricultural damage to American and Canadian prairie lands from 1930 to 1936 (in some areas until 1940). The phenomenon was caused by severe drought coupled with decades of extensive farming without crop rotation, fallow fields, cover crops or other techniques to prevent wind erosion. Deep plowing of the virgin topsoil of the Great Plains had displaced the natural deep-rooted grasses that normally kept the soil in place and trapped moisture even during periods of drought and high winds.
Drought	A drought is an extended period of months or years when a region notes a deficiency in its water supply whether surface or underground water. Generally, this occurs when a region receives consistently below average precipitation.

Soil conservation	Soil conservation is a set of management strategies for prevention of soil being eroded from the Earth's surface or becoming chemically altered by overuse, acidification, salinization or other chemical soil contamination. It is a component of environmental soil ience. Decisions regarding appropriate crop rotation, cover crops, and planted windbreaks are central to the ability of surface soils to retain their integrity, both with respect to erosive forces and chemical change from nutrient depletion.
Contour plowing	Contour plowing or contour farming is the farming practice of plowing across a slope following its elevation contour lines. The rows form slow water run-off during rainstorms to prevent soil erosion and allow the water time to settle into the soil. In contour plowing, the ruts made by the plow run perpendicular rather than parallel to slopes, generally resulting in furrows that curve around the land and are level.
Crop rotation	Crop rotation is the practice of growing a series of dissimilar types of crops in the same area in sequential seasons. Crop rotation confers various benefits to the soil. A traditional element of crop rotation is the replenishment of nitrogen through the use of green manure in sequence with cereals and other crops.
Windbreak	A windbreak is a plantation usually made up of one or more rows of trees or shrubs planted in such a manner as to provide shelter from the wind and to protect soil from erosion. They are commonly planted around the edges of fields on farms. If designed properly, windbreaks around a home can reduce the cost of heating and cooling and save energy.
Agroforestry	Agroforestry is an integrated approach of using the interactive benefits from combining trees and shrubs with crops and/or livestock. It combines agricultural and forestry technologies to create more diverse, productive, profitable, healthy and sustainable land-use systems. According to the World Agroforestry Centre, Agroforestry is a collective name for land use systems and practices in which woody perennials are deliberately integrated with crops and/or animals on the same land management unit.
Conservation Reserve Program	The Conservation Reserve Program is a cost-share and rental payment program under the United States Department of Agriculture (USDA), and is administered by the USDA Farm Service Agency (FSA). Technical assistance for is provided by the USDA Forest Service and the USDA Natural Resources Conservation Service (NRCS).

Chapter 14. Soil Resources

1. _____ Many Biological organic and inorganic substances occur in a mixture of different components in a solid. In order to separate the desired solute constituent or remove an undesirable solute component from the solid phase, the solid is brought into contact with a liquid. The solid and liquid are in contact and the solute or solutes can diffuse from the solid into the solvent, resulting in separation of the components originally in the solid.

   a. Leakage
   b. Leaching
   c. Limiting oxygen concentration
   d. Mercury silvering

2. _____ is the degradation of land in any drylands. Caused by a variety of factors, such as climate change and human activities, _____ is one of the most significant global environmental problems.

   Considerable controversy exists over the proper definition of the term '_____' for which Helmut Geist (2005) has identified more than 100 formal definitions.

   a. Desertification
   b. Genetically modified food
   c. Global distillation
   d. Hot stain

3. A _____ is a meteorological phenomenon common in arid and semi-arid regions. _____s arise when a gust front or other strong wind blows loose sand and dirt from a dry surface. Particles are transported by saltation and suspension, a process that moves soil from one place and deposits it in another.

   a. Juglone
   b. Genetically modified food
   c. Global distillation
   d. Dust storm

4. A _____ is a large persistent body of ice that forms where the accumulation of snow exceeds its ablation (melting and sublimation) over many years, often centuries. At least 0.1 km² in area and 50 m thick, but often much larger, a _____ slowly deforms and flows due to stresses induced by its weight. Crevasses, seracs, and other distinguishing features of a _____ are due to its flow.

   a. Glacier
   b. Genetically modified food
   c. Global distillation
   d. Hot stain

5. . In soil science, _____ refers to any organic matter that has reached a point of stability, where it will break down no further and might, if conditions do not change, remain as it is for centuries, if not millennia.

In agriculture, _____ is sometimes also used to describe mature compost, or natural compost extracted from a forest or other spontaneous source for use to amend soil. It is also used to describe a topsoil horizon that contains organic matter (_____ type, _____ form, _____ profile).

a. Low-flow irrigation systems

b. Servicios Ecoforestales para Agricultores

c. Humus

d. That Should Not Be: Our Children Will Accuse Us

1. b
2. a
3. d
4. a
5. c

You can take the complete Chapter Practice Test

for Chapter 14. Soil Resources
on all key terms, persons, places, and concepts.

Online 99 Cents

http://www.epub89.6.20924.14.cram101.com/

Use www.Cram101.com for all your study needs

including Cram101's online interactive problem solving labs in

chemistry, statistics, mathematics, and more.

Chapter 15. Mineral Resources

CHAPTER OUTLINE: KEY TERMS, PEOPLE, PLACES, CONCEPTS

Mineral

Igneous rock

Rock cycle

Sedimentary rock

Sedimentation

Blast furnace

Smelting

Acid mine drainage

Cost-benefit analysis

Tailings

Phytoremediation

Aluminium

Chromium

Polymetallic nodules

Biomining

Conservation

Industrial ecology

Chapter 15. Mineral Resources

Mineral	A mineral is a naturally occurring solid chemical substance formed through biogeochemical processes, having characteristic chemical composition, highly ordered atomic structure, and specific physical properties. By comparison, a rock is an aggregate of minerals and/or mineraloids and does not have a specific chemical composition. Minerals range in composition from pure elements and simple salts to very complex silicates with thousands of known forms.
Igneous rock	Igneous rock is one of the three main rock types, the others being sedimentary and metamorphic rock. Igneous rock is formed through the cooling and solidification of magma or lava. Igneous rock may form with or without crystallization, either below the surface as intrusive (plutonic) rocks or on the surface as extrusive (volcanic) rocks.
Rock cycle	The rock cycle is a fundamental concept in geology that describes the dynamic transitions through geologic time among the three main rock types: sedimentary, metamorphic, and igneous. As the diagram to the right illustrates, each type of rock is altered or destroyed when it is forced out of its equilibrium conditions. An igneous rock such as basalt may break down and dissolve when exposed to the atmosphere, or melt as it is subducted under a continent.
Sedimentary rock	Sedimentary rock is a type of rock that is formed by sedimentation of material at the Earth's surface and within bodies of water. Sedimentation is the collective name for processes that cause mineral and/or organic particles (detritus) to settle and accumulate or minerals to precipitate from a solution. Particles that form a sedimentary rock by accumulating are called sediment.
Sedimentation	Sedimentation is the tendency for particles in suspension to settle out of the fluid in which they are entrained, and come to rest against a barrier. This is due to their motion through the fluid in response to the forces acting on them: these forces can be due to gravity, centrifugal acceleration or electromagnetism. In geology sedimentation is often used as the polar opposite of erosion, i.e., the terminal end of sediment transport.
Blast furnace	A blast furnace is a type of metallurgical furnace used for smelting to produce industrial metals, generally iron. In a blast furnace, fuel, ore, and flux (limestone) are continuously supplied through the top of the furnace, while air (sometimes with oxygen enrichment) is blown into the bottom of the chamber, so that the chemical reactions take place throughout the furnace as the material moves downward. The end products are usually molten metal and slag phases tapped from the bottom, and flue gases exiting from the top of the furnace.
Smelting	Smelting is a form of extractive metallurgy; its main use is to produce a metal from its ore. This includes production of silver, iron, copper and other base metals from their ores.

Chapter 15. Mineral Resources

Acid mine drainage	Acid mine drainage or acid rock drainage (ARD), refers to the outflow of acidic water from (usually abandoned) metal mines or coal mines. However, other areas where the earth has been disturbed (e.g. construction sites, subdivisions, transportation corridors, etc). may also contribute acid rock drainage to the environment.
Cost-benefit analysis	Cost-benefit analysis sometimes called benefit-cost analysis (BCA), is a systematic process for calculating and comparing benefits and costs of a project, decision or government policy (hereafter, 'project'). Cost benefit analysis has two purposes:•To determine if it is a sound investment/decision (justification/feasibility),•To provide a basis for comparing projects. It involves comparing the total expected cost of each option against the total expected benefits, to see whether the benefits outweigh the costs, and by how much
	Cost benefit analysis is related to, but distinct from cost-effectiveness analysis.
Tailings	Tailings, slimes, tails, refuse, leach residue, or slickens, are the materials left over after the process of separating the valuable fraction from the uneconomic fraction (gangue) of an ore. Tailings are distinct from overburden or waste rock, which are the materials overlying an ore or mineral body that are displaced during mining without being processed.
	The extraction of minerals from ore can be done two ways: placer mining, which uses water and gravity to extract the valuable minerals, or hard rock mining, which uses pulverization of rock, then chemicals.
Phytoremediation	Phytoremediation (from the Ancient Greek φυτο (phyto, plant), and Latin remedium (restoring balance or remediation) describes the treatment of environmental problems (bioremediation) through the use of plants that mitigate the environmental problem without the need to excavate the contaminant material and dispose of it elsewhere.
	Phytoremediation consists in mitigating pollutant concentrations in contaminated soils, water, or air, with plants able to contain, degrade, or eliminate metals, pesticides, solvents, explosives, crude oil and its derivatives, and various other contaminants from the media that contain them.
	Application
	Phytoremediation may be applied wherever the soil or static water environment has become polluted or is suffering ongoing chronic pollution.
Aluminium	Aluminium is a chemical element in the boron group with symbol Al and atomic number 13. It is silvery white, and it is not soluble in water under normal circumstances.

Chapter 15. Mineral Resources

Chromium

Chromium is a chemical element which has the symbol Cr and atomic number 24. It is the first element in Group 6. It is a steely-gray, lustrous, hard metal that takes a high polish and has a high melting point. It is also odorless, tasteless, and malleable. The name of the element is derived from the Greek word 'chroma' , meaning colour, because many of its compounds are intensely coloured.

Polymetallic nodules

Polymetallic nodules, also called manganese nodules, are rock concretions on the sea bottom formed of concentric layers of iron and manganese hydroxides around a core. The core may be microscopically small and is sometimes completely transformed into manganese minerals by crystallization. When visible to the naked eye, it can be a small test (shell) of a microfossil (radiolarian or foraminifer), a phosphatized shark tooth, basalt debris or even fragments of earlier nodules.

Biomining

Biomining is a new approach to the extraction of desired minerals from ores being explored by the mining industry in the past few years. Microorganisms are used to leach out the minerals, rather than the traditional methods of extreme heat or toxic chemicals, which have a deleterious effect on the environment.

The development of industrial mineral processing has been established now in several countries including South Africa, Brazil and Australia.

Conservation

Conservation is an ethic of resour use, allocation, and protection. Its primary focus is upon maintaining the health of the natural world: its, fisheries, habitats, and biological diversity. Secondary focus is on materials conservation and energy conservation, which are seen as important to protect the natural world.

Industrial ecology

Industrial Ecology is the study of material and energy flows through industrial systems. The global industrial economy can be modeled as a network of industrial processes that extract resources from the Earth and transform those resources into commodits which can be bought and sold to meet the needs of humanity. Industrial ecology seeks to quantify the material flows and document the industrial processes that make modern socty function.

1. _____ is the tendency for particles in suspension to settle out of the fluid in which they are entrained, and come to rest against a barrier. This is due to their motion through the fluid in response to the forces acting on them: these forces can be due to gravity, centrifugal acceleration or electromagnetism. In geology _____ is often used as the polar opposite of erosion, i.e., the terminal end of sediment transport.

   a. Solvent Impregnated Resins
   b. Solvophobic
   c. Spinning cone
   d. Sedimentation

2. _____ is an ethic of resour use, allocation, and protection. Its primary focus is upon maintaining the health of the natural world: its, fisheries, habitats, and biological diversity. Secondary focus is on materials _____ and energy _____, which are seen as important to protect the natural world.

   a. Conservation movement
   b. Biodiversity hotspot
   c. Conservation
   d. Bonn Convention

3. A _____ is a naturally occurring solid chemical substance formed through biogeochemical processes, having characteristic chemical composition, highly ordered atomic structure, and specific physical properties. By comparison, a rock is an aggregate of _____ s and/or mineraloids and does not have a specific chemical composition. _____ s range in composition from pure elements and simple salts to very complex silicates with thousands of known forms.

   a. Mineral
   b. Mineral cycle
   c. Mineralientage
   d. Mineralization

4. _____ is one of the three main rock types, the others being sedimentary and metamorphic rock. _____ is formed through the cooling and solidification of magma or lava. _____ may form with or without crystallization, either below the surface as intrusive (plutonic) rocks or on the surface as extrusive (volcanic) rocks.

   a. Igneous rock
   b. Andesite line
   c. Ashstone
   d. East Australia hotspot

5. . _____ is a type of rock that is formed by sedimentation of material at the Earth's surface and within bodies of water. Sedimentation is the collective name for processes that cause mineral and/or organic particles (detritus) to settle and accumulate or minerals to precipitate from a solution. Particles that form a _____ by accumulating are called sediment.

   a. Shonkinite

b. Sovite

c. Spherulite

d. Sedimentary rock

ANSWER KEY
Chapter 15. Mineral Resources

1. d
2. c
3. a
4. a
5. d

You can take the complete Chapter Practice Test

for Chapter 15. Mineral Resources
on all key terms, persons, places, and concepts.

Online 99 Cents

http://www.epub89.6.20924.15.cram101.com/

Use www.Cram101.com for all your study needs

including Cram101's online interactive problem solving labs in

chemistry, statistics, mathematics, and more.

Chapter 16. Biological Resources

CHAPTER OUTLINE: KEY TERMS, PEOPLE, PLACES, CONCEPTS

_____ | Tiger

_____ | Ecosystem services

_____ | Species richness

_____ | Extinction

_____ | Endangered Species

_____ | International Union for Conservation of Nature

_____ | Threatened species

_____ | Blue whale

_____ | Habitat fragmentation

_____ | Biodiversity

_____ | Millennium Ecosystem Assessment

_____ | Invasive species

_____ | Brown tree snake

_____ | Carolina Parakeet

_____ | Bushmeat

_____ | Passenger Pigeon

_____ | Poaching

_____ | Amphibian

_____ | Indicator species

Conservation Biology

National park

Protected area

Habitat corridor

Restoration ecology

Wildlife corridor

Artificial insemination

Embryo transfer

Flagship species

Conservation reliant species

Endangered Species Act

Convention on Biological Diversity

Habitat Conservation Plan

Wildlife management

North Atlantic right whale

Tiger	The tiger is the largest cat species, reaching a total body length of up to 3.3 metres (11 ft) and weighing up to 306 kg (670 lb). Their most recognizable feature is a pattern of dark vertical stripes on reddish-orange fur with lighter underparts. They have exceptionally stout teeth, and their canines are the longest among living felids with a crown height of as much as 74.5 mm (2.93 in) or even 90 mm (3.5 in).
Ecosystem services	Humankind benefits from a multitude of resources and processes that are supplied by natural ecosystems. Collectively, these benefits are known as ecosystem services and include products like clean drinking water and processes such as the decomposition of wastes. While scientists and environmentalists have discussed ecosystem services for decades, these services were popularized and their definitions formalized by the United Nations 2004 Millennium Ecosystem Assessment (MA), a four-year study involving more than 1,300 scientists worldwide.
Species richness	Species richness is the number of different species in a given area. It is represented in equation form as S. Species richness is the fundamental unit in which to assess the homogeneity of an environment. Typically, species richness is used in conservation studies to determine the sensitivity of ecosystems and their resident species. The actual number of species calculated alone is largely an arbitrary number. These studies, therefore, often develop a rubric or measure for valuing the species richness number(s) or adopt one from previous studies on similar ecosystems.
Extinction	In biology and ecology, extinction is the end of an organism or of a group of organisms (taxon), normally a species. The moment of extinction is generally considered to be the death of the last individual of the species, although the capacity to breed and recover may have been lost before this point. Because a species' potential range may be very large, determining this moment is difficult, and is usually done retrospectively.
Endangered Species	An endangered species is a species of organisms facing a very high risk of extinction. The phrase is used vaguely in common parlance for any species fitting this description, but its use by conservation biologists typically refers to those deigned Endangered in the IUCN Red List, where it is the second most severe conservation status for wild populations, following Critically Endangered. There are currently 3079 animals and 2655 plants classified as Endangered worldwide, compared with 1998 levels of 1102 and 1197, respectively.
International Union for Conservation of Nature	The International Union for Conservation of Nature and Natural Resources (IUCN) is an international organization dedicated to finding 'pragmatic solutions to our most pressing environment and development challenges.' The organization publishes the IUCN Red List, compiling information from a network of conservation organizations to rate which species are most endangered.

Chapter 16. Biological Resources

The IUCN supports scientific research, manages field projects all over the world and brings governments, non-government organizations, United Nations agencies, companies and local communities together to develop and implement policy, laws and best practice. IUCN is the world's oldest and largest global environmental network - a democratic membership union with more than 1,000 government and NGO member organizations, and almost 11,000 volunteer scientists in more than 160 countries.

Threatened species	Threatened species are any species (including animals, plan, fungi, etc). which are vulnerable to endangerment in the near future. The World Conservation Union (IUCN) is the foremost authority on threatened species, and trea threatened species not as a single category, but as a group of three categories, depending on the degree to which they are threatened:•Vulnerable species•Endangered species•Critically endangered species Species that are threatened are sometimes characterised by the population dynamics measure of critical depensation, a mathematical measure of biomass related to population growth rate.
Blue whale	The blue whale is a marine mammal belonging to the suborder of baleen whales (called Mysticeti). At 30 metres (98 ft) in length and 180 metric tons (200 short tons) or more in weight, it is the largest known animal to have ever existed. Long and slender, the blue whale's body can be various shades of bluish-grey dorsally and somewhat lighter underneath.
Habitat fragmentation	Habitat fragmentation as the name implies, describes the emergence of discontinuities (fragmentation) in an organism's preferred environment (habitat), causing population fragmentation. Habitat fragmentation can be caused by geological processes that slowly alter the layout of the physical environment (suspected of being one of the major causes of speciation), or by human activity such as land conversion, which can alter the environment much faster and causes extinctions of many species. The term habitat fragmentation includes five discrete phenomena:•Reduction in the total area of the habitat•Decrease of the interior : edge ratio•Isolation of one habitat fragment from other areas of habitat•Breaking up of one patch of habitat into several smaller patches•Decrease in the average size of each patch of habitatNatural causes and effects Evidence of habitat destruction through natural processes such as volcanism, fire, and climate change is found in the fossil record.

Biodiversity	Biodiversity is the degree of variation of life forms within a given species, ecosystem, biome, or an entire planet. Biodiversity is a measure of the health of ecosystems. Biodiversity is in part a function of climate.
Millennium Ecosystem Assessment	The Millennium Ecosystem Assessment, released in 2005, is an international synthesis by over 1000 of the world's leading biological scientists that analyses the state of the Earth's ecosystems and provides summaries and guidelines for decision-makers. It concludes that human activity is having a significant and escalating impact on the biodiversity of world ecosystems, reducing both their resilience and biocapacity. The report refers to natural systems as humanity's 'life-support system', providing essential 'ecosystem services'.
Invasive species	Invasive species, a nomenclature term and categorization phrase used for flora and fauna, and for specific restoration-preservation processes in native habitats, with several definitions. •The first definition, the most used, applies to introduced species (also called 'non-indigenous' or 'non-native') that adversely affect the habitats and bioregions they invade economically, environmentally, and/or ecologically. Such invasive species may be either plants or animals and may drupt by dominating a region, wilderness areas, particular habitats, or wildland-urban interface land from loss of natural controls (such as predators or herbivores).
Brown tree snake	The brown tree snake is an arboreal rear-fanged colubrid snake native to eastern and northern coastal Australia, Papua New Guinea, and a large number of islands in northwestern Melanesia. This snake is infamous for being an invasive species responsible for devastating the majority of the native bird population on Guam.
Carolina Parakeet	The Carolina Parakeet was the only parrot species native to the eastern United States. It was found from the Ohio Valley to the Gulf of Mexico, and lived in old forests along rivers. It was the only species at the time classified in the genus Conuropsis.
Bushmeat	Bushmeat is meat from wild animals hunted in Africa and Asia, especially from endangered or protected species. The term has particularly been used refer to meat from animals in West and Central Africa. Today the term is often used to refer to a wider range of countries and especially in reference to the hunting of endangered ape species. Many conservation organizations have come together to address the bushmeat phenomenon through the formation of the Bushmeat Crisis Task Force, whose mission is to build a public, professional and government constituency aimed at identifying and supporting solutions that effectively respond to the bushmeat crisis in Africa and around the world.
Passenger Pigeon	The Passenger Pigeon or Wild Pigeon (Ectopistes migratorius) was a bird that existed in North America until the early 20th century when it went extinct due to hunting and habitat destruction. The species lived in enormous migratory flocks.

Chapter 16. Biological Resources

Poaching	Poaching is the illegal taking of wild plants or animals contrary to local and international conservation and wildlife management laws. Violations of hunting laws and regulations are normally punishable by law and, collectively, such violations are known as poaching.
	Poaching, like smuggling, has a long counter-cultural history, dispassionately reported for England in 'Pleas of the Forest', transgressions of the rigid Anglo-Norman Forest Law.
Amphibian	Amphibians are ectothermic, tetrapod vertebrates of the class Amphibia. They inhabit a wide variety of habitats with most species living within terrestrial, fossorial, arboreal or freshwater aquatic ecosystems. Amphibians typically start out as larva living in water, but some species have developed behavioural adaptations to bypass this.
Indicator species	An indicator species is any biological species that defines a trait or characteristic of the environment. For example, a species may delineate an ecoregion or indicate an environmental condition such as a disease outbreak, pollution, species competition or climate change. Indicator species can be among the most sensitive species in a region, and sometimes act as an early warning to monitoring biologists.
Conservation Biology	Conservation Biology is a peer-reviewed academic journal of the Society for Conservation Biology, published by Wiley-Blackwell.
	Conservation Biology publishes articles covering the science and practice of conserving Earth's biological diversity. Coverage includes issues concerning any of the Earth's ecosystems or regions, and that apply different approaches to solving problems in this area.
National park	A national park is a reserve of natural, semi-natural, or developed land that a sovereign state declares or owns. Although individual nations designate their own national parks differently , an international organization, the International Union for Conservation of Nature (IUCN), and its World Commission on Protected Areas, has defined National Parks as its category II type of protected areas.
Protected area	Protected areas are locations which receive protection because of their recognised natural, ecological and/or cultural values. There are several kinds of protected areas, which vary by level of protection depending on the enabling laws of each country or the regulations of the international organisations involved. The term 'protected area' also includes Marine Protected Areas, the boundaries of which will include some area of ocean.
Habitat corridor	A habitat corridor is a strip of land that aids in the movement of species between disconnected areas of their natural habitat. An animal's natural habitat would typically include a number of areas necessary to thrive, such as wetlands, burrowing sites, food, and breeding grounds.

| Restoration ecology | Restoration ecology is the scientific study and practice of renewing and restoring degraded, damaged, or destroyed ecosystems and habitats in the environment by active human intervention and action. Restoration ecology emerged as a separate field in ecology in the 1980s.

History

Land managers, laypeople, and stewards have been practicing restoration for many hundreds, if not thousands of years, yet the scientific field of 'restoration ecology' was first identified and coined in the late 1980s by John Aber and William Jordan. |
|---|---|
| Wildlife corridor | A wildlife corridor is an area of habitat connecting wildlife populations separated by human activities (such as roads, development, or logging). This allows an exchange of individuals between populations, which may help prevent the negative effects of inbreeding and reduced genetic diversity (via genetic drift) that often occur within isolated populations. Corridors may also help facilitate the re-establishment of populations that have been reduced or eliminated due to random events (such as fires or disease). |
| Artificial insemination | Artificial insemination, is the process by which sperm is placed into the reproductive tract of a female for the purpose of impregnating the female by using means other than sexual intercourse or natural insemination. In humans, it is used as assisted reproductive technology, using either sperm from the woman's male partner or sperm from a sperm donor (donor sperm) in cases where the male partner produces no sperm or the woman has no male partner (i.e., single women, lesbian couples). In cases where donor sperm is used the woman is the gestational and genetic mother of the child produced, and the sperm donor is the genetic or biological father of the child. |
| Embryo transfer | Embryo transfer refers to a step in the process of assisted reproduction in which embryos are placed into the uterus of a female with the intent to establish a pregnancy. This technique (which is often used in connection with in vitro fertilization (IVF)), may be used in humans or in animals, in which situations the goals may vary.

Embryos can be either 'fresh' from fertilized egg cells of the same menstrual cycle, or 'frozen', that is they have been generated in a preceding cycle and undergone embryo cryopreservation, and are thawed just prior to the transfer. |
| Flagship species | The concept of flagship species is a surrogate species concept with its genesis in the field of conservation biology. |

Chapter 16. Biological Resources

The flagship species concept holds that by raising the profile of a particular species, it can successfully leverage more support for biodiversity conservation at large in a particular context.

Several definitions have been advanced for the flagship species concept although the concept has for some time been immerse in confusion even in the academic literature.

Conservation reliant species	Conservation reliant species are endangered or threatened animal or plant species that require continuing species specific wildlife management intervention such as predator control, habitat management and parasite control to survive even when self-sustaining population recovery goals are achieved.

The term Conservation reliant species grew out of the conservation biology work of 'The Endangered Species Act at Thirty Project ', begun in 2001, and has been popularized by the leader of that project, J. Michael Scott This is a new wildlife management term, first published in Frontiers in Ecology and the Environmentin 2005. Worldwide application of the term has not yet developed and it has not yet appeared in a non-USA or Canadian authored publication.

Passage of the 1973 Endangered Species Act (ESA) carried with it the assumption that endangered species would be delisted as their populations recovered.

Endangered Species Act	The Endangered Species Act of 1973 (Endangered Species Act; 7 U.S.C. § 136, 16 U.S.C. § 1531 et seq). is one of the dozens of United States environmental laws passed in the 1970s. Signed into law by President Richard Nixon on December 28, 1973, it was designed to protect critically imperiled species from extinction as a 'consequence of economic growth and development untempered by adequate concern and conservation.'

The Act is administered by two federal agencies, the United States Fish and Wildlife Service (FWS) and the National Oceanic and Atmospheric Administration (NOAA).

Convention on Biological Diversity	The Convention on Biological Diversity known informally as the Biodiversity Convention, is an international legally binding treaty. The Convention has three main goals:•conservation of biological diversity (or biodiversity);•sustainable use of its components; and•fair and equitable sharing of benefits arising from genetic resources

In other words, its objective is to develop national strategies for the conservation and sustainable use of biological diversity. It is often seen as the key document regarding sustainable development.

Habitat Conservation Plan	A Habitat conservation plan is a plan prepared under the Endangered Species Act (ESA) by nonfederal parties wishing to obtain permits for incidental taking of threatened and endangered species.

	In 1982, Congress amended the ESA to enhance the permitting provisions of the act in Section 10 and intended, in part, to provide landowners with incentives to participate in endangered species conservation. A landowner prepares a 'Habitat Conservation Plan' that meets statutory criteria and can then obtain the 'incidental take permits' that allow otherwise prohibited impacts to endangered, threatened and other species covered in the permitting documents.
Wildlife management	Wildlife management attempts to balance the needs of wildlife with the needs of people using the best available science. Wildlife management can include game keeping, wildlife conservation and pest control. Wildlife management has become an integrated science using disciplines such as mathematics, chemistry, biology, ecology, climatology and geography to gain the best results.
North Atlantic right whale	The North Atlantic right whale which means 'good, or true, whale of the ice', is a baleen whale, one of three right whale species belonging to the genus Eubalaena, formerly classified as a single species. With only 400 in existence, North Atlantic right whales are among the most endangered whales in the world. They are protected under the U.S. Endangered Species Act of 1973 and the Marine Mammal Protection Act of 1972. Vessel strikes and entanglement in fixed fishing gear are the two greatest threats to their recovery.

CHAPTER QUIZ: KEY TERMS, PEOPLE, PLACES, CONCEPTS

1. The _____ is a marine mammal belonging to the suborder of baleen whales (called Mysticeti). At 30 metres (98 ft) in length and 180 metric tons (200 short tons) or more in weight, it is the largest known animal to have ever existed.

    Long and slender, the _____'s body can be various shades of bluish-grey dorsally and somewhat lighter underneath.

    a. Habitat conservation
    b. Blue whale
    c. Population fragmentation
    d. Project Elephant

2. . A _____ is a plan prepared under the Endangered Species Act (ESA) by nonfederal parties wishing to obtain permits for incidental taking of threatened and endangered species.

    In 1982, Congress amended the ESA to enhance the permitting provisions of the act in Section 10 and intended, in part, to provide landowners with incentives to participate in endangered species conservation. A landowner prepares a '_____' that meets statutory criteria and can then obtain the 'incidental take permits' that allow otherwise prohibited impacts to endangered, threatened and other species covered in the permitting documents.

Visit Cram101.com for full Practice Exams

a. Habitat destruction
b. Landscape limnology
c. Habitat Conservation Plan
d. Litterfall

3. _____s are ectothermic, tetrapod vertebrates of the class Amphibia. They inhabit a wide variety of habitats with most species living within terrestrial, fossorial, arboreal or freshwater aquatic ecosystems. _____s typically start out as larva living in water, but some species have developed behavioural adaptations to bypass this.

a. Odyssey
b. Pollution
c. Amphibian
d. Secondary forest

4. _____ are any species (including animals, plan, fungi, etc). which are vulnerable to endangerment in the near future.

The World Conservation Union (IUCN) is the foremost authority on _____, and trea _____ not as a single category, but as a group of three categories, depending on the degree to which they are threatened:•Vulnerable species•Endangered species•Critically endangered species

Species that are threatened are sometimes characterised by the population dynamics measure of critical depensation, a mathematical measure of biomass related to population growth rate.

a. Threatened species
b. IUCN Red List
c. Gibbons v. Ogden
d. Krakatoa

5. . The _____ and Natural Resources (IUCN) is an international organization dedicated to finding 'pragmatic solutions to our most pressing environment and development challenges.' The organization publishes the IUCN Red List, compiling information from a network of conservation organizations to rate which species are most endangered.

The IUCN supports scientific research, manages field projects all over the world and brings governments, non-government organizations, United Nations agencies, companies and local communities together to develop and implement policy, laws and best practice. IUCN is the world's oldest and largest global environmental network - a democratic membership union with more than 1,000 government and NGO member organizations, and almost 11,000 volunteer scientists in more than 160 countries.

a. Extinction
b. IUCN Red List
c. International Union for Conservation of Nature

ANSWER KEY
Chapter 16. Biological Resources

1. b
2. c
3. c
4. a
5. c

You can take the complete Chapter Practice Test

for Chapter 16. Biological Resources
on all key terms, persons, places, and concepts.

Online 99 Cents

http://www.epub89.6.20924.16.cram101.com/

Use www.Cram101.com for all your study needs

including Cram101's online interactive problem solving labs in

chemistry, statistics, mathematics, and more.

Chapter 17. Land Resources

CHAPTER OUTLINE: KEY TERMS, PEOPLE, PLACES, CONCEPTS

_____ | Audubon Society

_____ | Congaree National Park

_____ | National park

_____ | Land use

_____ | National Wilderness Preservation System

_____ | Wilderness Act

_____ | Invasive species

_____ | Transpiration

_____ | Forest management

_____ | Monoculture

_____ | Deforestation

_____ | Extinction

_____ | Habitat corridor

_____ | Ocean acidification

_____ | Forest Legacy Program

_____ | Temperate deciduous forest

_____ | Tongass National Forest

_____ | Population growth

_____ | Tropics

Chapter 17. Land Resources

	Subsistence agriculture
	Slash-and-burn
	Rangeland
	Taiga
	Carrying capacity
	Desertification
	Federal Land Policy and Management Act
	Land degradation
	Sahara
	Prime farmland
	Urban sprawl
	Wetland
	Clean Water Act
	Emergency Wetlands Resources Act
	Demographic
	Wetlands Reserve Program
	Restoration ecology
	Conservation

Audubon Society	The National Audubon Society is an American, non-profit, environmental organization dedicated to conservation. Incorporated in 1905, Audubon is one of the oldest of such organizations in the world and uses science, education and grassroots advocacy to advance its conservation mission. It is named in honor of John James Audubon, a Franco-American ornithologist and naturalist who painted, cataloged, and described the birds of North America in his famous book Birds of America published in sections between 1827 and 1838.
Congaree National Park	Congaree National Park preserves the largest tract of old growth bottomland hardwood forest left in the United States. Located in South Carolina, the 26,546-acre (107.43 km^2; 41.48 sq mi) national park received that designation in 2003 as the culmination of a grassroots campaign which had started in 1969. The lush trees growing in this floodplain forest are some of the tallest in the Eastern U.S., forming one of the highest temperate deciduous forest canopies remaining in the world. The Congaree River flows through the park.
National park	A national park is a reserve of natural, semi-natural, or developed land that a sovereign state declares or owns. Although individual nations designate their own national parks differently , an international organization, the International Union for Conservation of Nature (IUCN), and its World Commission on Protected Areas, has defined National Parks as its category II type of protected areas.
Land use	'Land use' is also often used to refer to the distinct land use types in zoning. Land use is the human use of land. Land use involves the management and modification of natural environment or wilderness into built environment such as fields, pastures, and settlements. It also has been defined as 'the arrangements, activities and inputs people undertake in a certain land cover type to produce, change or maintain it' (FAO, 1997a; FAO/UNEP, 1999).
National Wilderness Preservation System	The National Wilderness Preservation System of the United States protects federally managed wilderness areas designated for preservation in their natural condition. Activity on formally designated wilderness areas is coordinated by the National Wilderness Preservation System. Wilderness areas are managed by four federal land management agencies: the National Park Service, the U.S. Forest Service, the U.S. Fish and Wildlife Service, and the Bureau of Land Management.
Wilderness Act	The Wilderness Act of 1964 (Pub.L. 88-577) was written by Howard Zahniser of The Wilderness Society. It created the legal definition of wilderness in the United States, and protected some 9 million acres (36,000 km²) of federal land. The result of a long effort to protect federal wilderness, the Wilderness Act was signed into law by President Lyndon B. Johnson on September 3, 1964.

Chapter 17. Land Resources

Invasive species	Invasive species, a nomenclature term and categorization phrase used for flora and fauna, and for specific restoration-preservation processes in native habitats, with several definitions. •The first definition, the most used, applies to introduced species (also called 'non-indigenous' or 'non-native') that adversely affect the habitats and bioregions they invade economically, environmentally, and/or ecologically. Such invasive species may be either plants or animals and may drupt by dominating a region, wilderness areas, particular habitats, or wildland-urban interface land from loss of natural controls (such as predators or herbivores).
Transpiration	Transpiration is a process similar to evaporation. It is a part of the water cycle, and it is the loss of water vapor from parts of plants (similar to sweating), especially in leaves but also in stems, flowers and roots. Leaf surfaces are dotted with openings which are collectively called stomata, and in most plants they are more numerous on the undersides of the foliage.
Forest management	Forest management is the branch of forestry concerned with the overall administrative, economic, legal, and social aspects and with the essentially scientific and technical aspects, especially silviculture, protection, and forest regulation. This includes management for aesthetics, fish, recreation, urban values, water, wilderness, wildlife, wood products, forest genetic resources and other forest resource values. Management can be based on conservation, economics, or a mixture of the two.
Monoculture	Monoculture is the agricultural practice of producing or growing one single crop over a wide area. It is also known as a way of farming practice of growing large stands of a single species. It is widely used in modern industrial agriculture and its implementation has allowed for large harvests from minimal labor.
Deforestation	Deforestation is the removal of a forest or stand of trees where the land is thereafter converted to a nonforest use. Examples of deforestation include conversion of forestland to farms, ranches, or urban use. The term deforestation is often misused to describe any activity where all trees in an area are removed.
Extinction	In biology and ecology, extinction is the end of an organism or of a group of organisms (taxon), normally a species. The moment of extinction is generally considered to be the death of the last individual of the species, although the capacity to breed and recover may have been lost before this point. Because a species' potential range may be very large, determining this moment is difficult, and is usually done retrospectively.
Habitat corridor	A habitat corridor is a strip of land that aids in the movement of species between disconnected areas of their natural habitat. An animal's natural habitat would typically include a number of areas necessary to thrive, such as wetlands, burrowing sites, food, and breeding grounds.

Chapter 17. Land Resources

Ocean acidification	Ocean acidification is the name given to the ongoing decrease in the pH and increase in acidity of the Earth's oceans, caused by the uptake of anthropogenic carbon dioxide (CO_2) from the atmosphere. About a quarter of the carbon dioxide in the atmosphere goes into the oceans, where it forms carbonic acid. As the amount of carbon has risen in the atmosphere there has been a corresponding rise of carbon going into the ocean.
Forest Legacy Program	The Forest Legacy Program was established in the 1990 Farm Bill to protect environmentally important forest lands that are threatened by conversion to nonforest uses. It provides federal funding for conservation easements and fee simple purchases. To ascertain and protect environmentally important forest areas that are threatened by conversion to nonforest uses Development of the nation's forested areas poses an increasing threat to maintaining the integrity of our country's valuable forest lands.
Temperate deciduous forest	A temperate deciduous forest, more precisely termed temperate broadleaf forest or temperate broadleaved forest, is a biome found in the eastern and western United States, Canada, central Mexico, southern South America, Europe, West Asia, China, Japan, North Korea, South Korea and parts of Russia. A temperate deciduous forest consists of trees that lose their leaves every year. Examples include oak, maple, beech, and elm.
Tongass National Forest	The Tongass National Forest in southeastern Alaska is the largest national forest in the United States at 17 million acres (69,000 km²). Most of its area is part of the temperate rain forest WWF ecoregion, itself part of the larger Pacific temperate rain forest WWF ecoregion, and is remote enough to be home to many species of endangered and rare flora and fauna. Tongass encompasses islands of the Alexander Archipelago, fjords, glaciers, and peaks of the Coast Mountains.
Population growth	Population growth is the change in a population over time, and can be quantified as the change in the number of individuals of any species in a population using 'per unit time' for measurement. Population growth is determined by four factors, births (B), deaths (D), immigrants (I), and emigrants (E). Using a formula expressed as $\Delta P \equiv (B-D)+(I-E)$

Visit Cram101.com for full Practice Exams

Chapter 17. Land Resources

	In other words, the population growth of a period can be calculated in two parts, natural growth of population (B-D) and mechanical growth of population (I-E), in which mechanical growth of population is mainly affected by social factors, e.g. the advanced economies are growing faster while the backward economies are growing slowly even with negative growth.
Tropics	The tropics is a region of the Earth surrounding the Equator. It is limited in latitude by the Tropic of Cancer in the northern hemisphere at approximately 23° 26′ 16″ (or 23.4378°) N and the Tropic of Capricorn in the southern hemisphere at 23° 26′ 16″ (or 23.4378°) S; these latitudes correspond to the axial tilt of the Earth. The tropics are also referred to as the tropical zone and the torrid zone .
Subsistence agriculture	Subsistence agriculture is self-sufficiency farming in which the farmers focus on growing enough food to feed their families. The typical subsistence farm has a range of crops and animals needed by the family to eat and clothe themselves during the year. Planting decisions are made with an eye toward what the family will need during the coming year, rather than market prices.
Slash-and-burn	Slash-and-burn is an agricultural technique which involves cutting and burning of forests or woodlands to create fields. It is subsistence agriculture that typically uses little technology or other tools. It is typically part of shifting cultivation agriculture, and of transhumance livestock herding.
Rangeland	Rangelands are vast natural landscapes in the form of grasslands, shrublands, woodlands, wetlands, and deserts. Types of rangelands include tallgrass and shortgrass prairies, desert grasslands and shrublands, woodlands, savannas, chaparrals, steppes, and tundras. Rangelands do not include barren desert, farmland, closed canopy forests, or land covered by solid rock, concrete and/or glaciers.
Taiga	Taiga, is a biome characterized by coniferous forests. Taiga is the world's largest terrestrial biome. In North America it covers most of inland Canada and Alaska as well as parts of the extreme northern continental United States and is known as the Northwoods.
Carrying capacity	The carrying capacity of a biological species in an environment is the maximum population size of the species that the environment can sustain indefinitely, given the food, habitat, water and other necessities available in the environment. In population biology, carrying capacity is defined as the environment's maximal load, which is different from the concept of population equilibrium.

Desertification	Desertification is the degradation of land in any drylands. Caused by a variety of factors, such as climate change and human activities, desertification is one of the most significant global environmental problems. Considerable controversy exists over the proper definition of the term 'desertification' for which Helmut Geist (2005) has identified more than 100 formal definitions.
Federal Land Policy and Management Act	The Federal Land Policy and Management Act, or FLPMA (Pub.L. 94-579), is a United States federal law that governs the way in which the public lands administered by the Bureau of Land Management are managed. The law was enacted in 1976 by the 94th Congress and is found in the United States Code under Title 43. Congress recognized the value of the public lands, declaring that these lands would remain in public ownership.
Land degradation	Land degradation is a process in which the value of the biophysical environment is affected by one or more combination of human-induced processes acting upon the land. It is viewed as any change or disturbance to the land perceived to be deleterious or undesirable. Natural hazards are excluded as a cause, however human activities can indirectly affect phenomena such as floods and bushfires.
Sahara	The Sahara is the world's hottest desert, the third largest desert after Antarctica and the Arctic. At over 9,400,000 square kilometres (3,600,000 sq mi), it covers most of North Africa, making it almost as large as China or the United States. The Sahara stretches from the Red Sea, including parts of the Mediterranean coasts, to the outskirts of the Atlantic Ocean.
Prime farmland	Prime farmland is a designation assigned by U.S. Department of Agriculture defining land that has the best combination of physical and chemical characteristics for producing food, feed, forage, fiber, and oilseed crops and is also available for these land uses. Prime farmland has the soil quality, growing season, and moisture supply needed for the agricultural productivity to sustainably produce high yields of crops when treated and managed according to acceptable farming methods (e.g. water management). In general, prime farmlands have an adequate and dependable water supply from precipitation or irrigation, a favorable temperature and growing season, acceptable acidity or alkalinity, acceptable salt and sodium content, and few or no rocks.
Urban sprawl	Urban sprawl, is a multifaceted concept, which includes the spreading outwards of a city and its suburbs to its outskirts to low-density and auto-dependent development on rural land, high segregation of es (e.g.

stores and residential), and vario design features that encourage car dependency.

Discsions and debates about sprawl are often obfcated by the ambiguity associated with the phrase. For example, some commentators measure sprawl only with the average number of residential units per acre in a given area.

Wetland	A wetland is a land area that is saturated with water, either permanently or seasonally, such that it takes on characteristics that distinguish it as a distinct ecosystem. The primary factor that distinguishes wetlands is the characteristic vegetation that is adapted to its unique soil conditions: Wetlands are made up primarily of hydric soil, which supports aquatic plants. The water found in wetlands can be saltwater, freshwater, or brackish.
Clean Water Act	The Clean Water Act is the primary federal law in the United States governing water pollution. Commonly abbreviated as the Clean Water Act, the act established the goals of eliminating releases of high amounts of toxic substances into water, eliminating additional water pollution by 1985, and ensuring that surface waters would meet standards necessary for human sports and recreation by 1983. The principal body of law currently in effect is based on the Federal Water Pollution Control Amendments of 1972 and was significantly expanded from the Federal Water Pollution Control Amendments of 1948. Major amendments were enacted in the Clean Water Act of 1977 and the Water Quality Act of 1987.
Emergency Wetlands Resources Act	The Emergency Wetlands Resources Act of 1986 became a United States federal law (P.L). 99-645 (100 Stat. 3582) on November 10, 1986. Prior to the Act the purchase of wetlands by the Federal Government had been prohibited. The Act allocated funds from the Land and Water Conservation Fund (LWCF) for the purchase of wetlands by the Secretary of Interior, who is head of the United States Department of the Interior.
Demographic	Demographics are statistical characteristics of a population. These types of data are used widely in public opinion polling and marketing. Commonly examined demographics include gender, age, ethnicity, knowledge of languages, disabilities, mobility, home ownership, employment status, and even location.
Wetlands Reserve Program	The Wetlands Reserve Program is a voluntary program offering landowners the opportunity to protect, restore, and enhance wetlands on their property. The USDA Natural Resources Conservation Service (NRCS) administers the program with funding from the Commodity Credit Corporation.

Restoration ecology	
	Restoration ecology is the scientific study and practice of renewing and restoring degraded, damaged, or destroyed ecosystems and habitats in the environment by active human intervention and action. Restoration ecology emerged as a separate field in ecology in the 1980s.
	History
	Land managers, laypeople, and stewards have been practicing restoration for many hundreds, if not thousands of years, yet the scientific field of 'restoration ecology' was first identified and coined in the late 1980s by John Aber and William Jordan.
Conservation	Conservation is an ethic of resour use, allocation, and protection. Its primary focus is upon maintaining the health of the natural world: its, fisheries, habitats, and biological diversity. Secondary focus is on materials conservation and energy conservation, which are seen as important to protect the natural world.

1. _____ is an agricultural technique which involves cutting and burning of forests or woodlands to create fields. It is subsistence agriculture that typically uses little technology or other tools. It is typically part of shifting cultivation agriculture, and of transhumance livestock herding.

   a. Slaughter tapping
   b. Slash-and-burn
   c. Sustainable Forestry Initiative
   d. Variable retention

2. . _____, a nomenclature term and categorization phrase used for flora and fauna, and for specific restoration-preservation processes in native habitats, with several definitions. •The first definition, the most used, applies to introduced species (also called 'non-indigenous' or 'non-native') that adversely affect the habitats and bioregions they invade economically, environmentally, and/or ecologically. Such _____ may be either plants or animals and may drupt by dominating a region, wilderness areas, particular habitats, or wildland-urban interface land from loss of natural controls (such as predators or herbivores).

   a. Juglone
   b. Invasive species
   c. Natural landscaping

Chapter 17. Land Resources

3. The _____ is the world's hottest desert, the third largest desert after Antarctica and the Arctic. At over 9,400,000 square kilometres (3,600,000 sq mi), it covers most of North Africa, making it almost as large as China or the United States. The _____ stretches from the Red Sea, including parts of the Mediterranean coasts, to the outskirts of the Atlantic Ocean.

   a. Juglone
   b. Land recycling
   c. Sahara
   d. Land use, land-use change and forestry

4. A _____ is a strip of land that aids in the movement of species between disconnected areas of their natural habitat. An animal's natural habitat would typically include a number of areas necessary to thrive, such as wetlands, burrowing sites, food, and breeding grounds. Urbanization can split up such areas, causing animals to lose both their natural habitat and the ability to move between regions to use all of the resources they need to survive.

   a. Habitat destruction
   b. Habitat fragmentation
   c. Natural heritage
   d. Habitat corridor

5. In biology and ecology, _____ is the end of an organism or of a group of organisms (taxon), normally a species. The moment of _____ is generally considered to be the death of the last individual of the species, although the capacity to breed and recover may have been lost before this point. Because a species' potential range may be very large, determining this moment is difficult, and is usually done retrospectively.

   a. IUCN Red List
   b. Genetic pollution
   c. Genetically modified food
   d. Extinction

ANSWER KEY
Chapter 17. Land Resources

1. b
2. b
3. c
4. d
5. d

You can take the complete Chapter Practice Test

for Chapter 17. Land Resources
on all key terms, persons, places, and concepts.

Online 99 Cents

http://www.epub89.6.20924.17.cram101.com/

Use www.Cram101.com for all your study needs

including Cram101's online interactive problem solving labs in

chemistry, statistics, mathematics, and more.

Chapter 18. Food Resources

CHAPTER OUTLINE: KEY TERMS, PEOPLE, PLACES, CONCEPTS

_____ | Kwashiorkor

_____ | Malnutrition

_____ | Overnutrition

_____ | Demographic transition

_____ | Food security

_____ | Famine

_____ | Globalization

_____ | Poverty

_____ | Shifting cultivation

_____ | Subsistence agriculture

_____ | Crop yield

_____ | Domestication

_____ | Intercropping

_____ | Monoculture

_____ | Polyculture

_____ | Slash-and-burn

_____ | Biofuel

_____ | Golden rice

_____ | Cartagena Protocol on Biosafety

Chapter 18. Food Resources

_____ | Carbon footprint

_____ | Land degradation

_____ | Habitat fragmentation

_____ | Sustainable agriculture

_____ | Irrigation

_____ | Sustainable

_____ | Agroecosystem

_____ | Integrated pest management

_____ | Second Green Revolution

_____ | Bycatch

_____ | Fishery

_____ | Mediterranean sea

_____ | Pollution

_____ | Aquaculture

_____ | Fish farming

_____ | Mariculture

Kwashiorkor	Kwashiorkor is an acute form of childhood protein-energy malnutrition characterized by edema, irritability, anorexia, ulcerating dermatoses, and an enlarged liver with fatty infiltrates. The presence of edema caused by poor nutrition defines kwashiorkor. Kwashiorkor was thought to be caused by insufficient protein consumption but with sufficient calorie intake, distinguishing it from marasmus.
Malnutrition	Malnutrition is the condition that results from taking an unbalanced diet in which certain nutrients are lacking, in excess (too high an intake), or in the wrong proportions. A number of different nutrition disorders may arise, depending on which nutrients are under or overabundant in the diet. In most of the world, malnutrition is present in the form of undernutrition, which is caused by a diet lacking adequate calories and protein.
Overnutrition	Overnutrition is a form of malnutrition in which nutrients are oversupplied relative to the amounts required for normal growth, development, and metabolism. Overnutrition is a type of malnutrition where there are more nutrients than required for normal growth. The term can refer to:•obesity, brought on by general overeating of foods high in caloric content, as well as:•the oversupply of a specific nutrient or categories of nutrients, such as mineral or vitamin poisoning, due to excessive intake of dietary supplements or foods high in nutrients (such as liver), or nutritional imbalances caused by various fad diets. For mineral excess, see:•Iron poisoning, and•low sodium diet (excess sodium)..
Demographic transition	The demographic transition is the transition from high birth and death rates to low birth and death rates as a country develops from a pre-industrial to an industrialized economic system. The theory is based on an interpretation of demographic history developed in 1929 by the American demographer Warren Thompson (1887-1973). Thompson observed changes, or transitions, in birth and death rates in industrialized societies over the previous 200 years.
Food security	Food security refers to the availability of food and one's access to it. A household is considered food-secure when its occupants do not live in hunger or fear of starvation. According to the World Resources Institute, global per capita food production has been increasing substantially for the past several decades.
Famine	A famine is a widespread scarcity of food, caused by several factors including crop failure, population unbalance, or government policies. This phenomenon is usually accompanied or followed by regional malnutrition, starvation, epidemic, and increased mortality. Nearly every continent in the world has experienced a period of famine throughout history.
Globalization	Globalization is the process of international integration arising from the interchange of world views, products, ideas, and other aspects of culture.

Chapter 18. Food Resources

	Put in simple terms, globalization refers to processes that promote world-wide exchanges of national and cultural resources. Advances in transportation and telecommunications infrastructure, including the rise of the Internet, are major factors in globalization, generating further interdependence of economic and cultural activities.
Poverty	Poverty is the deprivation of food, shelter, money and clothing that occurs when people cannot satisfy their basic needs. Poverty can be understood simply as a lack of money, or more broadly in terms of barriers to everyday life. Absolute poverty or destitution refers to the state of severe deprivation of basic human needs, which commonly includes food, water, sanitation, clothing, shelter, health care, education and information.
Shifting cultivation	Shifting cultivation is an agricultural system in which plots of land are cultivated temporarily, then abandoned. This system often involves clearing of a piece of land followed by several years of wood harvesting or farming, until the soil loses fertility. Once the land becomes inadequate for crop production, it is left to be reclaimed by natural vegetation, or sometimes converted to a different long-term cyclical farming practice.
Subsistence agriculture	Subsistence agriculture is self-sufficiency farming in which the farmers focus on growing enough food to feed their families. The typical subsistence farm has a range of crops and animals needed by the family to eat and clothe themselves during the year. Planting decisions are made with an eye toward what the family will need during the coming year, rather than market prices.
Crop yield	In agriculture, crop yield refers to both the measure of the yield of a crop per unit area of land cultivation, and the seed generation of the plant itself (e.g. one wheat grain produces a stalk yielding three grain, or 1:3). The figure, 1:3 is considered by agronomists as the minimum required to sustain human life. One of the three seeds must be set aside for the next planting season, the remaining two either consumed by the grower, or one for human consumption and the other for livestock feed.
Domestication	Domestication is the process whereby a population of animals or plants, through a process of selection, becomes accustomed to human provision and control. A defining characteristic of domestication is artificial selection by humans. Humans have brought these populations under their control and care for a wide range of reasons: to produce food or valuable commodities (such as wool, cotton, or silk), for help with various types of work (such as transportation, protection, and warfare), scientific research, or simply to enjoy as companions or ornaments.
Intercropping	Intercropping is the practice of growing two or more crops in proximity.

The most common goal of intercropping is to produce a greater yield on a given piece of land by making use of resources that would otherwise not be utilized by a single crop. Careful planning is required, taking into account the soil, climate, crops, and varieties.

| Monoculture | Monoculture is the agricultural practice of producing or growing one single crop over a wide area. It is also known as a way of farming practice of growing large stands of a single species. It is widely used in modern industrial agriculture and its implementation has allowed for large harvests from minimal labor. |

| Polyculture | Polyculture is agriculture using multiple crops in the same space, in imitation of the diversity of natural ecosystems, and avoiding large stands of single crops, or monoculture. It includes crop rotation, multi-cropping, intercropping, companion planting, beneficial weeds, and alley cropping.

Polyculture, though it often requires more labor, has several advantages over monoculture:•The diversity of crops avoids the susceptibility of monocultures to disease. |

| Slash-and-burn | Slash-and-burn is an agricultural technique which involves cutting and burning of forests or woodlands to create fields. It is subsistence agriculture that typically uses little technology or other tools. It is typically part of shifting cultivation agriculture, and of transhumance livestock herding. |

| Biofuel | A biofuel is a type of fuel whose energy is derived from biological carbon fixation. Biofuels include fuels derived from biomass conversion, as well as solid biomass, liquid fuels and various biogases. Biofuels are gaining increased public and scientific attention, driven by factors such as oil price hikes and the need for increased energy security. |

| Golden rice | Golden rice is a variety of Oryza sativa rice produced through genetic engineering to biosynthesize beta-carotene, a precursor of vitamin A, in the edible parts of rice. The research was conducted with the goal of producing a fortified food to be grown and consumed in areas with a shortage of dietary vitamin A, which is estimated to kill 670,000 children under 5 each year.

Golden rice differs from its parental strain by the addition of two beta-carotene biosynthesis genes. |

| Cartagena Protocol on Biosafety | The Cartagena Protocol on Biosafety is an international agreement on biosafety, as a supplement to the Convention on Biological Diversity. The Biosafety Protocol seeks to protect biological diversity from the potential risks posed by living modified organisms resulting from modern biotechnology. |

Chapter 18. Food Resources

Carbon footprint	A carbon footprint has historically been defined as 'the total set of greenhouse gas (GHG) emissions caused by an organization, event, product or person.'. However, calculating a carbon footprint which conforms to this definition is often impracticable due to the large amount of data required, which is often time consuming to obtain. A more practicable definition has been suggested, which is gaining acceptance within the field: 'A measure of the total amount of carbon dioxide (CO_2) and methane (CH_4) emissions of a defined population, system or activity, considering all relevant sources, sinks and storage within the spatial and temporal boundary of the population, system or activity of interest.
Land degradation	Land degradation is a process in which the value of the biophysical environment is affected by one or more combination of human-induced processes acting upon the land. It is viewed as any change or disturbance to the land perceived to be deleterious or undesirable. Natural hazards are excluded as a cause, however human activities can indirectly affect phenomena such as floods and bushfires.
Habitat fragmentation	Habitat fragmentation as the name implies, describes the emergence of discontinuities (fragmentation) in an organism's preferred environment (habitat), causing population fragmentation. Habitat fragmentation can be caused by geological processes that slowly alter the layout of the physical environment (suspected of being one of the major causes of speciation), or by human activity such as land conversion, which can alter the environment much faster and causes extinctions of many species. The term habitat fragmentation includes five discrete phenomena:•Reduction in the total area of the habitat•Decrease of the interior : edge ratio•Isolation of one habitat fragment from other areas of habitat•Breaking up of one patch of habitat into several smaller patches•Decrease in the average size of each patch of habitatNatural causes and effects Evidence of habitat destruction through natural processes such as volcanism, fire, and climate change is found in the fossil record.
Sustainable agriculture	Sustainable agriculture is the practice of farming using principles of ecology, the study of relationships between organisms and their environment. It has been defined as 'an integrated system of plant and animal production practices having a site-specific application that will last over the long term:•tisfy human food and fiber needs•Enhance environmental quality and the natural resource base upon which the agricultural economy depends•Make the most efficient use of non-renewable resources and on-farm resources and integrate, where appropriate, natural biological cycles and controls•Sustain the economic viability of farm operations•Enhance the quality of life for farmers and society as a whole.' Sustainable agriculture in the United States was addressed by the 1990 farm bill.

Irrigation	Irrigation is the artificial application of water to the land or soil. It is used to assist in the growing of agricultural crops, maintenance of landscapes, and revegetation of disturbed soils in dry areas and during periods of inadequate rainfall. Additionally, irrigation also has a few other uses in crop production, which include protecting plants against frost, suppressing weed growing in grain fields and helping in preventing soil consolidation.
Sustainable	Sustainability is the capacity to endure. In ecology the word describes how biological systems remain diverse and productive over time. Long-lived and healthy wetlands and forests are examples of sustainable biological systems.
Agroecosystem	An agroecosystem is the basic unit of study for an agroecologist, and is somewhat arbitrarily defined as a spatially and functionally coherent unit of agricultural activity, and includes the living and nonliving components involved in that unit as well as their interactions.
	An agroecosystem can be viewed as a subset of a conventional ecosystem. As the name implies, at the core of an agroecosystem lies the human activity of agriculture.
Integrated pest management	Integrated pest management is a broad based ecological approach to agricultural pest control that integrates pesticides/herbicides into a management system incorporating a range of practices for economic control of a pest. In , one attempts to prevent infestation, to observe patterns of infestation when they occur, and to intervene (without poisons) when one deems necessary. is the intelligent selection and use of pest control actions that will ensure favourable economic, ecological and sociological consequences.
Second Green Revolution	The Second Green Revolution is a change in agricultural production widely thought necessary to feed and sustain the growing population on Earth These calls have precipitated in part, as a response to rising food commodity prices, and fears of peak oil among other factors.
	It is thought that genetic engineering of new crops and foods will take the lead in producing increased crop yield and nutrition. Proponents
	Bill Gates has been among the proponents of a second green revolution, saying:'
	Three quarters of the world's poorest people get their food and income by farming small plots of land...if we can make smallholder farming more productive and more profitable, we can have a massive impact on hunger and nutrition and poverty...the charge is clear--we have to develop crops that can grow in a drought; that can survive in a flood; that can resist pests and disease...we need higher yields on the same land in harsher weather."
	Biello, David (Oct 16, 2009).

Chapter 18. Food Resources

Bycatch	The term 'bycatch' is usually used for fish caught unintentionally in a fishery while intending to catch other fish. It may however also indicate untargeted catch in other forms of animal harvesting or collecting. Bycatch is of a different species, undersized individuals of the target species, or juveniles of the target species.
Fishery	Generally, a fishery is an entity engaged in raising or harvesting fish which is determined by some authority to be a fishery. According to the FAO, a fishery is typically defined in terms of the 'people involved, species or type of fish, area of water or seabed, method of fishing, class of boats, purpose of the activities or a combination of the foregoing features'. The definition often includes a combination of fish and fishers in a region, the latter fishing for similar species with similar gear types.
Mediterranean sea	In oceanography, a mediterranean sea is a mostly enclosed sea that has limited exchange of water with outer oceans and where the water circulation is dominated by salinity and temperature differences rather than winds. The mediterranean seas of the Atlantic Ocean •The Mediterranean Sea (or the Eurafrican Mediterranean Sea or the European Mediterranean Sea): including the Black Sea, the Sea of Azov, the Aegean Sea, the Adriatic Sea, the Ligurian Sea, the Balearic Sea, the Tyrrhenian Sea, the Ionian Sea, and the Sea of Marmara.•The Arctic Ocean (or the Arctic Mediterranean Sea, considered an ocean by many)•The American Mediterranean Sea: the combination of the Gulf of Mexico and the Caribbean Sea.•The Baltic Sea•Baffin BayThe mediterranean seas of the Indian Ocean •The Persian Gulf•The Red SeaThe mediterranean sea between the Indian and Pacific Oceans •The Australasian Mediterranean Sea: the sea enclosed by the Sunda Islands and the Philippines, including the Banda Sea, the Sulu Sea, the Sulawesi Sea, the Java Sea, etc.Types of mediterranean seas There are two types of mediterranean seaConcentration basin •A concentration basin has a higher salinity than the outer ocean due to evaporation, and its water exchange consists of inflow of the fresher oceanic water in the upper layer and outflow of the saltier mediterranean water in the lower layer of the connecting channel.
Pollution	Pollution is the introduction of contaminants into a natural environment that causes instability, disorder, harm or discomfort to the ecosystem i.e. physical systems or living organisms. Pollution can take the form of chemical substances or energy, such as noise, heat or light. Pollutants, the components of pollution, can be either foreign substances/energies or naturally occurring contaminants.
Aquaculture	Aquaculture, is the farming of aquatic organisms such as fish, crustaceans, molluscs and aquatic plants. Aquaculture involves cultivating freshwater and saltwater populations under controlled conditions, and can be contrasted with commercial fishing, which is the harvesting of wild fish. Mariculture refers to aquaculture practised in marine environments.

Fish farming	Fish farming is the principal form of aquaculture, while other methods may fall under mariculture. Fish farming involves raising fish commercially in tanks or enclosures, usually for food. A facility that releases young (juvenile) fish into the wild for recreational fishing or to supplement a species' natural numbers is generally referred to as a fish hatchery.
Mariculture	Mariculture is a specialized branch of aquaculture involving the cultivation of marine organisms for food and other products in the open ocean, an enclosed section of the ocean, or in tanks, ponds or raceways which are filled with seawater. An example of the latter is the farming of marine fish, including finfish and shellfish e.g.prawns, or oysters and seaweed in saltwater ponds. Non-food products produced by mariculture include: fish meal, nutrient agar, jewellery (e.g. cultured pearls), and cosmetics.

CHAPTER QUIZ: KEY TERMS, PEOPLE, PLACES, CONCEPTS

1. A _____ is a type of fuel whose energy is derived from biological carbon fixation. _____s include fuels derived from biomass conversion, as well as solid biomass, liquid fuels and various biogases. _____s are gaining increased public and scientific attention, driven by factors such as oil price hikes and the need for increased energy security.

    a. Juglone
    b. Sustainable forest management
    c. Sustainable Forestry Initiative
    d. Biofuel

2. _____ is the process whereby a population of animals or plants, through a process of selection, becomes accustomed to human provision and control. A defining characteristic of _____ is artificial selection by humans. Humans have brought these populations under their control and care for a wide range of reasons: to produce food or valuable commodities (such as wool, cotton, or silk), for help with various types of work (such as transportation, protection, and warfare), scientific research, or simply to enjoy as companions or ornaments.

    a. Domestication
    b. Gibbons v. Ogden
    c. Krakatoa
    d. Pesticide residue

3. . A _____ is a widespread scarcity of food, caused by several factors including crop failure, population unbalance, or government policies. This phenomenon is usually accompanied or followed by regional malnutrition, starvation, epidemic, and increased mortality. Nearly every continent in the world has experienced a period of _____ throughout history.

a. Juglone
b. Famine
c. Food waste in the United Kingdom
d. Pesticide residue

4. _____ refers to the availability of food and one's access to it. A household is considered food-secure when its occupants do not live in hunger or fear of starvation. According to the World Resources Institute, global per capita food production has been increasing substantially for the past several decades.

a. Food waste
b. Food security
c. Food waste in the United Kingdom
d. Pesticide residue

5. _____ is the practice of growing two or more crops in proximity. The most common goal of _____ is to produce a greater yield on a given piece of land by making use of resources that would otherwise not be utilized by a single crop. Careful planning is required, taking into account the soil, climate, crops, and varieties.

a. International Centre for Integrated Mountain Development
b. International Organization for Biological Control
c. Intercropping
d. Irish Seed Savers Association

ANSWER KEY
Chapter 18. Food Resources

1. d
2. a
3. b
4. b
5. c

You can take the complete Chapter Practice Test

for Chapter 18. Food Resources
on all key terms, persons, places, and concepts.

Online 99 Cents

http://www.epub89.6.20924.18.cram101.com/

Use www.Cram101.com for all your study needs

including Cram101's online interactive problem solving labs in

chemistry, statistics, mathematics, and more.

Chapter 19. Air Pollution

CHAPTER OUTLINE: KEY TERMS, PEOPLE, PLACES, CONCEPTS

_____ Air pollution

_____ Wildfire

_____ Cellular respiration

_____ Hydrocarbon

_____ Nitrogen

_____ Pollutant

_____ Sulfur trioxide

_____ Carbon monoxide

_____ Methane

_____ Ozone

_____ Stratosphere

_____ Troposphere

_____ Smog

_____ Crop yield

_____ Health effect

_____ Electrostatic precipitator

_____ Scrubber

_____ Ozone depletion

_____ Ultraviolet

Chapter 19. Air Pollution

Carbon tetrachloride

Chlorofluorocarbon

1,1,1-Trichloroethane

Montreal Protocol

Acid rain

Robert Angus Smith

Development

Hubbard Brook Experimental Forest

Arctic haze

Stockholm Convention on Persistent Organic Pollutants

Radon

Air pollution	Air pollution is the introduction of chemicals, particulate matter, or biological materials that cause harm or discomfort to humans or other living organisms, or cause damage to the natural environment or built environment, into the atmosphere.
	The atmosphere is a complex dynamic natural gaseous system that is essential to support life on planet Earth. Stratospheric ozone depletion due to air pollution has long been recognized as a threat to human health as well as to the Earth's ecosystems.
Wildfire	A wildfire is any uncontrolled fire in combustible vegetation that occurs in the countryside or a wilderness area.

Other names such as brush fire, bushfire, forest fire, desert fire, grass fire, hill fire, peat fire, vegetation fire, and veldfire may be used to describe the same phenomenon depending on the type of vegetation being burned. A wildfire differs from other fires by its extensive size, the speed at which it can spread out from its original source, its potential to change direction unexpectedly, and its ability to jump gaps such as roads, rivers and fire breaks.

Cellular respiration	Cellular respiration is the set of the metabolic reactions and processes that take place in the cells of organisms to convert biochemical energy from nutrients into adenosine triphosphate (ATP), and then release waste products. The reactions involved in respiration are catabolic reactions that involve the redox reaction (oxidation of one molecule and the reduction of another). Respiration is one of the key ways a cell gains useful energy to fuel cellular changes.
Hydrocarbon	In organic chemistry, a hydrocarbon is an organic compound consisting entirely of hydrogen and carbon. Hydrocarbons from which one hydrogen atom has been removed are functional groups, called hydrocarbyls. Aromatic hydrocarbons (arenes), alkanes, alkenes, cycloalkanes and alkyne-based compounds are different types of hydrocarbons.
Nitrogen	Nitrogen is a chemical element with symbol N and atomic number 7. Elemental nitrogen is a colorless, odorless, tasteless, and mostly inert diatomic gas at standard conditions, constituting 78.09% by volume of Earth's atmosphere. The element nitrogen was discovered as a separable component of air, by Scottish physician Daniel Rutherford, in 1772. It belongs to the pnictogen family. Nitrogen is a common element in the universe, estimated at about seventh in total abundance in our galaxy and the Solar System.
Pollutant	A pollutant is a waste material that pollutes air, water or soil, and is the cause of pollution. Three factors determine the severity of a pollutant: its chemical nature, its concentration and its persistence. Some pollutants are biodegradable and therefore will not persist in the environment in the long term.
Sulfur trioxide	Sulfur trioxide is the chemical compound with the formula SO_3. In the gaseous form, this species is a significant pollutant, being the primary agent in acid rain. It is prepared on massive scales as a precursor to sulfuric acid.
Carbon monoxide	Carbon monoxide also called carbonous oxide, is a colorless, odorless and tasteless gas which is slightly lighter than air. It is highly toxic to humans and animals in higher quantities, although it is also produced in normal animal metabolism in low quantities, and is thought to have some normal biological functions.

Chapter 19. Air Pollution

Methane	Appendix: extraterrestrial methane
	Methane has been detected or is believed to exist in several locations of the solar system. In most cases, it is believed to have been created by abiotic processes. Possible exceptions are Mars and Titan.
Ozone	Ozone (O_3) is a constituent of the troposphere (it is also an important constituent of some regions of the stratosphere commonly known as the Ozone layer). Photochemical and chemical reactions involving it drive many of the chemical processes that occur in the atmosphere by day and by night. At abnormally high concentrations brought about by human activities (largely incomplete combustion of fossil fuels, such as gasoline, diesel, etc)., it is a pollutant, and a constituent of smog.
Stratosphere	The stratosphere is the second major layer of Earth's atmosphere, just above the troposphere, and below the mesosphere. It is stratified in temperature, with warmer layers higher up and cooler layers farther down. This is in contrast to the troposphere near the Earth's surface, which is cooler higher up and warmer farther down.
Troposphere	The troposphere is the lowest portion of Earth's atmosphere. It contains approximately 75% of the atmosphere's mass and 99% of its water vapor and aerosols.
	The average depth of the troposphere is approximately 17 km (11 mi) in the middle latitudes.
Smog	Smog is a type of air pollution; the word 'smog' was coined in the early 20th century as a portmanteau of the words smoke and fog to refer to smoky fog. The word was then intended to refer to what was sometimes known as pea soup fog, a familiar and serious problem in London from the 19th century to the mid 20th century. This kind of smog is caused by the burning of large amounts of coal within a city; this smog contains soot particulates from smoke, sulfur dioxide and other components.
Crop yield	In agriculture, crop yield refers to both the measure of the yield of a crop per unit area of land cultivation, and the seed generation of the plant itself (e.g. one wheat grain produces a stalk yielding three grain, or 1:3). The figure, 1:3 is considered by agronomists as the minimum required to sustain human life.
	One of the three seeds must be set aside for the next planting season, the remaining two either consumed by the grower, or one for human consumption and the other for livestock feed.
Health effect	Health effects are changes in health resulting from exposure to a source. Health effects are an important consideration in many areas, such as hygiene, pollution studies, occupational safety and health, nutrition and health sciences in general.

Chapter 19. Air Pollution

Electrostatic precipitator	An electrostatic precipitator or electrostatic air cleaner is a particulate collection device that removes particles from a flowing gas (such as air) using the force of an induced electrostatic charge. Electrostatic precipitators are highly efficient filtration devices that minimally impede the flow of gases through the device, and can easily remove fine particulate matter such as dust and smoke from the air stream. In contrast to wet scrubbers which apply energy directly to the flowing fluid medium, an ESP applies energy only to the particulate matter being collected and therefore is very efficient in its consumption of energy (in the form of electricity).
Scrubber	'Scrubber' systems are a diverse group of air pollution control devices that can be used to remove some particulates and/or gases from industrial exhaust streams. Traditionally, the term 'scrubber' has referred to pollution control devices that use liquid to wash unwanted pollutants from a gas stream. Recently, the term is also used to describe systems that inject a dry reagent or slurry into a dirty exhaust stream to 'wash out' acid gases.
Ozone depletion	Ozone depletion describes two distinct but related phenomena observed since the late 1970s: a steady decline of about 4% per decade in the total volume of ozone in Earth's stratosphere (the ozone layer), and a much larger springtime decrease in stratospheric ozone over Earth's polar regions. The latter phenomenon is referred to as the ozone hole. In addition to these well-known stratospheric phenomena, there are also springtime polar tropospheric ozone depletion events.
Ultraviolet	Ultraviolet light is electromagnetic radiation with a wavelength shorter than that of visible light, but longer than X-rays, that is, in the range 10 nm to 400 nm, corresponding to photon energies from 3 eV to 124 eV. It is so-named because the spectrum consists of electromagnetic waves with frequencies higher than those that humans identify as the colour violet. These frequencies are invisible to humans, but visible to a number of insects and birds.

UV light is found in sunlight (where it constitutes about 10% of the energy in vacuum) and is emitted by electric arcs and specialized lights such as black lights. |
Carbon tetrachloride	Carbon tetrachloride, also known by many other names is the organic compound with the formula CCl_4. It was formerly widely used in fire extinguishers, as a precursor to refrigerants, and as a cleaning agent. It is a colourless liquid with a 'sweet' smell that can be deteed at low levels.
Chlorofluorocarbon	A chlorofluorocarbon is an organic compound that contains carbon, chlorine, and fluorine, produced as a volatile derivative of methane and ethane. A common subclass are the hydrochlorofluorocarbons (HCFCs), which contain hydrogen, as well. They are also commonly known by the DuPont trade name Freon.
1,1,1-Trichloroethane	The organic compound 1,1,1-trichloroethane, is a chloroalkane. This colourless, sweet-smelling liquid was once produced industrially in large quantities for use as a solvent.

Chapter 19. Air Pollution

Montreal Protocol	The Montreal Protocol on Substances That Deplete the Ozone Layer (a protocol to the Vienna Convention for the Protection of the Ozone Layer) is an international treaty designed to protect the ozone layer by phasing out the production of numerous substances believed to be responsible for ozone depletion. The treaty was opened for signature on September 16, 1987, and entered into force on January 1, 1989, followed by a first meeting in Helsinki, May 1989. Since then, it has undergone seven revisions, in 1990 (London), 1991 (Nairobi), 1992 (Copenhagen), 1993 (Bangkok), 1995 (Vienna), 1997 (Montreal), and 1999 (Beijing). It is believed that if the international agreement is adhered to, the ozone layer is expected to recover by 2050. Due to its widespread adoption and implementation it has been hailed as an example of exceptional international co-operation, with Kofi Annan quoted as saying that 'perhaps the single most successful international agreement to date has been the Montreal Protocol'.
Acid rain	Acid rain is a rain or any other form of precipitation that is unusually acidic, meaning that it possesses elevated levels of hydrogen ions (low pH). It can have hmful effects on plants, aquatic animals, and infrastructure. Acid rain is caused by emissions of cbon dioxide, sulfur dioxide and nitrogen oxides which react with the water molecules in the atmosphere to produce acids.
Robert Angus Smith	Robert Angus Smith was a Scottish chemist, who investigated numerous environmental issues. He is famous for his research on air pollution in 1852, in the course of which he discovered what came to be known as acid rain. He is sometimes referred to as the 'Father of Acid Rain'.
Development	In classical differential geometry, development refers to the simple idea of rolling one smooth surface over another in Euclidean space. For example, the tangent plane to a surface (such as the sphere or the cylinder) at a point can be rolled around the surface to obtain the tangent-plane at other points.
	The tangential contact between the surfaces being rolled over one another provides a relation between points on the two surfaces.
Hubbard Brook Experimental Forest	Hubbard Brook Experimental Forest is an area of land in the White Mountains of New Hampshire that functions as an outdoor laboratory for ecological studies. It was initially established in 1955 by the United States Forest Service for the study of the relationship between forest cover and water quality and supply.
	In 1955 the first tract was dedicated, in the Hubbard Brook watershed, just west of the village of West Thornton, New Hampshire.
Arctic haze	Arctic haze is the phenomenon of a visible reddish-brown springtime haze in the atmosphere at high latitudes in the Arctic due to anthropogenic air pollution.

A major distinguishing factor of Arctic haze is the ability of its chemical ingredients to persist in the atmosphere for an extended period of time compared to other pollutants. Due to limited amounts of snow, rain, or turbulent air to displace pollutants from the polar air mass in spring, Arctic haze can linger for more than a month in the northern atmosphere.

Stockholm Convention on Persistent Organic Pollutants	Stockholm Convention on Persistent Organic Pollutants is an international environmental treaty, signed in 2001 and effective from May 2004, that aims to eliminate or restrict the production and use of persistent organic pollutants (POPs).
	In 1995, the Governing Council of the United Nations Environment Programme (UNEP) called for global action to be taken on POPs, which it defined as 'chemical substances that persist in the environment, bio-accumulate through the food web, and pose a risk of causing adverse effects to human health and the environment'.
	Following this, the Intergovernmental Forum on Chemical Safety (IFCS) and the International Programme on Chemical Safety (IPCS) prepared an assessment of the 12 worst offenders, known as the dirty dozen.
Radon	Radon is a chemical element with the atomic number 86, and is represented by the symbol Rn. It is a radioactive, colorless, odorless, tasteless noble gas, occurring naturally as the decay product of uranium or thorium. Its most stable isotope, ^{222}Rn, has a half-life of 3.8 days.

1. _____s are changes in health resulting from exposure to a source. _____s are an important consideration in many areas, such as hygiene, pollution studies, occupational safety and health, nutrition and health sciences in general. Some of the major environmental sources of _____s are air pollution, water pollution, soil contamination, noise pollution and over-illumination.

   a. Juglone
   b. Health effect
   c. Krakatoa
   d. thermal

2. . A _____ is an organic compound that contains carbon, chlorine, and fluorine, produced as a volatile derivative of methane and ethane. A common subclass are the hydro_____s (HCFCs), which contain hydrogen, as well.

They are also commonly known by the DuPont trade name Freon.

a. Chlorofluorocarbon
b. Dibromodifluoromethane
c. Dibromofluoromethane
d. Dichlorodifluoromethane

3. _____ is a rain or any other form of precipitation that is unusually acidic, meaning that it possesses elevated levels of hydrogen ions (low pH). It can have hmful effects on plants, aquatic animals, and infrastructure. _____ is caused by emissions of cbon dioxide, sulfur dioxide and nitrogen oxides which react with the water molecules in the atmosphere to produce acids.

a. Agricultural pollution
b. Environmental impact of paint
c. In situ chemical reduction
d. Acid rain

4. _____ is the set of the metabolic reactions and processes that take place in the cells of organisms to convert biochemical energy from nutrients into adenosine triphosphate (ATP), and then release waste products. The reactions involved in respiration are catabolic reactions that involve the redox reaction (oxidation of one molecule and the reduction of another). Respiration is one of the key ways a cell gains useful energy to fuel cellular changes.

a. Beta oxidation
b. 1,3-Bisphosphoglyceric acid
c. Cellular respiration
d. Citric acid cycle

5. The _____ is the second major layer of Earth's atmosphere, just above the troposphere, and below the mesosphere. It is stratified in temperature, with warmer layers higher up and cooler layers farther down. This is in contrast to the troposphere near the Earth's surface, which is cooler higher up and warmer farther down.

a. Stratosphere
b. Tropical Atlantic Variability
c. Vapor pressure
d. Weather window

1. b
2. a
3. d
4. c
5. a

You can take the complete Chapter Practice Test

for Chapter 19. Air Pollution
on all key terms, persons, places, and concepts.

Online 99 Cents

http://www.epub89.6.20924.19.cram101.com/

Use www.Cram101.com for all your study needs

including Cram101's online interactive problem solving labs in

chemistry, statistics, mathematics, and more.

Chapter 20. Global Climate Change

CHAPTER OUTLINE: KEY TERMS, PEOPLE, PLACES, CONCEPTS

- Carbon capture and storage
- Climate change
- Anthropogenic
- Chlorofluorocarbon
- Global warming
- Intergovernmental Panel on Climate Change
- Methane
- Nitrous oxide
- Carbon tetrachloride
- Chlorodifluoromethane
- 1,1,1-Trichloroethane
- Radiative forcing
- Sulfur hexafluoride
- Global cooling
- Greenhouse effect
- Albedo
- Climate model
- Mount Pinatubo
- Negative feedback

_____ Antarctic ice sheet

_____ Gangotri Glacier

_____ Glacier

_____ Greenland ice sheet

_____ Ice sheet

_____ Thermal expansion

_____ Inuit

_____ Permafrost

_____ Hurricane

_____ Krill

_____ Zooplankton

_____ Coral bleaching

_____ Coral reef

_____ Extinction

_____ Agricultural productivity

_____ Ozone depletion

_____ Ultraviolet

_____ Carbon tax

_____ Carbon sequestration

	Earth Summit
	Geoengineering
	Kyoto Protocol
	Saltwater intrusion

CHAPTER HIGHLIGHTS & NOTES: KEY TERMS, PEOPLE, PLACES, CONCEPTS

Carbon capture and storage	Carbon capture and storage is the process of capturing waste carbon dioxide (CO_2) from large point sources, such as fossil fuel power plants, transporting it to a storage site, and depositing it where it will not enter the atmosphere, normally an underground geological formation. The aim is to prevent the release of large quantities of CO_2 into the atmosphere (from fossil fuel use in power generation and other industries). It is a potential means of mitigating the contribution of fossil fuel emissions to global warming and ocean acidification.
Climate change	Climate change is a significant and lasting change in the statistical distribution of weather patterns over periods ranging from decades to millions of years. It may be a change in average weather conditions or the distribution of events around that average (e.g., more or fewer extreme weather events). Climate change may be limited to a specific region or may our across the whole Earth.
Anthropogenic	Human impact on the environment or anthropogenic impact on the environment includes impacts on biophysical environments, biodiversity and other resources. The term anthropogenic designates an effect or object resulting from human activity. The term was first used in the technical sense by Russian geologist A. P. Pavlov, and was first used in English by British ecologist Arthur Tansley in reference to human influences on climax plant communities.
Chlorofluorocarbon	A chlorofluorocarbon is an organic compound that contains carbon, chlorine, and fluorine, produced as a volatile derivative of methane and ethane. A common subclass are the hydrochlorofluorocarbons (HCFCs), which contain hydrogen, as well. They are also commonly known by the DuPont trade name Freon.

Chapter 20. Global Climate Change

Global warming	Global warming refers to the rising average temperature of Earth's atmosphere and oceans, which began to increase in the late 19th century and is projected to continue rising. Since the early 20th century, Earth's average surface temperature has increased by about 0.8 °C (1.4 °F), with about two thirds of the increase occurring since 1980. Warming of the climate system is unequivocal, and scientists are more than 90% certain that most of it is caused by increasing concentrations of greenhouse gases produced by human activities such as deforestation and the burning of fossil fuels. These findings are recognized by the national science academies of all major industrialized nations.[A] Climate model projections are summarized in the 2007 Fourth Assessment Report (AR4) by the Intergovernmental Panel on Climate Change (IPCC).
Intergovernmental Panel on Climate Change	The Intergovernmental Panel on Climate Change is a scientific intergovernmental body, set up at the request of member governments. It was first established in 1988 by two United Nations organizations, the World Meteorological Organization (WMO) and the United Nations Environment Programme (UNEP), and later endorsed by the United Nations General Assembly through Resolution 43/53. Its mission is to provide comprehensive scientific assessments of current scientific, technical and socio-economic information worldwide about the risk of climate change caused by human activity, its potential environmental and socio-economic consequences, and possible options for adapting to these consequences or mitigating the effects. It is chaired by Rajendra K. Pachauri.
Methane	Appendix: extraterrestrial methane Methane has been detected or is believed to exist in several locations of the solar system. In most cases, it is believed to have been created by abiotic processes. Possible exceptions are Mars and Titan.
Nitrous oxide	Nitrous oxide, commonly kwn as laughing gas or sweet air, is a chemical compound with the formula N_2O. It is an oxide of nitrogen. At room temperature, it is a colorless n-flammable gas, with a slightly sweet odor and taste.
Carbon tetrachloride	Carbon tetrachloride, also known by many other names is the organic compound with the formula CCl_4. It was formerly widely used in fire extinguishers, as a precursor to refrigerants, and as a cleaning agent. It is a colourless liquid with a 'sweet' smell that can be deteed at low levels.
Chlorodifluoromethane	Chlorodifluoromethane is a hydrochlorofluorocarbon (HCFC). This colorless gas is better known as HCFC-22, or R-22. It was once commonly used as a propellant and in air conditioning applications.

Chapter 20. Global Climate Change

1,1,1-Trichloroethane	The organic compound 1,1,1-trichloroethane, is a chloroalkane. This colourless, sweet-smelling liquid was once produced industrially in large quantities for use as a solvent. It is regulated by the Montreal Protocol as an ozone-depleting substance and its use is being rapidly phased out.
Radiative forcing	In climate science, radiative forcing is loosely defined as the change in net irradiance at atmospheric boundaries between different layers of the atmosphere, namely the troposphere and the stratosphere (the tropopause). Net irradiance is the difference between the incoming radiation energy and the outgoing radiation energy in a given climate system and is measured in Watts per square meter. The change is computed based on 'unperturbed' values, defined by the Intergovernmental Panel on Climate Change (IPCC) as the measured difference relative to a base period.
Sulfur hexafluoride	Sulfur hexafluoride is an inorganic, colorless, odorless, and non-flammable greenhouse gas. SF_6 has an octahedral geometry, consisting of six fluorine atoms attached to a central sulfur atom. It is a hypervalent molecule.
Global cooling	Global cooling was a conjecture during the 1970s of imminent cooling of the Earth's surface and atmosphere along with a posited commencement of glaciation. This hypothesis had little support in the scientific community, but gained temporary popular attention due to a combination of a slight downward trend of temperatures from the 1940s to the early 1970s and press reports that did not accurately reflect the scientific understanding of ice age cycles. In contrast to the global cooling conjecture, the current scientific opinion on climate change is that the Earth has not durably cooled, but undergone global warming throughout the twentieth century.
Greenhouse effect	The greenhouse effect is a process by which thermal radiation from a planetary surface is absorbed by atmospheric greenhouse gases, and is re-radiated in all directions. Since part of this re-radiation is back towards the surface, energy is transferred to the surface and the lower atmosphere. As a result, the avera surface temperature is higher than it would be if direct heating by solar radiation were the only warming mechanism.
Albedo	Albedo or reflection coefficient, derived from Latin albedo 'whiteness' (or reflected sunlight), in turn from albus 'white', is the diffuse reflectivity or reflecting power of a surface. It is defined as the ratio of reflected radiation from the surface to incident radiation upon it. Being a dimensionless fraction, it may also be expressed as a percentage, and is measured on a scale from zero for no reflecting power of a perfectly black surface, to 1 for perfect reflection of a white surface.
Climate model	Climate models use quantitative methods to simulate the interactions of the atmosphere, oceans, land surface, and ice. They are used for a variety of purposes from study of the dynamics of the climate system to projections of future climate.

Chapter 20. Global Climate Change

Mount Pinatubo	Mount Pinatubo is an active stratovolcano located on the island of Luzon, at the intersection of the borders of the Philippine provinces of Zambales, Tarlac, and Pampanga. It is located in the Tri-Cabusilan Mountain range separating the west coast of Luzon from the central plains, and is 42 km (26 mi) west of the dormant and more prominent Mount Arayat, occasionally mistaken for Pinatubo. Ancestral Pinatubo was a stratovolcano made of andesite and dacite.
Negative feedback	Negative feedback occurs when the output of a system acts to oppose changes to the input of the system, with the result that the changes are attenuated. If the overall feedback of the system is negative, then the system will tend to be stable. In many physical and biological systems, qualitatively different iluences can oppose each other.
Antarctic ice sheet	The Antarctic ice sheet is one of the two polar ice caps of the Earth. It covers about 98% of the Antarctic continent and is the largest single mass of ice on Earth. It covers an area of almost 14 million square km and contains 30 million cubic km of ice.
Gangotri Glacier	Gangotri Glacier is located in Uttarkashi District, Uttarakhand, India in a region bordering China. This glacier, source of the Ganges, is one of the largest in the Himalayas with an estimated volume of over 27 cubic kilometers. The glacier is about 30 kilometres long (19 miles) and 2 to 4 km (1 to 2 mi) wide.
Glacier	A glacier is a large persistent body of ice that forms where the accumulation of snow exceeds its ablation (melting and sublimation) over many years, often centuries. At least 0.1 km² in area and 50 m thick, but often much larger, a glacier slowly deforms and flows due to stresses induced by its weight. Crevasses, seracs, and other distinguishing features of a glacier are due to its flow.
Greenland ice sheet	The Greenland Ice Sheet is a vast body of ice covering 1,710,000 square kilometres (660,235 sq mi), roughly 80% of the surface of Greenland. It is the second largest ice body in the world, after the Antarctic Ice Sheet. The ice sheet is almost 2,400 kilometres (1,500 mi) long in a north-south direction, and its greatest width is 1,100 kilometres (680 mi) at a latitude of 77°N, near its northern margin.
Ice sheet	An ice sheet a mass of glacier ice that covers surrounding terrain and greater than 50,000 km^2 (19,000 sq mi), thus also known as continental glacier. The only current ice sheets are in Antarctica and Greenland; during the last glacial period at Last Glacial Maximum (LGM) the Laurentide ice sheet covered much of North America, the Weichselian ice sheet covered northern Europe and the Patagonian Ice Sheet covered southern South America. Ice sheets are bigger than ice shelves or alpine glaciers. Masses of ice covering less than 50,000 km^2 are termed an ice cap.

Thermal expansion	ImgProperty databaseimg Thermal expansion is the ndency of matr to change in volume in response to a change in mperature. When a substance is head, its particles begin moving more and thus usually maintain a grear average separation. Marials which contract with increasing mperature are rare; this effect is limid in size, and only occurs within limid mperature ranges .
Inuit	The Inuit are a group of culturally similar indigenous peoples inhabiting the Arctic regions of Greenland, Canada, the United States, and eastern Siberia. Inuit is a plural noun; the singular is 'Inuk'. The Inuit languages are classified in the Eskimo-Aleut family.
Permafrost	In geology, permafrost is soil at or below the freezing point of water 0 °C (32 °F) for two or more years. Ice is not always present, as may be in the case of nonporous bedrock, but it frequently occurs and it may be in amounts exceeding the potential hydraulic saturation of the ground material. Most permafrost is located in high latitudes (i.e. land close to the North and South poles), but alpine permafrost may exist at high altitudes in much lower latitudes.
Hurricane	Hurricane! (episode: 1616 (308)) is a Nova episode that aired on November 7, 1989 on PBS. The episode describes the fury of a hurricane and the history of hurricane forecasting. The episode features footage of Hurricane Camille of 1969 and Hurricane Gilbert of 1988 and behind the scenes footage at the National Hurricane Center as forecasters tracked Hurricane Gilbert from its formation to its landfall in northern Mexico. Notable meteorologists, Hugh Willoughby, Bob Sheets (then director of the National Hurricane Center) and Jeff Masters were shown in the episode.
Krill	Krill are small crustaceans of the order Euphausiacea, and are found in all the world's oceans. The name krill comes from the Norwegian word, meaning 'young fry of fish', which is also often attributed to other species of fish. Krill are considered an important trophic level connection - near the bottom of the food chain - because they feed on phytoplankton and to a lesser extent zooplankton, converting these into a form suitable for many larger animals for whom krill makes up the largest part of their diet.
Zooplankton	Zooplankton are heterotrophic (sometimes detritivorous) plankton. Plankton are organisms drifting in oceans, seas, and bodies of fresh water. Zooplankton is a categorisation spanning a range of organism sizes including small protozoans and large metazoans.

Chapter 20. Global Climate Change

Coral bleaching	Coral bleaching is the loss of intracellular endosymbionts (Symbiodinium, also known as zooxanthellae) through either expulsion or loss of algal pigmentation. The corals that form the structure of the great reef ecosystems of tropical seas depend upon a symbiotic relationship with unicellular flagellate protozoa that are photosynthetic and live within their tissues. Zooxanthellae give coral its coloration, with the specific color depending on the particular clade.
Coral reef	Coral reefs are underwater structures made from calcium carbonate secreted by corals. Corals are colonies of tiny living animals found in marine waters that contain few nutrients. Most coral reefs are built from stony corals, which in turn consist of polyps that cluster in groups.
Extinction	In biology and ecology, extinction is the end of an organism or of a group of organisms (taxon), normally a species. The moment of extinction is generally considered to be the death of the last individual of the species, although the capacity to breed and recover may have been lost before this point. Because a species' potential range may be very large, determining this moment is difficult, and is usually done retrospectively.
Agricultural productivity	Agricultural productivity is measured as the ratio of agricultural outputs to agricultural inputs. While individual products are usually measured by weight, their varying densities make measuring overall agricultural output difficult. Therefore, output is usually measured as the market value of final output, which excludes intermediate products such as corn feed used in the meat industry.
Ozone depletion	Ozone depletion describes two distinct but related phenomena observed since the late 1970s: a steady decline of about 4% per decade in the total volume of ozone in Earth's stratosphere (the ozone layer), and a much larger springtime decrease in stratospheric ozone over Earth's polar regions. The latter phenomenon is referred to as the ozone hole. In addition to these well-known stratospheric phenomena, there are also springtime polar tropospheric ozone depletion events.
Ultraviolet	Ultraviolet light is electromagnetic radiation with a wavelength shorter than that of visible light, but longer than X-rays, that is, in the range 10 nm to 400 nm, corresponding to photon energies from 3 eV to 124 eV. It is so-named because the spectrum consists of electromagnetic waves with frequencies higher than those that humans identify as the colour violet. These frequencies are invisible to humans, but visible to a number of insects and birds. UV light is found in sunlight (where it constitutes about 10% of the energy in vacuum) and is emitted by electric arcs and specialized lights such as black lights.
Carbon tax	A carbon tax is an environmental tax levied on the carbon content of fuels. It is a form of carbon pricing. Carbon is present in every hydrocarbon fuel (coal, petroleum, and natural gas) and is released as carbon dioxide (CO_2) when they are burnt.

Carbon sequestration	Carbon sequestration is the capture of carbon dioxide (CO_2) and may refer specifically to:•'The process of removing carbon from the atmosphere and depositing it in a reservoir.' When carried out deliberately, this may also be referred to as carbon dioxide removal, which is a form of geoengineering.•The process of carbon capture and storage, where carbon dioxide is removed from flue gases, such as on power stations, before being stored in underground reservoirs.•Natural biogeochemical cycling of carbon between the atmosphere and reservoirs, such as by chemical weathering of rocks. Carbon sequestration describes long-term storage of carbon dioxide or other forms of carbon to either mitigate or defer global warming. It has been proposed as a way to slow the atmospheric and marine accumulation of greenhouse gases, which are released by burning fossil fuels. Carbon dioxide is naturally captured from the atmosphere through biological, chemical or physical processes.
Earth Summit	The United Nations Conference on Environment and Development (UNCED), also known as the Rio Earth Summit, Rio Conference, Earth Summit was a major United Nations conference held in Rio de Janeiro from 3 June to 14 June 1992. In 2012, the United Nations Conference on Sustainable Development was also held in Rio, and is also commonly called Rio+20 or Rio Earth Summit 2012. was held June 20-22nd. Overview 255 governments participated, with 144 sending their heads of state or government.
Geoengineering	The concept of geoengineering refers to the deliberate large-scale engineering and manipulation of the planetary environment to combat or counteract anthropogenic changes in atmospheric chemistry. The Intergovernmental Panel on Climate Change concluded in 2007 that geoengineering options, such as ocean fertilization to remove CO_2 from the atmosphere, remained largely unproven. It was judged that reliable cost estimates for geoengineering had not yet been published.
Kyoto Protocol	The Kyoto Protocol is a protocol to the United Nations Framework Convention on Climate Change (UNFCCC or FCCC), aimed at fighting global warming. The UNFCCC is an international environmental treaty with the goal of achieving the 'stabilisation of greenhouse gas concentrations in the atmosphere at a level that would prevent dangerous anthropogenic interference with the climate system.' The Protocol was initially adopted on 11 December 1997 in Kyoto, Japan, and entered into force on 16 February 2005. As of September 2011, 191 states have signed and ratified the protocol. The only remaining signatory not to have ratified the protocol is the United States.

Saltwater intrusion	Saltwater intrusion is the movement of saline water into freshwater aquifers. Most often, it is caused by ground-water pumping from coastal wells, or from construction of navigation channels or oil field canals. The channels and canals provide conduits for salt water to be brought into fresh water marshes.

1. Appendix: extraterrestrial _____

   _____ has been detected or is believed to exist in several locations of the solar system. In most cases, it is believed to have been created by abiotic processes. Possible exceptions are Mars and Titan.

   a. Nitrogen trifluoride
   b. Methane
   c. Perfluorocarbon tracer
   d. R-410A

2. _____ was a conjecture during the 1970s of imminent cooling of the Earth's surface and atmosphere along with a posited commencement of glaciation. This hypothesis had little support in the scientific community, but gained temporary popular attention due to a combination of a slight downward trend of temperatures from the 1940s to the early 1970s and press reports that did not accurately reflect the scientific understanding of ice age cycles. In contrast to the _____ conjecture, the current scientific opinion on climate change is that the Earth has not durably cooled, but undergone global warming throughout the twentieth century.

   a. Global cooling
   b. Global warming
   c. Greenhouse effect
   d. Polar amplification

3. A _____ is an environmental tax levied on the carbon content of fuels. It is a form of carbon pricing. Carbon is present in every hydrocarbon fuel (coal, petroleum, and natural gas) and is released as carbon dioxide (CO_2) when they are burnt.

   a. Carbon tax
   b. ClientEarth
   c. Container deposit legislation
   d. Critical habitat

4. . _____, also known by many other names is the organic compound with the formula CCl_4. It was formerly widely used in fire extinguishers, as a precursor to refrigerants, and as a cleaning agent.

It is a colourless liquid with a 'sweet' smell that can be deteed at low levels.

a. Carbon tetrachloride
b. Chloromethane
c. Halomethane
d. Hexafluoroethane

5. The _____ is a scientific intergovernmental body, set up at the request of member governments. It was first established in 1988 by two United Nations organizations, the World Meteorological Organization (WMO) and the United Nations Environment Programme (UNEP), and later endorsed by the United Nations General Assembly through Resolution 43/53. Its mission is to provide comprehensive scientific assessments of current scientific, technical and socio-economic information worldwide about the risk of climate change caused by human activity, its potential environmental and socio-economic consequences, and possible options for adapting to these consequences or mitigating the effects. It is chaired by Rajendra K. Pachauri.

a. Intergovernmental Panel on Climate Change
b. Carbon dioxide equivalent
c. Carbon dioxide flooding
d. Carbon lock-in

1. b
2. a
3. a
4. a
5. a

You can take the complete Chapter Practice Test

for Chapter 20. Global Climate Change
on all key terms, persons, places, and concepts.

Online 99 Cents

http://www.epub89.6.20924.20.cram101.com/

Use www.Cram101.com for all your study needs

including Cram101's online interactive problem solving labs in

chemistry, statistics, mathematics, and more.

Chapter 21. Water Pollution

——————————— | Fly ash

——————————— | Water pollution

——————————— | Biochemical oxygen demand

——————————— | Cellular respiration

——————————— | Estuary

——————————— | Eutrophication

——————————— | Cultural eutrophication

——————————— | Dead zone

——————————— | Hypoxia

——————————— | Nitrogen

——————————— | Phosphorus

——————————— | Groundwater

——————————— | Volatile organic compound

——————————— | Thermal pollution

——————————— | Pollutant

——————————— | Clean Water Act

——————————— | Nonpoint source pollution

——————————— | Urban runoff

——————————— | Green chemistry

Chapter 21. Water Pollution

CHAPTER OUTLINE: KEY TERMS, PEOPLE, PLACES, CONCEPTS

_____ Pollution

_____ Lake Maracaibo

_____ Arsenic poisoning

_____ Cholera

_____ Sludge

_____ Activated sludge

_____ Trickling filter

_____ Constructed wetland

_____ Refuse Act

_____ Water quality

CHAPTER HIGHLIGHTS & NOTES: KEY TERMS, PEOPLE, PLACES, CONCEPTS

Fly ash	Fly ash is one of the residues generated in combustion, and comprises the fine particles that rise with the flue gases. Ash which does not rise is termed bottom ash. In an industrial context, fly ash usually refers to ash produced during combustion of coal.
Water pollution	Water pollution is the contamination of water bodies (e.g. lakes, rivers, oceans, aquifers and groundwater). Water pollution occurs when pollutants are discharged directly or indirectly into water bodies without adequate treatment to remove harmful compounds. Water pollution affects plants and organisms living in these bodies of water.
Biochemical oxygen demand	Biochemical oxygen demand or B.O.D.

is the amount of dissolved oxygen needed by aerobic biological organisms in a y of water to break down organic material present in a given water sample at certain temperature over a specific time period. The term also refers to a chemical procedure for determining this amount. This is not a precise quantitative test, although it is widely used as an indication of the organic quality of water.

Cellular respiration	Cellular respiration is the set of the metabolic reactions and processes that take place in the cells of organisms to convert biochemical energy from nutrients into adenosine triphosphate (ATP), and then release waste products. The reactions involved in respiration are catabolic reactions that involve the redox reaction (oxidation of one molecule and the reduction of another). Respiration is one of the key ways a cell gains useful energy to fuel cellular changes.
Estuary	An estuary is a partly enclosed coastal body of water with one or more rivers or streams flowing into it, and with a free connection to the open sea. Estuaries form a transition zone between river environments and ocean environments and are subject to both marine influences, such as tides, waves, and the influx of saline water; and riverine influences, such as flows of fresh water and sediment. The inflow of both seawater and freshwater provide high levels of nutrients in both the water column and sediment, making estuaries among the most productive natural habitats in the world.
Eutrophication	Eutrophication, is the ecosystem response to the addition of artificial or natural substances, such as nitrates and phosphates, through fertilizers or sewage, to an aquatic system. One example is the 'bloom' or great increase of phytoplankton in a water body as a response to increased levels of nutrients. Negative environmental effects include hypoxia, the depletion of oxygen in the water, which induces reductions in specific fish and other animal populations.
Cultural eutrophication	Cultural eutrophication is the pross that speeds up natural eutrophication because of human activity. Due to clearing of land and building of towns and cities, land runoff is aclerated and more nutrients such as phosphates and nitrate are supplied to lakes and rivers, and then to coastal estuaries and bays. Extra nutrients are also supplied by treatment plants, golf courses, fertilizers, and farms.
Dead zone	Dead zones are hypoxic (low-oxygen) areas in the world's oceans, the observed incidences of which have been increasing since oceanographers began noting them in the 1970s. These occur near inhabited coastlines, where aquatic life is most concentrated. (The vast middle portions of the oceans which naturally have little life are not considered 'dead zones'). The term can also be applied to the identical phenomenon in large lakes.

Hypoxia	Hypoxia, is a phenomenon that occurs in aquatic environments as dissolved oxygen (DO; molecular oxygen dissolved in the water) becomes reduced in concentration to a point where it becomes detrimental to aquatic organisms living in the system. Dissolved oxygen is typically expressed as a percentage of the oxygen that would dissolve in the water at the prevailing temperature and salinity . An aquatic system lacking dissolved oxygen (0% saturation) is termed anaerobic, reducing, or anoxic; a system with low concentration--in the range between 1 and 30% saturation--is called hypoxic or dysoxic.
Nitrogen	Nitrogen is a chemical element with symbol N and atomic number 7. Elemental nitrogen is a colorless, odorless, tasteless, and mostly inert diatomic gas at standard conditions, constituting 78.09% by volume of Earth's atmosphere. The element nitrogen was discovered as a separable component of air, by Scottish physician Daniel Rutherford, in 1772. It belongs to the pnictogen family.

Nitrogen is a common element in the universe, estimated at about seventh in total abundance in our galaxy and the Solar System. |
| Phosphorus | Phosphorus is a chemical element with symbol P and atomic number 15. A multivalent nonmetal of the nitrogen group, phosphorus as a mineral is almost always present in its maximally oxidised state, as inorganic phosphate rocks. Elemental phosphorus exists in two major forms-white phosphorus and red phosphorus-but due to its high reactivity, phosphorus is never found as a free element on Earth.

The first form of elemental phosphorus to be produced (white phosphorus, in 1669) emits a faint glow upon exposure to oxygen - hence its name given from Greek mythology, meaning 'light-bearer', referring to the 'Morning Star', the planet Venus. |
Groundwater	Groundwater is water located beneath the ground surface in soil pore spaces and in the fractures of rock formations. A unit of rock or an unconsolidated deposit is called an aquifer when it can yield a usable quantity of water. The depth at which soil pore spaces or fractures and voids in rock become completely saturated with water is called the water table.
Volatile organic compound	Volatile organic compounds (s) are organic chemicals that have a high vapor pressure at ordinary, room-temperature conditions. Their high vapor pressure results from a low boiling point, which causes large numbers of molecules to evaporate or sublimate from the liquid or solid form of the compound and enter the surrounding air. An example is formaldehyde, with a boiling point of -19 ° C (-2 °F), slowly exiting paint and getting into the air.
Thermal pollution	Thermal pollution is the degradation of water quality by any process that changes ambient water temperature.

Chapter 21. Water Pollution

	A common cause of thermal pollution is the use of water as a coolant by power plants and industrial manufacturers. When water used as a coolant is returned to the natural environment at a higher temperature, the change in temperature decreases oxygen supply, and affects ecosystem composition.
Pollutant	A pollutant is a waste material that pollutes air, water or soil, and is the cause of pollution.
	Three factors determine the severity of a pollutant: its chemical nature, its concentration and its persistence. Some pollutants are biodegradable and therefore will not persist in the environment in the long term.
Clean Water Act	The Clean Water Act is the primary federal law in the United States governing water pollution. Commonly abbreviated as the Clean Water Act, the act established the goals of eliminating releases of high amounts of toxic substances into water, eliminating additional water pollution by 1985, and ensuring that surface waters would meet standards necessary for human sports and recreation by 1983.
	The principal body of law currently in effect is based on the Federal Water Pollution Control Amendments of 1972 and was significantly expanded from the Federal Water Pollution Control Amendments of 1948. Major amendments were enacted in the Clean Water Act of 1977 and the Water Quality Act of 1987.
Nonpoint source pollution	Nonpoint source (NPS) pollution refers to both water and air pollution from diffuse sources. Nonpoint source water pollution affects a water body from sources such as polluted runoff from agricultural areas draining into a river, or wind-borne debris blowing out to sea. Nonpoint source air pollution affects air quality from sources such as smokestacks or car tailpipes. Although these pollutants have originated from a point source, the long-range transport ability and multiple sources of the pollutant make it a nonpoint source of pollution. Nonpoint source pollution can be contrasted with point source pollution, where discharges occur to a body of water or into the atmosphere at a single location.
Urban runoff	Urban runoff is surface runoff of rainwater created by urbanization. This runoff is a major source of water pollution in many parts of the United States and other urban communities worldwide.
	Overview
	Impervious surfaces (roads, parking lots and sidewalks) are constructed during land development.

Chapter 21. Water Pollution

CHAPTER HIGHLIGHTS & NOTES: KEY TERMS, PEOPLE, PLACES, CONCEPTS

Green chemistry	Green chemistry, is a philosophy of chemical research and engineering that encourages the design of products and processes that minimize the use and generation of hazardous substances. Whereas environmental chemistry is the chemistry of the natural environment, and of pollutant chemicals in nature, green chemistry seeks to reduce and prevent pollution at its source. In 1990 the Pollution Prevention Act was passed in the United States.
Pollution	Pollution is the introduction of contaminants into a natural environment that causes instability, disorder, harm or discomfort to the ecosystem i.e. physical systems or living organisms. Pollution can take the form of chemical substances or energy, such as noise, heat or light. Pollutants, the components of pollution, can be either foreign substances/energies or naturally occurring contaminants.
Lake Maracaibo	Lake Maracaibo is a large brackish bay in Venezuela. It is connected to the Gulf of Venezuela by Tablazo Strait (55km) at the northern end, and fed by numerous rivers, the largest being the Catatumbo. It is commonly considered a lake rather than a bay or lagoon, and at 13,210 km² it would be the largest lake in South America. The geological record shows that it has been a true lake in the past, and as such is one of the oldest lakes on Earth at 20-36 million years old.
Arsenic poisoning	Arsenic poisoning is a medical condition caused by elevated levels of the element arsenic. The dominant basis of arsenic poisoning is from ground water that naturally contains high concentrations of arsenic. A 2007 study found that over 137 million people in more than 70 countries are probably affected by arsenic poisoning of drinking water.
Cholera	Cholera is an infection of the small intestine that is caused by the bacterium Vibrio cholerae. The main symptoms are profuse watery diarrhea and vomiting. Transmission is primarily through consuming contaminated drinking water or food.
Sludge	Sludge refers to the residual, semi-solid material left from industrial wastewater, or sewage treatment processes. It can also refer to the settled suspension obtained from conventional drinking water treatment, and numerous other industrial processes. The term is also sometimes used as a generic term for solids separated from suspension in a liquid; this 'soupy' material usually contains significant quantities of 'interstitial' water (between the solid particles).
Activated sludge	Activated sludge is a process for treating sewage and industrial wtewaters using air and a biological floc composed of bacteria and protozoans.

Chapter 21. Water Pollution

In a sewage (or industrial wtewater) treatment plant, the activated sludge process can be used for one or several of the following purposes:•oxidizing carbonaceous matter: biological matter.•oxidizing nitrogeneous matter: mainly ammonium and nitrogen in biological materials.•removing phosphate.•driving off entrained ges carbon dioxide, ammonia, nitrogen, etc.•generating a biological floc that is ey to settle.•generating a liquor that is low in dissolved or suspended material.The process

The process involves air or oxygen being introduced into a mixture of primary treated or screened sewage or industrial wtewater (called wtewater from now on) combined with organisms to develop a biological floc which reduces the organic content of the sewage. This material, which in healthy sludge is a brown floc, is largely composed of saprotrophic bacteria but also h an important protozoan flora mainly composed of amoebae, Spirotrichs, Peritrichs including Vorticellids and a range of other filter feeding species.

Trickling filter

A trickling filter consists of a fixed bed of rocks, lava, coke, gravel, slag, polyurethane foam, sphagnum peat moss, ceramic, or plastic media over which sewage or other wastewater flows downward and causes a layer of microbial slime (biofilm) to grow, covering the bed of media. Aerobic conditions are maintained by splashing, diffusion, and either by forced air flowing through the bed or natural convection of air if the filter medium is porous.

The terms trickle filter, trickling biofilter, biofilter, biological filter and biological trickling filter are often used to refer to a trickling filter.

Constructed wetland

A constructed wetland is an artificial wetland, marsh or swamp created as a new or restored habitat for native and migratory wildlife, for anthropogenic discharge such as wastewater, stormwater runoff, or sewage treatment, for land reclamation after mining, refineries, or other ecological disturbances such as required mitigation for natural wetlands lost to a development.

Natural wetlands act as a biofilter, removing sediments and pollutants such as heavy metals from the water, and constructed wetlands can be designed to emulate these features. Biofiltration

Vegetation in a wetland provides a substrate (roots, stems, and leaves) upon which microorganisms can grow as they break down organic materials.

Refuse Act

The Refuse Act is a United States federal statute governing use of waterways. The Act, a section of the Rivers and Harbors Act of 1899, prohibited 'dumping of refuse' into navigable waters, except by permit.

Implementation history

Chapter 21. Water Pollution

Water quality	Water quality is the physical, chemical and biological characteristics of water. It is a measure of the condition of water relative to the requirements of one or more biotic species and or to any human need or purpose. It is most frequently used by reference to a set of standards against which compliance can be assessed.

1. _____ is a process for treating sewage and industrial wtewaters using air and a biological floc composed of bacteria and protozoans.

In a sewage (or industrial wtewater) treatment plant, the _____ process can be used for one or several of the following purposes:•oxidizing carbonaceous matter: biological matter.•oxidizing nitrogeneous matter: mainly ammonium and nitrogen in biological materials.•removing phosphate.•driving off entrained ges carbon dioxide, ammonia, nitrogen, etc.•generating a biological floc that is ey to settle.•generating a liquor that is low in dissolved or suspended material.The process

The process involves air or oxygen being introduced into a mixture of primary treated or screened sewage or industrial wtewater (called wtewater from now on) combined with organisms to develop a biological floc which reduces the organic content of the sewage. This material, which in healthy sludge is a brown floc, is largely composed of saprotrophic bacteria but also h an important protozoan flora mainly composed of amoebae, Spirotrichs, Peritrichs including Vorticellids and a range of other filter feeding species.

a. Aerobic granular reactor
b. Agricultural wastewater treatment
c. Activated sludge
d. Air stripping

2. . _____ is a chemical element with symbol P and atomic number 15. A multivalent nonmetal of the nitrogen group, _____ as a mineral is almost always present in its maximally oxidised state, as inorganic phosphate rocks. Elemental _____ exists in two major forms-white _____ and red _____-but due to its high reactivity, _____ is never found as a free element on Earth.

The first form of elemental _____ to be produced (white _____, in 1669) emits a faint glow upon exposure to oxygen - hence its name given from Greek mythology, meaning 'light-bearer', referring to the 'Morning Star', the planet Venus.

a. Phosphorus
b. Sinibaldo I Ordelaffi

c. Rowland Hill

d. Convention for the Protection of the Marine Environment of the North-East Atlantic

3. _____s are hypoxic (low-oxygen) areas in the world's oceans, the observed incidences of which have been increasing since oceanographers began noting them in the 1970s. These occur near inhabited coastlines, where aquatic life is most concentrated. (The vast middle portions of the oceans which naturally have little life are not considered '_____s'). The term can also be applied to the identical phenomenon in large lakes.

a. Dead zone

b. Barcelona Convention

c. Coal Oil Point seep field

d. Convention for the Protection of the Marine Environment of the North-East Atlantic

4. _____s (s) are organic chemicals that have a high vapor pressure at ordinary, room-temperature conditions. Their high vapor pressure results from a low boiling point, which causes large numbers of molecules to evaporate or sublimate from the liquid or solid form of the compound and enter the surrounding air. An example is formaldehyde, with a boiling point of -19 °C (-2 °F), slowly exiting paint and getting into the air.

a. Xenobiotic

b. Volatile organic compound

c. Hydrological code

d. Land reclamation

5. _____ is one of the residues generated in combustion, and comprises the fine particles that rise with the flue gases. Ash which does not rise is termed bottom ash. In an industrial context, _____ usually refers to ash produced during combustion of coal.

a. Food waste

b. Great Stink

c. Green waste

d. Fly ash

ANSWER KEY
Chapter 21. Water Pollution

---

1. c
2. a
3. a
4. b
5. d

You can take the complete Chapter Practice Test

for Chapter 21. Water Pollution
on all key terms, persons, places, and concepts.

Online 99 Cents

http://www.epub89.6.20924.21.cram101.com/

Use www.Cram101.com for all your study needs

including Cram101's online interactive problem solving labs in

chemistry, statistics, mathematics, and more.

Chapter 22. Pest Management

CHAPTER OUTLINE: KEY TERMS, PEOPLE, PLACES, CONCEPTS

_____ | Pesticide

_____ | Herbicide

_____ | Insecticide

_____ | Rachel Carson

_____ | Silent Spring

_____ | Malaria

_____ | Monoculture

_____ | Pesticide resistance

_____ | Bioaccumulation

_____ | Intercropping

_____ | Famine

_____ | Natural selection

_____ | Bacillus thuringiensis

_____ | Selective breeding

_____ | Integrated pest management

_____ | Food irradiation

_____ | Federal Insecticide, Fungicide, and Rodenticide Act

_____ | Food Quality Protection Act

_____ | Stockholm Convention on Persistent Organic Pollutants

| | Persistent organic pollutant |

Pesticide	Pesticides are substances or mixture of substances intended for preventing, destroying, repelling or mitigating any pest. A pesticide may be a chemical, biological agent (such as a virus or bacterium), antimicrobial, disinfectant or device used against any pest. Pests include insects, plant pathogens, weeds, molluscs, birds, mammals, fish, nematodes (roundworms), and microbes that destroy property, spread disease or are vectors for disease or cause nuisance.
Herbicide	Herbicides, also commonly known as weedkillers, are pesticides used to kill unwanted plants. Selective herbicides kill specific targets while leaving the desired crop relatively unharmed. Some of these act by interfering with the growth of the weed and are often synthetic 'imitations' of plant hormones.
Insecticide	An insecticide is a pesticide used against insects. They include ovicides and larvicides used against the eggs and larvae of insects respectively. Insecticides are used in agriculture, medicine, industry and the household.
Rachel Carson	Rachel Carson was an American marine biologist and conservationist whose book Silent Spring and other writings are credited with advancing the global environmental movement.

Rachel Carson began her career as an aquatic biologist in the U.S. Bureau of Fisheries, and became a full-time nature writer in the 1950s. Her widely praised 1951 bestseller The Sea Around Us won her a U.S. National Book Award, recognition as a gifted writer, and financial security. |
| Silent Spring | Silent Spring is a book written by Rachel Carson and published by Houghton Mifflin on 27 September 1962. The book is widely credited with helping launch the environmental movement.

The New Yorker started serializing Silent Spring in June 1962, and it was published in book form (with illustrations by Lois and Louis Darling) by Houghton Mifflin later that year. When the book Silent Spring was published, Rachel Carson was already a well-known writer on natural history, but had not previously been a social critic. |

Malaria	Malaria is a mosquito-borne infectious disease of humans and other animals caused by protists (a type of microorganism) of the genus Plasmodium. It begins with a bite from an infected female mosquito (Anopheles Mosquito), which introduces the protists via its saliva into the circulatory system, and ultimately to the liver where they mature and reproduce. The disease causes symptoms that typically include fever and headache, which in severe cases can progress to coma or death.
Monoculture	Monoculture is the agricultural practice of producing or growing one single crop over a wide area. It is also known as a way of farming practice of growing large stands of a single species. It is widely used in modern industrial agriculture and its implementation has allowed for large harvests from minimal labor.
Pesticide resistance	Pesticide resistance is the adaptation of pest population targeted by a pesticide resulting in decreased susceptibility to that chemical. In other words, pests develop a resistance to a chemical through natural selection: the most resistant organisms are the ones to survive and pass on their genetic traits to their offspring. Manufacturers of pesticides tend to prefer a definition that is dependent on failure of a product in a real situation, sometimes called field resistance.
Bioaccumulation	Bioaccumulation refers to the accumulation of substances, such as pesticides, or other organic chemicals in an organism. Bioaccumulation occurs when an organism absorbs a toxic substance at a rate greater than that at which the substance is lost. Thus, the longer the biological half-life of the substance the greater the risk of chronic poisoning, even if environmental levels of the toxin are not very high.
Intercropping	Intercropping is the practice of growing two or more crops in proximity. The most common goal of intercropping is to produce a greater yield on a given piece of land by making use of resources that would otherwise not be utilized by a single crop. Careful planning is required, taking into account the soil, climate, crops, and varieties.
Famine	A famine is a widespread scarcity of food, caused by several factors including crop failure, population unbalance, or government policies. This phenomenon is usually accompanied or followed by regional malnutrition, starvation, epidemic, and increased mortality. Nearly every continent in the world has experienced a period of famine throughout history.
Natural selection	Natural selection is the gradual, non-random, process by which biological traits become either more or less common in a population as a function of differential reproduction of their bearers. It is a key mechanism of evolution.

Chapter 22. Pest Management

Bacillus thuringiensis	Bacillus thuringiensis is a Gram-positive, soil-dwelling bacterium, commonly used as a biological pesticide; alternatively, the Cry toxin may be extracted and used as a pesticide. B. thuringiensis also occurs naturally in the gut of caterpillars of various types of moths and butterflies, as well as on the dark surfaces of plants. During sporulation, many strains produce crystal proteins (proteinaceous inclusions), called δ-endotoxins, that have insecticidal action.
Selective breeding	Selective breeding is the process of breeding plants and animals for particular genetic traits. Typically, strains that are selectively bred are domesticated, and the breeding is sometimes done by a professional breeder. Bred animals are known as breeds, while bred plants are known as varieties, cultigens, or cultivars.
Integrated pest management	Integrated pest management is a broad based ecological approach to agricultural pest control that integrates pesticides/herbicides into a management system incorporating a range of practices for economic control of a pest. In , one attempts to prevent infestation, to observe patterns of infestation when they occur, and to intervene (without poisons) when one deems necessary. is the intelligent selection and use of pest control actions that will ensure favourable economic, ecological and sociological consequences.
Food irradiation	Food irradiation is the process of exposing food to ionizing radiation to destroy microorganisms, bacteria, viruses, or insects that might be present in the food. Further applications include sprout inhibition, delay of ripening, increase of juice yield, and improvement of re-hydration. Irradiated food does not become radioactive, but in some cases there may be subtle chemical changes.
Federal Insecticide, Fungicide, and Rodenticide Act	The Federal Insecticide, Fungicide, and Rodenticide Act (P.L. 80-104) 7 U.S.C. § 136 et seq. is a United States federal law that set up the basic U.S. system of pesticide regulation to protect applicators, consumers, and the environment. It is administered and regulated by the United States Environmental Protection Agency (EPA) and the appropriate environmental agencies of the respective states.
Food Quality Protection Act	The Food Quality Protection Act or H.R.1627, was passed unanimously by Congress in 1996 and was signed into law by former U.S. President Bill Clinton on August 3, 1996. The Food Quality Protection Act standardized the way the Environmental Protection Agency (EPA) would manage the use of pesticides and amended the Federal Insecticide, Fungicide, and Rodenticide Act and the Federal Food Drug and Cosmetic Act. It mandated a health-based standard for pesticides used in foods, provided special protections for babies and infants, streamlined the approval of safe pesticides, established incentives for the creation of safer pesticides, and required that pesticide registrations remain current.

Chapter 22. Pest Management

Stockholm Convention on Persistent Organic Pollutants	Stockholm Convention on Persistent Organic Pollutants is an international environmental treaty, signed in 2001 and effective from May 2004, that aims to eliminate or restrict the production and use of persistent organic pollutants (POPs).
	In 1995, the Governing Council of the United Nations Environment Programme (UNEP) called for global action to be taken on POPs, which it defined as 'chemical substances that persist in the environment, bio-accumulate through the food web, and pose a risk of causing adverse effects to human health and the environment'.
	Following this, the Intergovernmental Forum on Chemical Safety (IFCS) and the International Programme on Chemical Safety (IPCS) prepared an assessment of the 12 worst offenders, known as the dirty dozen.
Persistent organic pollutant	Persistent organic pollutants (s) are organic compounds that are resistant to environmental degradation through chemical, biological, and photolytic processes. Because of this, they have been observed to persist in the environment, to be capable of long-range transport, bioaccumulate in human and animal tissue, biomagnify in food chains, and to have potential significant impacts on human health and the environment.
	Many s are currently or were in the past used as pesticides.

1. _____ is the gradual, non-random, process by which biological traits become either more or less common in a population as a function of differential reproduction of their bearers. It is a key mechanism of evolution.

   Variation exists within all populations of organisms.

   a. Differential reproduction
   b. Juglone
   c. Natural selection
   d. Irish Seed Savers Association

2. . _____s are substances or mixture of substances intended for preventing, destroying, repelling or mitigating any pest. A _____ may be a chemical, biological agent (such as a virus or bacterium), antimicrobial, disinfectant or device used against any pest. Pests include insects, plant pathogens, weeds, molluscs, birds, mammals, fish, nematodes (roundworms), and microbes that destroy property, spread disease or are vectors for disease or cause nuisance.

    a. Pesticide residue

    b. Pneumatic fracturing

    c. Polychlorinated biphenyl

    d. Pesticide

3. _____ is a book written by Rachel Carson and published by Houghton Mifflin on 27 September 1962. The book is widely credited with helping launch the environmental movement.

The New Yorker started serializing _____ in June 1962, and it was published in book form (with illustrations by Lois and Louis Darling) by Houghton Mifflin later that year. When the book _____ was published, Rachel Carson was already a well-known writer on natural history, but had not previously been a social critic.

    a. Juglone

    b. Lead

    c. Silent Spring

    d. Methyl tert-butyl ether

4. _____s, also commonly known as weedkillers, are pesticides used to kill unwanted plants. Selective _____s kill specific targets while leaving the desired crop relatively unharmed. Some of these act by interfering with the growth of the weed and are often synthetic 'imitations' of plant hormones.

    a. Hydrocarbon

    b. Lead

    c. Maximum Residue Limit

    d. Herbicide

5. An _____ is a pesticide used against insects. They include ovicides and larvicides used against the eggs and larvae of insects respectively. _____s are used in agriculture, medicine, industry and the household.

    a. Odyssey

    b. Lead

    c. Insecticide

    d. Methyl tert-butyl ether

1. c
2. d
3. c
4. d
5. c

You can take the complete Chapter Practice Test

for Chapter 22. Pest Management
on all key terms, persons, places, and concepts.

Online 99 Cents

http://www.epub89.6.20924.22.cram101.com/

Use www.Cram101.com for all your study needs

including Cram101's online interactive problem solving labs in

chemistry, statistics, mathematics, and more.

CHAPTER OUTLINE: KEY TERMS, PEOPLE, PLACES, CONCEPTS

	Heavy metal
	Fresh Kills Landfill
	Landfill
	Incineration
	Electrostatic precipitator
	Fly ash
	Source reduction
	Materials recovery facility
	Aluminium
	Hazardous waste
	Love Canal
	Polychlorinated biphenyl
	Nuclear weapon
	Bioremediation
	Phytoremediation
	Green chemistry

Heavy metal	A heavy metal is a member of a loosely-defined subset of elements that exhibit metallic properties. It mainly includes the transition metals, some metalloids, lanthanides, and actinides. Many different definitions have been proposed--some based on density, some on atomic number or atomic weight, and some on chemical properties or toxicity.
Fresh Kills Landfill	The Fresh Kills Landfill was a landfill covering 2,200 acres (890 ha) in the New York City borough of Staten Island in the United States. The name comes from the landfill's location along the banks of the Fresh Kills estuary in western Staten Island. The landfill was opened in 1947 as a temporary landfill, but eventually became New York City's principal landfill in the second half of the 20th century, and it was once the largest landfill, as well as man-made structure, in the world.
Landfill	A landfill site (also known as tip, dump or rubbish dump and historically as a midden) is a site for the disposal of waste materials by burial and is the oldest form of waste treatment. Historically, landfills have been the most common methods of organized waste disposal and remain so in many places around the world. Landfills may include internal waste disposal sites (where a producer of waste carries out their own waste disposal at the place of production) as well as sites used by many producers.
Incineration	Incineration is a waste treatment process that involves the combustion of organic substances contained in waste materials. Incineration and other high temperature waste treatment systems are described as 'thermal treatment'. Incineration of waste materials converts the waste into ash, flue gas, and heat.
Electrostatic precipitator	An electrostatic precipitator or electrostatic air cleaner is a particulate collection device that removes particles from a flowing gas (such as air) using the force of an induced electrostatic charge. Electrostatic precipitators are highly efficient filtration devices that minimally impede the flow of gases through the device, and can easily remove fine particulate matter such as dust and smoke from the air stream. In contrast to wet scrubbers which apply energy directly to the flowing fluid medium, an ESP applies energy only to the particulate matter being collected and therefore is very efficient in its consumption of energy (in the form of electricity).
Fly ash	Fly ash is one of the residues generated in combustion, and comprises the fine particles that rise with the flue gases. Ash which does not rise is termed bottom ash. In an industrial context, fly ash usually refers to ash produced during combustion of coal.
Source reduction	Source reduction refers to any change in the design, manufacture, purchase, or use of materials or products (including packaging) to reduce their amount or toxicity before they become municipal solid waste.

CHAPTER HIGHLIGHTS & NOTES: KEY TERMS, PEOPLE, PLACES, CONCEPTS

	Synonyms
	Pollution Prevention (or P2) and Toxics use reduction are also called source reduction because they address the use of hazardous substances at the source.
	Procedures
	Source Reduction is achieved through improvements in production and product design, or through Environmentally Preferable Purchasing (EPP).
Materials recovery facility	A materials recovery facility is a specialized plant that receives, separates and prepares recyclable materials for marketing to end-user manufacturers. Generally, there are two different types: clean and dirty s.
	A clean accepts recyclable commingled materials that have already been separated at the source from municipal solid waste generated by either residential or commercial sources.
Aluminium	Aluminium is a chemical element in the boron group with symbol Al and atomic number 13. It is silvery white, and it is not soluble in water under normal circumstances.
	Aluminium is the third most abundant element (after oxygen and silicon), and the most abundant metal, in the Earth's crust.
Hazardous waste	A Hazardous waste is waste that poses substantial or potential threats to public health or the environment. In the United States, the treatment, storage and disposal of hazardous waste is regulated under the Resource Conservation and Recovery Act (RCRA). Hazardous wastes are defined under RCRA in 40 CFR 261 where they are divided into two major categories: characteristic wastes and listed wastes.
Love Canal	Love Canal was a neighborhood in Niagara Falls, New York, located in the white collar LaSalle section of the city. It officially covers 36 square blocks in the far southeastern corner of the city, along 99th Street and Read Avenue. Two bodies of water define the northern and southern boundaries of the neighborhood: Bergholtz Creek to the north and the Niagara River one-quarter mile (400 m) to the south.
Polychlorinated biphenyl	A polychlorinated biphenyl is any of the 209 configurations of organochlorides with 2 to 10 chlorine atoms attached to biphenyl, which is a molecule composed of two benzene rings. The chemical formula for a PCB is $C_{12}H_{10-x}Cl_x$. 130 of the 209 different PCB arrangements and orientations are used commercially.

Chapter 23. Solid and Hazardous Wastes

Nuclear weapon	A nuclear weapon is an explosive device that derives its destructive force from nuclear reactions, either fission or a combination of fission and fusion. Both reactions release vast quantities of energy from relatively small amounts of matter. The first fission ('atomic') bomb test released the same amount of energy as approximately 20,000 tons of TNT. The first thermonuclear ('hydrogen') bomb test released the same amount of energy as approximately 10,000,000 tons of TNT.
Bioremediation	Bioremediation is the use of microorganismal metabolism to remove pollutants. Technologies can be generally classified as in situ or ex situ. In situ bioremediation involves treating the contaminated material at the site, while ex situ involves the removal of the contaminated material to be treated elsewhere.
Phytoremediation	Phytoremediation (from the Ancient Greek φυτο (phyto, plant), and Latin remedium (restoring balance or remediation) describes the treatment of environmental problems (bioremediation) through the use of plants that mitigate the environmental problem without the need to excavate the contaminant material and dispose of it elsewhere.
	Phytoremediation consists in mitigating pollutant concentrations in contaminated soils, water, or air, with plants able to contain, degrade, or eliminate metals, pesticides, solvents, explosives, crude oil and its derivatives, and various other contaminants from the media that contain them.
	Application
	Phytoremediation may be applied wherever the soil or static water environment has become polluted or is suffering ongoing chronic pollution.
Green chemistry	Green chemistry, is a philosophy of chemical research and engineering that encourages the design of products and processes that minimize the use and generation of hazardous substances. Whereas environmental chemistry is the chemistry of the natural environment, and of pollutant chemicals in nature, green chemistry seeks to reduce and prevent pollution at its source. In 1990 the Pollution Prevention Act was passed in the United States.

1. A _____ is waste that poses substantial or potential threats to public health or the environment. In the United States, the treatment, storage and disposal of _____ is regulated under the Resource Conservation and Recovery Act (RCRA). _____s are defined under RCRA in 40 CFR 261 where they are divided into two major categories: characteristic wastes and listed wastes.

   a. Metabolic waste
   b. Hazardous waste
   c. Municipal solid waste
   d. Planned obsolescence

2. _____ was a neighborhood in Niagara Falls, New York, located in the white collar LaSalle section of the city. It officially covers 36 square blocks in the far southeastern corner of the city, along 99th Street and Read Avenue. Two bodies of water define the northern and southern boundaries of the neighborhood: Bergholtz Creek to the north and the Niagara River one-quarter mile (400 m) to the south.

   a. Love Canal
   b. Minamata disease
   c. Mobro 4000
   d. Saint John, New Brunswick harbour cleanup

3. _____ refers to any change in the design, manufacture, purchase, or use of materials or products (including packaging) to reduce their amount or toxicity before they become municipal solid waste.

   Synonyms

   Pollution Prevention (or P2) and Toxics use reduction are also called _____ because they address the use of hazardous substances at the source.

   Procedures

   _____ is achieved through improvements in production and product design, or through Environmentally Preferable Purchasing (EPP).

   a. Juglone
   b. Source reduction
   c. Green waste
   d. Hazardous waste

4. . _____, is a philosophy of chemical research and engineering that encourages the design of products and processes that minimize the use and generation of hazardous substances. Whereas environmental chemistry is the chemistry of the natural environment, and of pollutant chemicals in nature, _____ seeks to reduce and prevent pollution at its source. In 1990 the Pollution Prevention Act was passed in the United States.

a. Bio-based material

b. California Green Chemistry Initiative

c. Green chemistry

d. Reductive dechlorination

5. A _____ site (also known as tip, dump or rubbish dump and historically as a midden) is a site for the disposal of waste materials by burial and is the oldest form of waste treatment. Historically, _____s have been the most common methods of organized waste disposal and remain so in many places around the world.

_____s may include internal waste disposal sites (where a producer of waste carries out their own waste disposal at the place of production) as well as sites used by many producers.

a. Landfill

b. Municipal solid waste

c. NERV

d. Priority product

ANSWER KEY
Chapter 23. Solid and Hazardous Wastes

1. b
2. a
3. b
4. c
5. a

You can take the complete Chapter Practice Test

for Chapter 23. Solid and Hazardous Wastes
on all key terms, persons, places, and concepts.

Online 99 Cents

http://www.epub89.6.20924.23.cram101.com/

Use www.Cram101.com for all your study needs

including Cram101's online interactive problem solving labs in

chemistry, statistics, mathematics, and more.

Chapter 24. Tomorrow`s World

CHAPTER OUTLINE: KEY TERMS, PEOPLE, PLACES, CONCEPTS

_____	Climate change
_____	Malnutrition
_____	Poverty
_____	Carrying capacity
_____	Sustainable development
_____	Reforestation
_____	Aquaculture
_____	Integrated pest management
_____	Sustainable city
_____	Fossil fuel
_____	Sustainable consumption

CHAPTER HIGHLIGHTS & NOTES: KEY TERMS, PEOPLE, PLACES, CONCEPTS

Climate change	Climate change is a significant and lasting change in the statistical distribution of weather patterns over periods ranging from decades to millions of years. It may be a change in average weather conditions or the distribution of events around that average (e.g., more or fewer extreme weather events). Climate change may be limited to a specific region or may our across the whole Earth.
Malnutrition	Malnutrition is the condition that results from taking an unbalanced diet in which certain nutrients are lacking, in excess (too high an intake), or in the wrong proportions. A number of different nutrition disorders may arise, depending on which nutrients are under or overabundant in the diet.

Visit Cram101.com for full Practice Exams

Chapter 24. Tomorrow's World

Poverty	Poverty is the deprivation of food, shelter, money and clothing that occurs when people cannot satisfy their basic needs. Poverty can be understood simply as a lack of money, or more broadly in terms of barriers to everyday life. Absolute poverty or destitution refers to the state of severe deprivation of basic human needs, which commonly includes food, water, sanitation, clothing, shelter, health care, education and information.
Carrying capacity	The carrying capacity of a biological species in an environment is the maximum population size of the species that the environment can sustain indefinitely, given the food, habitat, water and other necessities available in the environment. In population biology, carrying capacity is defined as the environment's maximal load, which is different from the concept of population equilibrium. For the human population, more complex variables such as sanitation and medical care are sometimes considered as part of the necessary establishment.
Sustainable development	Sustainable development is a pattern of growth in which resource use aims to meet human needs while preserving the environment so that these needs can be met not only in the present, but also for generations to come (sometimes taught as ELF-Environment, Local people, Future). The term sustainable development was used by the Brundtland Commission which coined what has become the most often-quoted definition of sustainable development as development that 'meets the needs of the present without compromising the ability of future generations to meet their own needs.' Sustainable development ties together concern for the carrying capacity of natural systems with the social challenges facing humanity. As early as the 1970s 'sustainability' was employed to describe an economy 'in equilibrium with basic ecological support systems.' Ecologists have pointed to The Limits to Growth, and presented the alternative of a 'steady state economy' in order to address environmental concerns.
Reforestation	Reforestation is the natural or intentional restocking of existing forests and woodlands that have been depleted, usually through deforestation. Reforestation can be used to improve the quality of human life by soaking up pollution and dust from the air, rebuild natural habitats and ecosystems, mitigate global warming since forests facilitate biosequestration of atmospheric carbon dioxide, and harvest for resources, particularly timber. The term reforestation is similar to afforestation, the process of restoring and recreating areas of woodlands or forests that may have existed long ago but were deforested or otherwise removed at some point in the past.

Aquaculture	Aquaculture, is the farming of aquatic organisms such as fish, crustaceans, molluscs and aquatic plants. Aquaculture involves cultivating freshwater and saltwater populations under controlled conditions, and can be contrasted with commercial fishing, which is the harvesting of wild fish. Mariculture refers to aquaculture practised in marine environments.
Integrated pest management	Integrated pest management is a broad based ecological approach to agricultural pest control that integrates pesticides/herbicides into a management system incorporating a range of practices for economic control of a pest. In , one attempts to prevent infestation, to observe patterns of infestation when they occur, and to intervene (without poisons) when one deems necessary. is the intelligent selection and use of pest control actions that will ensure favourable economic, ecological and sociological consequences.
Sustainable city	A sustainable city is a city designed with consideration of environmental impact, inhabited by people dedicated to minimization of required inputs of energy, water and food, and waste output of heat, air pollution - CO_2, methane, and water pollution. Richard Register first coined the term 'ecocity' in his 1987 book, Ecocity Berkeley: building cities for a healthy future. Other leading figures who envisioned the sustainable city are architect Paul F Downton, who later founded the company Ecopolis Pty Ltd, and authors Timothy Beatley and Steffen Lehmann, who have written extensively on the subject.
Fossil fuel	Fossil fuels are fuels formed by natural processes such as anaerobic decomposition of buried dead organisms. The age of the organisms and their resulting fossil fuels is typically millions of years, and sometimes exceeds 650 million years. Fossil fuels contain high percentages of carbon and include coal, petroleum, and natural gas.
Sustainable consumption	Definitions of sustainable consumption share a number of common features, and to an extent build in the characteristics of sustainable production, its twin sister concept and inherit much of from the idea of sustainable development:•Quality of life;•Wise use of resources, and minimisation of waste and pollution;•Use of renewable resources within their capacity for renewal;•Fuller product life-cycles; and•Intergenerational and intragenerational equity.The Oslo Definition The definition proposed by the 1994 Oslo Symposium on Sustainable Consumption defines it as 'the use of services and related products which respond to basic needs and bring a better quality of life while minimizing the use of natural resources and toxic materials as well as emissions of waste and pollutants over the life cycle of the service or product so as not to jeopardize the needs of future generations.' Institutionalising sustainable consumption

Chapter 24. Tomorrow`s World

During the 1990s, was mainly developed by the Organisation for Economic Co-operation and Development (OECD), the UN Commission on Sustainable Development (UNCSD), UN Environment Programme (UNEP), the Division of Sustainable Development of the UN's Department of Economic and Social Affairs (UNDESA) and the international non-governmental organization Consumers International.

Chapter 4.3 from Agenda 21 in from the UN Conference on Environment and Development (UNCED) in 1992 states:'The major cause of the continued deterioration of the global environment is the unsustainable pattern of consumption and production, particularly in industrialized countries, which is a matter of grave concern, aggravating poverty and imbalances.'Developments of sustainable consumption after Agenda 21 •1994 - At the UND it was decided there was a need to consider .•1995 - was requested to be incorporated by UN Economic and Social Council (ECOSOC) into the UN Guidelines on Consumer Protection.•1997 - A major report produced by OECD on .•1998 - UNEP program begins and diussion of in the Human Development Report of the UN Development Program (UNDP).•2002 - Creation of a ten-year program on sustainable consumption and production (P) in the Plan of Implementation at the World Summit on Sustainable Development (WSSD) in Johannesburg.•2003 - The 'Marrakech Process' was developed by co-ordination of a series a of meetings and other 'multi-stakeholder' processes by UNEP and UNDESA following the WSSD.

Sustainable consumption governance has developed from the Oslo definition to the present day implementation strategies and policies that were generated through these global meetings. Governance of sustainable consumption

Overall, governance is still at an early stage of development, but these institutions exhibit principles of network governance.

1. _____ is a significant and lasting change in the statistical distribution of weather patterns over periods ranging from decades to millions of years. It may be a change in average weather conditions or the distribution of events around that average (e.g., more or fewer extreme weather events). _____ may be limited to a specific region or may our across the whole Earth.

    a. Climate oscillation
    b. Climate change
    c. CLIWOC
    d. Cretaceous Thermal Maximum

2. _____ is the condition that results from taking an unbalanced diet in which certain nutrients are lacking, in excess (too high an intake), or in the wrong proportions. A number of different nutrition disorders may arise, depending on which nutrients are under or overabundant in the diet. In most of the world, _____ is present in the form of undernutrition, which is caused by a diet lacking adequate calories and protein.

    a. Juglone
    b. Climate: Long range Investigation, Mapping, and Prediction
    c. CLIWOC
    d. Malnutrition

3. The _____ of a biological species in an environment is the maximum population size of the species that the environment can sustain indefinitely, given the food, habitat, water and other necessities available in the environment. In population biology, _____ is defined as the environment's maximal load, which is different from the concept of population equilibrium.

For the human population, more complex variables such as sanitation and medical care are sometimes considered as part of the necessary establishment.

    a. Juglone
    b. Climate: Long range Investigation, Mapping, and Prediction
    c. CLIWOC
    d. Carrying capacity

4. . _____ is a broad based ecological approach to agricultural pest control that integrates pesticides/herbicides into a management system incorporating a range of practices for economic control of a pest. In , one attempts to prevent infestation, to observe patterns of infestation when they occur, and to intervene (without poisons) when one deems necessary. is the intelligent selection and use of pest control actions that will ensure favourable economic, ecological and sociological consequences.

    a. International Organization for Biological Control
    b. Integrated pest management
    c. Orange oil

5. _____, is the farming of aquatic organisms such as fish, crustaceans, molluscs and aquatic plants. _____ involves cultivating freshwater and saltwater populations under controlled conditions, and can be contrasted with commercial fishing, which is the harvesting of wild fish. Mariculture refers to _____ practised in marine environments.

    a. Aquaculture
    b. K5 Plan
    c. Paperless office
    d. Rainforest Shmainforest

1. b
2. d
3. d
4. b
5. a

You can take the complete Chapter Practice Test

for Chapter 24. Tomorrow`s World
on all key terms, persons, places, and concepts.

Online 99 Cents

http://www.epub89.6.20924.24.cram101.com/

Use www.Cram101.com for all your study needs

including Cram101's online interactive problem solving labs in

chemistry, statistics, mathematics, and more.